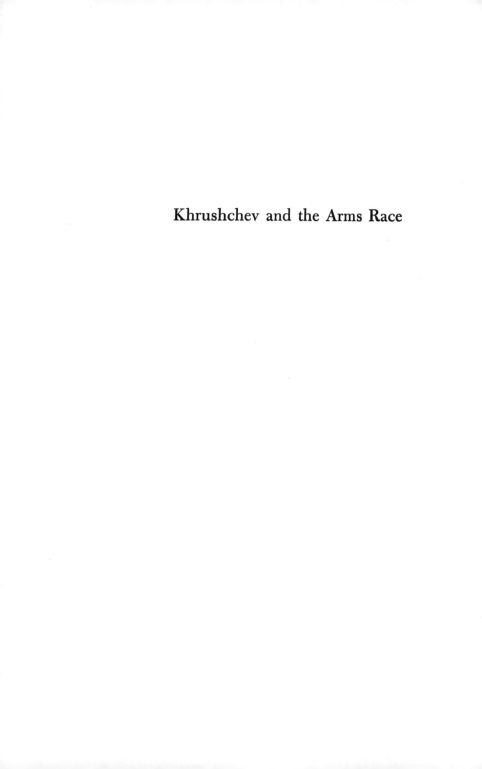

Khrushchev and the Arms Race

A Study from
THE ARMS CONTROL PROJECT

CENTER FOR INTERNATIONAL STUDIES
MASSACHUSETTS INSTITUTE OF TECHNOLOGY

This volume is based, in part, on material from a report prepared under contract with the United States Arms Control and Disarmament Agency. The judgments expressed in this study are those of the authors and do not necessarily reflect the views of the United States Arms Control and Disarmament Agency, or any other department or agency of the United States Government.

KHRUSHCHEV AND THE ARMS RACE

Soviet Interests in Arms Control and Disarmament 1954–1964

Lincoln P. Bloomfield, Walter C. Clemens, Jr., and Franklyn Griffiths

THE M.I.T. PRESS

Massachusetts Institute of Technology
Cambridge, Massachusetts, and London, England

144122

Foreword

The Center's Arms Control project has consistently sought its focus in the intersections between arms control and foreign policy, broadly conceived. The topic in question, combining as it does the Center's long-term concern for Soviet affairs with an obviously crucial aspect of the quest for moderation in the arms race, has been one of our major preoccupations. This book represents the result of almost two years of intensive study of Soviet interests and motivation regarding disarmament and arms control, within the time frame of the historical period that now can be designated "The Khrushchev Decade."

A number of individuals contributed to this book. Working on it full time during the whole period of research were Walter C. Clemens, Jr. and Franklyn Griffiths; contributing on a part-time basis were Fritz Ermarth, John Hoagland, Peter Kenez, Paul Marantz, and Joseph L. Nogee. Valuable advice was given by Franklyn D. Holzman, Herbert Levine, and Marshall Shulman.

Walter Clemens prepared the initial detailed analytical design for the study. He also conducted research on the negotiations and diplomatic aspects, and in addition was principally responsible for coordinating the work of the other contributors. Franklyn Griffiths was a resourceful and energetic collaborator on all phases of the study, and conducted research on propaganda, the political uses of arms control, and internal Soviet politics. Fritz Ermarth contributed the economic inputs, John Hoagland the military-strategic data, and Joseph Nogee the negotiating history for the 1962–1964 period.

Walter Clemens prepared the initial versions of Parts II and IV, Franklyn Griffiths Part III, and both contributed to Part I. Walter Clemens also prepared the bibliographical essay. The undersigned served as over-all supervisor and editor, and drafted certain portions of the book. Indispensable substantive and intellectual contributions were made at all stages of the study by Donald L. M. Blackmer, Morton Gorden, and Alexander Korol. The editing process was generously assisted by Jean Clark and Irirangi Bloomfield. Lisa Walford and Judith Tipton helpfully assisted with the typing and administration.

The representatives of the U.S. Arms Control and Disarmament Agency with whom we dealt during the period of research were uniformly courteous and cooperative, and we wish to record a particular debt of appreciation to Thomas C. Irvin, William C. Kinsey, and John F. Lippmann.

The authors are grateful to those Western government officials, past and present, who have given us the benefit of their informal comments, and regretful that the Soviet and East European officials whom we afforded the opportunity to do the same were not equally responsive.

LINCOLN P. BLOOMFIELD
Director, Arms Control Project
Center for International Studies
Massachusetts Institute of Technology

Cambridge, Massachusetts
January 1966

Contents

TABLES

FIGURES

Introduction

This book is about the interest of the contemporary Soviet Union in various forms of arms control and disarmament measures.[1] At a minimum it is useful to understand better why the Soviet Union behaved as it did over the past ten or so years in dealing with this range of issues. At a maximum it would be highly desirable for the West to put itself in a better position to make predictions about the forces that tend to favor or inhibit a serious Soviet approach to measures of arms control or disarmament.

One of the early (and more cynical) explanations of the predictive powers of the Delphic Oracle was that a vapor issuing from a cleft in the floor in the cave probably intoxicated the Pythian priestess. Later investigators discovered that there was neither cleft nor gas, so ruled instead in favor

---

[1] These two quite different things are generally lumped together under the loose phrase "arms control." But when we refer to disarmament we mean measures that significantly lower the levels of arms; when we speak precisely of arms control measures we mean steps aimed at reducing the risk of accidental, inadvertent, or miscalculated war, or at reducing the frightfulness of nuclear war if it should break out; these may of course — but not necessarily — include the lowering of levels.

of a trance. The interpreter of the complexities of Soviet foreign policy well might yearn for either method — intoxication or convulsion — as a short cut to deciphering the acts of the Kremlin's occupants.

When it comes to mastering the relative forces that shape U.S. foreign policy, the scholarly detective work involved, though demanding and even mysterious in its own ways, benefits inestimably from the fact that after a decent interval one can sometimes interview the significant participants. They can be asked what they intended, which elements in the government favored which policies, and how it all came out in the process of decision making.

The student of Soviet policy has none of these aids available to him. Typically, he makes educated guesses based on his deep immersion in the history and literature of Soviet affairs. If he wishes to be "scientific," he faces a massive and generally discouraging task of detection, the purpose of which is to reconstruct reality as best he can from fragments of circumstantial evidence that can be evaluated in only the shortest of historical perspectives.

The way in which we have tackled the question centers on the chief factors, both internal and external, that we believe go into the formulation of Soviet arms control policy. We have tried to look closely at these factors as they relate to periods of high and low apparent Soviet interest in arms control from 1954 to 1964. At the end we have sought to discern in more general terms the combinations of factors that seem to influence Soviet interests in limiting the arms race.

Soviet arms control and disarmament policy, as Russian diplomats express it in diplomatic forums and in propaganda organs, represents only a surface manifestation of real interests; in an admittedly Freudian vein we have labeled these overt expressions "manifest" policy. For we see these only as clues to understanding the "latent" policies that lie beneath. Soviet interest in steps aimed at directly affecting the arms competition with the West can no more be deciphered from public speeches alone than the shape of an elephant can be deduced by grasping its trunk. As the fabled blind man guessed he was dealing with a snake, so the analyst of arms control needs to see well beyond manifest and overt Soviet diplomacy and propaganda if he is to deduce the reality of Soviet interests. The real Soviet attitudes toward arms control and disarmament are to be found only in a complex synthesis of the perceptions, action plans, and expectations of Soviet leadership concerning domestic and external affairs.

In our view the significant source of Soviet arms control policy is to be found in "trade-offs" among several key underlying factors: externally, the military-strategic situation, and the general foreign policy situation featuring not only the more traditional view to the West but increasingly the view looking eastward toward China; internally, the pressures generated by the state of the Soviet economy, and the state of agreement or dissent among the Soviet leadership.

But what impulses actually moved Soviet leaders of the time? What were their purposes and expectations? In short, what did they really believe? The analysis of "manifest" policy in terms of the many conflicting opportunities and constraints that faced the Soviet leaders still does not enable the observer to see very far below the visible fraction of the iceberg of Soviet strategy and motivations. It is impossible, for example, to determine with any assurance the relationship between the drive for *détente* with the West and the dramatic shifts in the Soviet negotiating posture on questions of disarmament and arms control. They are obviously related. But which is cause, which effect? Is one strategic, the other merely tactical, one genuine, the other a ruse? Or both? Or neither?

Certainly, increased recognition of the dangers in a nuclear war underlay Soviet *détente* strategy during the decade. Disarmament or arms control might in that sense have seemed a rational means to lessen the dangers of such a war. But since a conciliatory stand on disarmament had the additional virtue of helping to reduce tension in general, it might have been viewed purely as a tactic to support the *détente* strategy with no real intention of accepting significant international inspection or other controls. Conversely, a lessening of East-West tensions would have a feedback effect into the arms competition, tending to abate it at least in the West. In sum, then, the same factors that may have impelled Moscow toward East-West measures of arms control also worked for a general softening of Soviet policy toward the West, and vice versa, and we cannot be certain of the exact relationship. What we can do is to examine such evidence as is available in order to form some judgments.

We have found it convenient to break the decade into three general subperiods, the first (1954–1956) a time of Soviet policy changes, the second the period of policy oscillations from Sputnik in 1957 to the Cuban missile crisis of 1962, and the third centering on limited agreements reached in 1963 and 1964. The historian's attempt to impose a scheme of his own upon history is, of course, always to some extent artificial and even misleading. History does sometimes cooperate to create natural boundaries of time, and Nikita Sergeievitch Khrushchev, by his emergence to a position of predominance in the Soviet Union by 1955, following the death of Stalin, supplied a natural starting point. By his unceremonious removal at the hands of resentful and ambitious colleagues in the fall of 1964 he provided the needful final punctuation mark, fortuitously giving us a sense that we had dealt with a self-contained "period" in time. Looking back to what we can now call the "Khrushchev decade" from the vantage point of the sudden end of that era, 1955 seen from 1966 acquires depth, breadth, and meaning; so do the other landmarks of Soviet arms control and disarmament policy in the Khrushchev era.

The decade in question was one of phenomenal change,

the extent of which becomes more apparent if measured against some of the basic continuities of Soviet and perhaps even Tsarist diplomacy regarding disarmament.

As to the Communists, the evidence suggests that there was little expectation of negotiated agreements either before or after the Revolution, and that after 1917 Lenin and then Stalin sought primarily to manipulate the political appeal of the disarmament issue in the West to Soviet advantage. There is also evidence that Tsarist diplomacy from the time Nicholas II called the 1899 Disarmament Conference had much the same outlook.[2]

The Russia of Nicholas, Lenin, and Stalin might well have profited strategically from disarmament agreements limiting the forces of their powerful adversaries. But Tsar and Commissar alike seem to have feared the political and long-term military restrictions inherent in such agreements. Because of this anxiety and also because agreements were deemed infeasible, Tsarist and then Bolshevik diplomacy utilized disarmament negotiations primarily as a device to manipulate the atmosphere of world politics. Under Khrushchev, as we shall see, Moscow's approach to the disarmament question

[2] For documents on the origins of the Hague Conference, see L. Teleshevskoi, ed., "K istorii pervoi Gaagskoi konferentsii 1899 g.," *Krasnyi arkhiv* (Moscow, 1932), Vol. LI-LII, pp. 64–96; and "Novye materialy o Gaagskoi mirnoi konferentsii 1899 g.," *Krasnyi arkhiv*, Vol. LIV–LV, pp. 49–70; also the other sources cited in Walter C. Clemens, Jr., *Soviet Disarmament Policy 1917–1963: An Annotated Bibliography of Soviet and Western Sources* (Stanford, Calif.: The Hoover Institution, 1965), p. xiii; on the origins of the Bolshevik position, see Walter C. Clemens, Jr., "Origins of the Soviet Campaign for Disarmament: the Soviet Position on Peace, Security and Revolution at the Genoa, Moscow and Lausanne Conferences, 1922–1923," unpublished Ph.D. dissertation, Columbia University, 1961; Franklyn Griffiths, "Origins of Peaceful Coexistence: A Historical Note," *Survey*, No. 50 (January 1964), pp. 195–207, reprinted in Walter Lacquer, ed., *The State of Soviet Studies* (Cambridge, Mass.: The M.I.T. Press, 1965), pp. 152–162; also Walter C. Clemens, Jr., "Lenin on Disarmament," *Slavic Review*, Vol. XXIII, No. 3 (September 1964), pp. 504–525; see also the documents and other interpretive works cited in *Soviet Disarmament Policy, op. cit.*, Parts I and II.

seemed to become more serious. While negotiations were still exploited for propaganda value, the Kremlin came also to believe that arms control (though probably not general disarmament) could be a feasible and useful object of Soviet strategy as well as a tactical political weapon.

The early Bolshevik view of disarmament differed from the Tsarist largely by reason of its ideological presupposition of inexorable conflict between political foes, a view deriving from the conspiratorial experience in which no quarter was given or expected.[3] *Kto, kogo* — "who, whom?" was the central question of survival and victory, one that permitted little room for the idea of "collaboration among adversaries" that later came to influence Khrushchev's version of peaceful coexistence. For the Bolsheviks, politics was indeed a zero-sum game: what one side wins, the other loses, and any "rules" are but temporary expedients.

Cooperation with the opponent for tactical gain, and the necessary moderation of Bolshevik conduct to that end, could be pursued only at the risk of dissipating the militancy and drive of the revolutionary sect. Communist ideology further postulated the inevitability of war between capitalist states, and the necessity of the revolutionary transformation of capitalist societies in order to assure a lasting peace. Hence, to suggest prior to 1917 that capitalist governments were capable of reaching agreements on disarmament, or to endorse the possibility of negotiated disarmament, was to do violence to ideology, to divert the "masses" away from "just" wars favoring the proletariat and toward reformist activity, and to impede efforts to harness the great potential of the peace issue in the revolutionary struggle.

These considerations led Lenin initially to oppose any suggestion of negotiations to reduce armaments. While the

[3] For elaboration, see Alexander Dallin *et al, The Soviet Union and Disarmament: An Appraisal of Soviet Attitudes and Intentions* (New York: Frederick A. Praeger, 1965), pp. 37–47; also Walter C. Clemens, Jr., "Ideology in Soviet Disarmament Policy," *Journal of Conflict Resolution*, Vol. VIII, No. 1 (March 1964), pp. 7–22.

Russian revolution of 1905 raged, he declared: "Let the hypocritical or sentimental bourgeoisie dream about disarmament. While there is still oppression and exploitation on earth, we must strive not for disarmament, but for universal, popular armament."[4] Lenin's chief works on the subject, written in 1916, made the same point: the slogan of the Communists, he declared, must not be "international disarmament," but rather "arming the proletariat in order to defeat, expropriate, and disarm the bourgeoisie."[5] His analysis of imperialism led him to reiterate that economic "contradictions" would continue inevitably to trigger intercapitalist wars, and after the revolution he also proclaimed the inevitability of a fight to the death between socialism and capitalism.[6] After 1919, however, Lenin began to view the short-term situation in terms of a socialist regime in one country successfully securing its existence in a network of capitalist states.[7] The necessity of coexistence was already beginning to have its effect on the prerevolutionary ideology, and would soon influence the Soviet approach to disarmament and arms limitation.

As late as 1920 Lenin reiterated that all Communist parties were to campaign actively against " 'social pacifism,' against the belief in the League of Nations, disarmament, and arbitration as a means of averting war."[8] But under the pressure of events the Soviet leaders adopted an increasingly conciliatory approach to Western governments on the diplomatic level. In the peace treaties that Soviet Russia signed

[4] V. I. Lenin, *Sochineniia* (2nd ed., 30 vols.; Moscow, 1926–1932), Vol. VIII, pp. 395–397.

[5] *Ibid.*, Vol. XIX, p. 314 *passim*.

[6] However, Lenin failed to define the nature of the "contradictions" responsible for the impending wars of Soviet Russia with the Western states. See Frederic S. Burin, "The Communist Doctrine of the Inevitability of War," *American Political Science Review*, Vol. LVII, No. 2 (June 1963), pp. 337–339.

[7] See E. H. Carr, *The Bolshevik Revolution, 1917–1923* (London: Macmillan & Co. Ltd., 1953), Vol. III, Chap. 27.

[8] Lenin, *Sochineniia* (2nd ed.), Vol. XXV, *op. cit.*, p. 281.

with its neighbors and with Imperial Germany from 1917 to 1921, the Bolshevik negotiators sought and received what Adolf Joffe termed "guarantees for peaceful coexistence" — arms control measures such as demilitarized zones and limitations on economic and propaganda warfare.[9] By mid-1921 acute economic stress at home and the ebbing tide of revolution abroad had pushed the Kremlin toward a more restrained posture vis-à-vis the capitalist governments. Lenin opted to take several steps "backward" in order to consolidate forces, in the belief that this would make it possible to expand the revolution forward — within and outside of Russia — at a later date.

Soviet and Comintern propaganda was therefore moderated to accord with the new tactics of the "united front," and Moscow's diplomatic posture was more closely attuned to the need for recognition, trade, and political and economic concessions from the West. Whereas Lenin had earlier condemned the very principle of disarmament negotiations as a snare and an illusion, in 1921–1922 he recognized the diplomatic usefulness of such talks, first as a way of strengthening the influence of the "pacifist bourgeoisie" in the political process of the various Western countries, and second as a means of dividing the bourgeois governments among themselves. Lenin thus instructed the Soviet delegation to the Genoa Economic Conference in 1922 that it should seek not only an agreement on trade with the Western bourgeoisie, but also an accord on policy, "as one of the few chances for the peaceful evolution of capitalism to a new structure, [an event] which we, as Communists have little faith in but are willing to help test and consider it our duty to do so. . . ."[10] The first Soviet disarmament proposal was thus put forward in the context of a broad effort to manipulate the politics of Western societies, particularly at the elite level.

[9] See Clemens, "Lenin on Disarmament," *op. cit.*, p. 209.
[10] First published in *Pravda*, April 12, 1964.

While a differentiated view of the class enemy reappeared in the mid-1930's, the dominant approach under Stalin was less conciliatory to Western elites. It tended to stress the dichotomy between the capitalist and proletarian classes in the West, and saw disarmament as a tool for deepening this cleavage through the "exposure" of Western unwillingness to disarm and the mobilization of Communist-led peace movements against Western foreign policies. Although the Soviet government claimed to be the only true supporter of disarmament throughout Stalin's lifetime, the Kremlin made clear that it continued to doubt the possibility that capitalist governments would agree voluntarily to disarmament. The Comintern warned its member parties that Soviet proposals were meant for agitation — not for agreements, which could only be counterrevolutionary.[11] These considerations do not rule out the possibility that the Soviet leadership might at times have regarded modest and transitory arms limitations as potentially beneficial. But the practical improbability of agreements, coupled with the highly politicized conception of security the Bolsheviks brought to the Kremlin, led the Soviet leaders to focus largely on the instrumental and propaganda uses of the disarmament issue.

From these basic attitudes to disarmament and arms control a number of corollaries followed for the Soviet approach to negotiations: the Soviets showed themselves highly suspicious of any capitalist proposal for the limitation (as opposed to the reduction or elimination) of arms. Thus they looked with a jaundiced eye upon the Washington Naval

[11] See Jane Degras, ed., *The Communist International, 1914–1943: Documents* (London: The Royal Institute for International Affairs, Oxford University Press, 1956), Vol. I, pp. 285 ff., Vol. II, p. 377; *Izvestiia*, December 5, 1922; *Pravda*, December 14, 1922; Bela Kun, ed., *Kommunisticheskii International v dokumentakh: resheniia, tezisy i vozvaniia kongressov kominterna i plenumov IKKI 1919–1932* (Moscow: Partinoe Izdatel'stvo, 1933), pp. 322–323; and *International Press Correspondence*, Vol. VIII, No. 58 (September 1, 1928), pp. 1006–1008, and No. 84 (November 28, 1928), pp. 1596–1597.

Conference quotas for capital ships, on the Lausanne Conference restrictions on military ships passing through the Black Sea Straits, and on the complicated ratios advocated by various participants in the League of Nations disarmament negotiations.

A major Soviet publication in 1930, looking back on these events, took pains to define what disarmament was *not*: it was not an increase, a preservation, an imperceptible, or a mock reduction of obsolete weapons; it was not a formula putting off actual disarmament for a distant or undefined moment; and it was not an effort to improve a state's power position by relating disarmament to "security" or "international obligations."[12] Against this background the Soviet rejection of the Baruch Plan after World War II formed part of a longer continuum. The American proposal for the international control of atomic energy represented for Moscow just one more scheme to freeze the balance of power to the disadvantage of the Soviet Union.

A corollary of the Soviet policy was its rejection of the "security-first" school, championed largely by France in the interwar disarmament negotiations and by the United States since 1945. The argument that security must precede disarmament was treated as a thinly veiled plot to put off disarmament indefinitely. Similarly, inspection before disarmament was depicted by Moscow as a device for espionage, although some Soviet proposals to the League of Nations provided for international inspection machinery.[13]

[12] E. A. Korovin and V. V. Egor'ev, *Razoruzhenie* (Moscow: Gosizdat, 1930), pp. 151–154.

[13] As early as 1922, however, a Soviet negotiator declared that inspection was not necessary, desirable, or even possible. See *Conférence de Moscou pour la limitation des armaments* (Moscow: NKID, 1923), p. 164. On the ambiguities of the interwar proposals, see Clemens, "Ideology in Soviet Disarmament Policy," *op. cit.*, p. 13. For a more general analysis of Soviet policy between the wars, see Franklyn Griffiths, "Proposals of Total Disarmament in Soviet Foreign Policy, 1927–1932 and 1959–1960," Russian Institute, Columbia University, unpublished certificate essay, 1962, pp. 85–95.

Another corollary took the form of rejection of Western proposals that disputed questions — whether political controversies or arms control procedures — be subject to majority vote resolution or arbitration; the grounds were the familiar ones that there exist no neutral men.[14] In organizations dominated by Westerners the vote was expected to run against Soviet interests. This attitude occasioned yet another Kremlin objection to the Baruch Plan, since the latter would have deprived Moscow of its Security Council veto over enforcement machinery — the more unacceptable given the absence in the plan of any deadline for the destruction of America's atomic weapons.

Against all this, the Soviet leaders have tended to favor rapid and "maximum" solutions to the disarmament problem. As Allen W. Dulles pointed out in 1947:

> On every possible occasion, from the Genoa Conference in 1922 to the Geneva Conference in 1932–34, the Soviet Union energetically pressed for total disarmament; and when she found that no states were prepared to follow her in such a radical step, she advocated a proportionate reduction of armaments.[15]

All of these positions were consistent not only with Communist ideological presuppositions, seemingly confirmed at times by Western actions, but with Soviet strategic interests as well. From the time that Nicholas II called the Hague Disarmament Conference in 1899 until roughly the beginning of the Khrushchev decade, Russia was confronted by two overriding problems. The first was her relative military and economic backwardness; the second was the vastness of the territory to be defended. Russia's basic strategic deficiencies meant that it would be advantageous militarily if all weapons were eliminated, but that a proportionate cut might leave the

[14] Jan F. Triska and Robert M. Slusser, *The Theory, Law and Policy of Soviet Treaties* (Stanford, Calif.: Stanford University Press, 1962), pp. 381–388.

[15] Allen W. Dulles, "Disarmament in the Atomic Age," *Foreign Affairs*, No. 2 (January 1947), p. 205.

country relatively less able to defend its broad frontiers. The total destruction of all armaments, of course, would put a greater premium on Russia's enormous human and material resources as factors of international power. But the Soviet leaders did not expect the Western governments to surrender their own advantages unless coerced.

These were the main lines of Russian policy under Lenin and Stalin, and, with certain qualifications, under Nicholas II as well. The extent to which the Khrushchev era continued or modified these trends will emerge more clearly in the pages that follow.[16] A few highlights may be suggested here. Whereas Russian disarmament proposals from 1899 to 1953 seemed intended primarily for propaganda effect, some proposals of the Khrushchev period appeared more calculated to achieve an agreement. "Exposure" tactics to embarrass the capitalist regimes were sometimes supplanted or at least paralleled by stratagems to strengthen what the Soviet leaders called "sober forces" in the West. Whereas Moscow once opposed a priori the "mere" limitation of arms, it came after 1955 to support "partial measures" such as a nuclear test ban, and in 1962–1963 to favor a "nuclear umbrella" that would, if accepted, perpetuate a Soviet-U.S. duopoly. Whereas Communist propagandists once held that capitalist business interests might collapse without the arms race, by 1959 the line had changed to one of warning the West that the defense burden was slowing its economic growth. And whereas Lenin held that war was inevitable and disarmament unattainable while capitalism endured, Khrushchev declared that the advent of the atomic bomb made war unthinkable and disarmament an objective necessity, even while peaceful competition of the two systems continued.

[16] On the extent to which Peking has since adopted and Moscow modified Lenin's views toward disarmament, see Walter C. Clemens, Jr., "The Sino-Soviet Dispute — Dogma and Dialectics on Disarmament," *International Affairs* (London), Vol. 41, No. 2 (April 1965), pp. 204–222.

To be sure, the changes that ensued in the Khrushchev decade by no means implied that the Soviet government was sincerely dedicated to the achievement of arms control in disregard of other priorities in its foreign and domestic policy. The Soviets continued to view capitalist motives with deep suspicion; to look askance at arms limitations that might freeze the balance of power to their disadvantage; to oppose inspection of armaments as contrasted to "inspection of disarmament"; and to propose comprehensive disarmament packages some of which were riddled with "jokers" and looked suspiciously like a mere updating of Litvinov's proposals of 1927 and 1932 to the League of Nations. In all, there were some powerfully fixed elements setting rigid limits to change.

The changes in Soviet policy under Khrushchev nevertheless seem on balance to have been more significant than the pre-1963 continuities that persisted. This judgment hinges not only on the surface manifestations of Soviet diplomacy from 1954 to 1964, but also on the fact that these manifest policies could be seen as a logical expression of fairly deep-seated objective changes in over-all Soviet strategy. For the first time in the twentieth century the Soviet leaders had cause to feel relatively safe from attack and to believe that they could bargain on a basis of parity with the West. They became seriously worried lest their advanced power position were to become threatened by the emergence of additional nuclear powers, especially China or Germany. The Soviet Union could sense that it had "arrived" in an economic sense, generating in turn a deeper stake in preserving a *status quo* in which Russia's material problems were being dealt with in a reasonably satisfactory manner. And finally there were new restraints arising from Soviet society itself, contributing to a weakening of the rigid totalitarian mold of the Stalinist period, even when signs of oppression remained.

There was paradox and irony in this extraordinary period of struggle between forces of innovation and forces of inertia; except in a literary sense it was not a struggle in the classic mode between nations representing *status quo* and revolution. In the decade under study there were revolutions struggling to be born both in the Soviet bloc and in the West, as well as in the "third world" to the south. Both East and West had *status quo*'s of their own to protect, and revolutions to foster in the other's camp.

The revolution in strategic thinking produced by nuclear weapons brought the United States and the Soviet Union to recognize that they had a stake in, and even crudely to share, an "established order" of sorts. Both came to find in Red China a threat to this order. Both had to face the diplomatic consequences of the end of general warfare as a rational means of resolving differences. Both grappled with the collapse of monopolistic positions within their alliance structures as the nuclear standoff bred the revival of independent politics around the world. As nuclear warfare came to look like a nonzero-sum enterprise, the prime antagonists — the United States and the Soviet Union — had to become the prime collaborators if any steps were to be taken to moderate the arms competition. These then were the key forces working for change in both strategy and policy.

But the forces of inertia were almost equally as strong. There was a perceived need on both sides to find ways of changing the ground rules of the conflict, however protracted that conflict might be. But the accumulated history of political warfare *à outrance* between Communists and capitalists left a towering obstacle to any such move. The pluralistic features of both societies — one pluralistic because pluralism was cherished, the other at least crudely pluralistic in spite of itself — set close political limits to the freedom of maneuver of those who would innovate; powerful men on both sides were ready to pounce at the first sign of major concessions. And the infernally complex nature of the arms problem itself posed obstacles both of a technical and an intellectual nature.

A final complication of the landscape we have sought to map is its shifting internal quality. Any one of our three slices of history reveals interesting interconnections between the several objective factors we have studied, as they influenced and were influenced by the political process. But the most crucial fact is that over time all of them were in motion, and in no way did their political relevance remain fixed and constant through the Khrushchev decade. All not only shifted; they interacted one with another, feeding back on the whole and continuously altering both reality and Moscow's perceptions of the world with which it had to deal.

PART I

THE SPIRIT OF GENEVA: A NEW ROUND AFTER STALIN 1954–1956

The year 1955 was a turning point in both the style and content of Soviet postwar disarmament diplomacy, following a frigid — and occasionally superheated — spell since 1946. In the 1954–1956 period, and particularly in the spring of 1955, the Soviet Union astonished not a few observers by announcing a series of apparent concessions: these in several important instances represented a clear acceptance, at least verbally, of positions that for some years had been vainly advocated by the Western powers.

The 1955 Soviet disarmament concessions were of course not made in a vacuum; they took place in the period of Soviet glacial thaw that followed Stalin's death. The atmosphere in which they were advanced reflected the process of internal "de-Stalinization" that came to a peak at the Twentieth Party Congress in 1956. It reflected revised notions about the relations of "fraternal" states within the Communist bloc. And it reflected a basic reappraisal of the hard external line that since the end of the war had helped sustain an unprecedented state of international tension. The

17

origins of the altered climate dated back to Stalin's death in 1953, and they were incipient in modifications of Soviet policy as early as 1949.[1] As it turned out, the "spirit of Geneva" ebbed quickly after the Conference of Heads of Governments in July 1955. But many of the factors that led to the Summit persisted, continuing to impel both Moscow and the West toward renewed attempts to modulate their conflicts and regulate their armaments.

The primary change in position in the 1954–1956 period was a significant shift toward accommodation with the West. For the first time since the cold war had set in, Soviet behavior suggested at least the possibility that Moscow sought and perhaps expected to bridge the gap separating its disarmament positions from those of the West. For the first time it was at least plausible to debate whether in fact East-West agreements on arms control were possible. The trends in Soviet policy were away from the Stalinist proclivity for sweeping and immediate measures that were crudely aimed at crippling the West militarily, and away from antagonistic propaganda designed to set the "masses" against the Western governments. The style of Soviet disarmament diplomacy became more conciliatory, less evasive, and more apparently oriented toward a narrowing of East-West differences instead of their "exposure."

Moscow's new proposals explicitly endorsed many of the principles and specific details espoused by the West. If Moscow did not accept aspects of the Western program, the Soviet proposals nevertheless showed greater apparent feasibility than in Stalin's time. Moscow seemed then to accept the Western concept of comprehensive disarmament in stages while simultaneously showing a new interest in a wide range of partial measures to safeguard peace and curb the arms race. Even on the delicate issue of inspection Moscow showed a new willingness to consider at least some international con-

[1] See Marshall D. Shulman, *Stalin's Foreign Policy Reappraised* (Cambridge, Mass.: Harvard University Press, 1963).

trols. *Formal Soviet recognition of the clandestine-weapon problem indicated a new readiness to weigh the hard realities and implications of nuclear technology.*

At the same time, even in the proposals advanced on international inspection and enforcement, the Soviet position remained ambiguous in some respects and restrictive in others, for example, in limiting inspection to unspecified "objects of control." The Kremlin's comprehensive disarmament proposals of May 10, 1955 posited a timetable that seemed unrealistic to Western observers. Moscow persisted in advancing proposals that would benefit only one side militarily — such as the early liquidation of overseas bases. Even more fundamentally, while Moscow may have perceived a certain "moderate" trend of opinion in the United States, its historically antagonistic expectations regarding the West were probably greatly reinforced by the calculation that the "moderate" Western forces were unlikely to prevail.

Which of these two opposing facets in the Soviet outlook had more potential strength cannot be measured. For the West did not after May 10, 1955 explore either the possibilities or ambiguities in the Soviet démarche, but shifted the axis of Western proposals toward various inspection measures and investigation of the technical problems of control. In September 1955, Washington placed a "reservation" on its previous disarmament positions. In the light of all this it seems fair to conclude that the full measure of Soviet policy was never actually taken.

It may be, of course, that the Soviet leaders had no intention of following through on any of their arms control proposals. Perhaps these proposals were purely tactical, serving the political purpose of promoting a détente and inhibiting Western armament, particularly in West Germany, by relaxing tensions. Or perhaps some — but not all — Soviet leaders argued successfully that nothing would be lost and much gained if the West were to accept the 1955 proposal. The fact is that we shall never know for sure.

At a minimum, however, the May 1955 change in Soviet arms control policy, even if meant as a tactical device at the time, became elongated over the years, at least suggesting the possibilities inherent in a strategy of limited collaboration between adversaries.[2]

[2] For elaboration of this concept, see Thomas C. Schelling and Morton H. Halperin, *Strategy and Arms Control* (New York: The Twentieth Century Fund, 1961).

1

Manifest Soviet Policy 1954–1956

Oscillation

The shift in manifest Soviet policies toward arms control can be dated from September 30, 1954, when Andrei Vyshinsky announced to the U.N. General Assembly that the Soviet government was now willing to negotiate on the basis of the principles laid out in the so-called Anglo-French memorandum of June 11, 1954 that Moscow had previously spurned. Since the Western memorandum provided for conventional and nuclear disarmament to proceed in stages, Vyshinsky's statement implied that Moscow had dropped its traditional insistence upon the unconditional prohibition of all nuclear weapons regardless of conventional arms reductions or control measures.[1]

This ostensible concession was retracted in February, only to be made again in March and expanded in May 1955. TASS on February 18, 1955 carried a statement proposing the immediate destruction of all nuclear stocks, the freezing

[1] The major diplomatic moves cited here are documented in U.S. Department of State, *Documents on Disarmament, 1945–1959* (2 vols., Washington, 1960), hereafter cited as *Documents on Disarmament, 1945–1959*.

21

of conventional forces and military budgets as of January 1, 1955, and the convening of a world disarmament conference forthwith. Thus when the Disarmament Commission Subcommittee (DCSC) reconvened on February 25, 1955, Soviet representative Andrei Gromyko, by insisting on priority for the position stated by TASS, appeared to renege on the position originally presented to the Assembly.

On March 11, 1955, however, Moscow again seemed to return to its previously stated willingness to negotiate on the basis of the Anglo-French memorandum. The details were spelled out in a Soviet proposal of March 18, 1955 that was in many ways similar to the French elaboration of the plan originally introduced by the Western nations on March 8. The Soviet and Western plans appeared to be in agreement that comprehensive disarmament should begin with a freeze on military forces and spending; reductions of military manpower and conventional armaments should take place in two stages; production of nuclear weapons should halt at the end of the first stage (Western proposal) or at the beginning of the second stage (Soviet proposal); following the latter two stages there might be a reduction of forces to the minimum levels needed for internal security and fulfillment of U.N. obligations; and "existing" stocks of nuclear materials should be used exclusively for peaceful purposes.

This set of proposals seemed to constitute a framework of consensus potentially broader than any East-West agreement since 1945. There were important differences, which Western proposals in mid-April of the same year helped to bridge. But the Soviet *démarche* of May 10, 1955 seemed to go still further toward narrowing the gap between East and West.

Démarche

The Soviet proposals of May 10, 1955 were particularly significant in three respects. First, they acknowledged that,

as the West had been insisting for years, hidden nuclear stockpiles were an undeniable possibility in the contemporary
world; this effectively put an end to Soviet demands for a
simple uninspected ban on nuclear weapons. Second, although they constituted a comprehensive package, the May
10 proposals also embodied the seeds of a partial-measures
approach that became increasingly explicit in the remainder
of 1955 and an ostensible principle of Soviet policy in March
1956. And third, they represented a movement toward Western positions on some of the details of disarmament, particularly in terms of the interrelationship between disarmament
and security, that was nothing short of dramatic by contrast
to the glacial pace of negotiations until then.

Specifically, the Soviet proposal of May 10 adopted the
Western position on force levels, the timing of nuclear disarmament, and the principle of a single control organ. It
also accepted the Western view that the base period for the
initial freeze of force levels should be 1954 rather than
1955. At the same time the major East-West differences on
inspection and control were still unresolved. Questions of
control were in fact discussed in a separate section of the May
10 document, which argued that international distrust did
not presently permit states to allow international inspection
of industrial and other facilities basic to their security. An
agreement that purported to authorize such inspection would
"create a false sense of security" because "there are possibilities beyond the reach of international control for evading
this control and for organizing the clandestine manufacture
of atomic and hydrogen weapons. . . ."[2]

Clearly an inner contradiction pervaded the Soviets' May
10 *démarche*, growing out of their acknowledgment of the
clandestine-weapon problem coupled with a call at the same
time for complete nuclear disarmament under what might
or might not be adequate international control. Moscow
offered two approaches in an apparent effort to overcome

2 *Ibid.*, Vol. I, p. 465.

this dilemma. The first comprised a "political declaration" listing the major cold war issues and calling for their early resolution in order to "create the requisite conditions for the execution of a broad disarmament program" with "international control over its implementation." Second, the May 10 statement on control proposed the establishment, during the first stage of conventional reductions, of static control posts to guard against surprise attack. These would be established "at large ports, at railway junctions, on main motor highways, and in aerodromes" in the territory of the states concerned. These posts would be supplemented by the single control organ with expanding powers and unlimited access to the objects subject to its jurisdiction.

Without wholly facing up to the many political and technical difficulties raised by its new proposals, Moscow implied that confidence-building measures — including measures to guard against certain types of surprise attack — would create a climate in which unrestricted inspection might either be allowed (though this was never specified by Moscow) or — more likely in the light of increased good will between states — become superfluous.

The elements of the partial-measures approach that Moscow pursued increasingly in the next two years existed in the comprehensive program of May 10, not only in the surprise attack posts but in another measure proposed for the first time by a great power, a nuclear test ban, to be implemented in the first stage of disarmament. The proposal posited that the test ban would be supervised by an international commission reporting to the General Assembly. (However, Moscow's position evolved in 1955 and 1956 to deny the need for special machinery to inspect a test ban.)[3]

This initiative involved other unresolved problems. One was its timetable, calling for only one year per stage. Another was the proposed liquidation of all overseas bases in

[3] See, e.g., Bulganin's letter of September 11, 1956 to Eisenhower in *ibid*, p. 692.

1956 and 1957. Also it postponed many vital details for consideration by a world disarmament conference to be called early in 1956. Finally, all measures of "prevention" and "suppression" regarding violations of the agreement were entrusted to the veto-ridden Security Council.

Despite the difficulties, the Soviet *démarche* appeared an oasis in the barren desert of ten years' disarmament negotiations. The response of the Western negotiators indicates the degree of at least verbal consensus that seemed suddenly to have been achieved. For example, U.S. delegate James Wadsworth on May 12 said he was "gratified to find that the concepts which we have put forward over a considerable length of time . . . have been accepted in a large measure by the Soviet Union."[4] Further exploration of the meaning of the May 10 proposal was put off as the Western delegates in the DCSC moved, over Soviet opposition, to suspend their deliberations on May 18, 1955 until after the Heads of Governments Conference expected in July.

The Geneva Summit

The chiefs of state met in Geneva from July 18 to 22, 1955. They discussed disarmament, European security and Germany, and cultural and economic exchange programs. Premier Bulganin introduced a modified version of the Soviets' May 10 proposal, dropping its "political declaration," its statement concerning clandestine weapons, and some of its less feasible features, such as the two-year timetable and the proposed liquidation of foreign bases. But some troublesome changes were also made. The most egregious of these was an additional specification that non-great-power armed forces be limited to 150,000–200,000 men — a provision obviously directed against the recently developed NATO plans to build a 500,000-man *Bundeswehr*. (The May 10 proposal

[4] U.N. Document DC/SC.1/PV.48 (United Nations, May 12, 1955), p. 43.

had said that limits on the forces of smaller powers would be fixed early in 1956 by a "World Disarmament Conference.")

At the Summit meeting there was however no real negotiation on disarmament. In fact, in Geneva the Western heads of government made no reference to the positions they had advanced and debated earlier that spring in the DCSC, nor did they reply to Bulganin's amended version of the Soviets' May 10 proposal except to assert that static control posts were insufficient to guard against surprise attack. Instead the Western leaders spoke in terms of control measures, each advocating an approach that would, they said, lead later to disarmament. President Eisenhower thus made his surprise "Open Skies" proposal for aerial inspection of the Soviet Union and the United States. British Prime Minister Anthony Eden pushed for an experimental zone of arms limitations and inspection in Central Europe. French Premier Faure espoused budgetary controls of armaments.[5]

The various issues and proposals dealing with control of armaments were soon overshadowed by the chief item of contention at the Summit: European security and Germany. Moscow renewed proposals that both NATO and the Warsaw Pact be replaced by an all-European security pact within the framework of which a presumably neutralized Germany might be reunited. The West, however, persisted in its refusal to disband NATO and insisted that Germany should be reunited on the basis of free elections and a free hand in foreign and military policy — conditions that Moscow quickly rejected.

Disarmament negotiations continued when the DCSC reconvened in New York late in August of 1955. Each delegation continued to press the basic line taken by its govern-

[5] See also Paul C. Davis, "The New Diplomacy: the 1955 Geneva Summit Meeting," in *Foreign Policy in the Sixties*, Roger Hilsman and Robert C. Good, eds. (Baltimore, Md.: The Johns Hopkins Press, 1965), pp. 159–190.

ment at Geneva. On September 6 the U.S. representative Harold Stassen announced that his government was placing a "reservation" on all American "pre-Summit" disarmament positions. The U.S. and the other Western delegates still espoused the control measures advocated by their governments at Geneva but called for additional research to overcome the difficulties of control alluded to in Moscow's statement of May 10.

From October 27 through November 16, 1955 the foreign ministers' meeting in Geneva wrestled with the same issues discussed at the Summit Conference in July. They finally admitted what the heads of government had not: that such new "spirit" as existed in East-West relations was not adequate to resolve divergent positions on European security and Germany, on economic and cultural exchange — and on disarmament and its control.

Détente *and Partial Measures*

The Summit meeting was followed by an exchange of letters between President Eisenhower and Premier Bulganin which was kept up throughout 1956. The Bulganin letters were particularly interesting for their circumspect and "reasonable" tone, and their emphasis on agreements already reached and on the common interests of the two superpowers. In letters of January 23 and February 1, 1956, for instance, Bulganin called for a U.S.-Soviet treaty of friendship and cooperation.

The major Soviet arms control proposal in 1956 was introduced in the DCSC on March 27, 1956. It was notable first for its emphasis on conventional rather than nuclear weapons disarmament; second for its explicit advocacy of a "partial-measures" approach; and third for its detailed provisions for inspection — not just over "disarmament" but over-all conventional armaments. The first part of the Soviet proposal provided for limiting and reducing conventional armaments and armed forces to the levels specified in the May 10 document, but in two rather than the three years proposed earlier. The control provisions were somewhat more specific and far-reaching than Moscow had proposed in 1955. Ground control posts were again suggested, but with the clarification that they would be enumerated in a special agreement that would also extend to the signatories' foreign bases. The control organ again was to have unlimited access to all objects of control, now spelled out as "military units, stores of military equipment and ammunition; land, naval, and air bases; factories manufacturing conventional armaments and ammunition." Since no ban on nuclear production was contained in the Soviet proposal, the problem of dealing with clandestine nuclear production did not arise. The 1956 draft even seemed to take a step toward the "prior positioning" of control by specifying that the control organ would be established within two months of the convention's entry into force and one month before the first reductions began.

The March 1956 proposal outlined a scheme for a zone of arms limitation and inspection in Central Europe that was similar to the 1954–1955 Eden Plan and the Rapacki Plans of 1957 and 1958. "Both parts of Germany and of states adjacent to them" would be included. First, ceilings would be placed on foreign forces in the zone. Second, the stationing of atomic formations and weapons in the zone would be prohibited — a move obviously designed to thwart U.S. plans for NATO. Third, "joint inspection of the armed forces and armaments" in the zone would be instituted.

The March 27 proposal also called for agreement on three partial measures, not contingent on progress in other problems of disarmament:

1. To discontinue forthwith tests of *thermonuclear* weapons.
2. To ensure that no atomic weapons are included in the armaments of troops in *German territory*. The states concerned shall take the necessary measures to carry out this provision within *three months*.

3. To reduce the military budgets of states by up to 15 per cent as against their military budgets for the previous year.[6]

The preamble of the Soviet document stated the hope that the proposed reduction of conventional weapons would "facilitate . . . agreement on the prohibition of atomic and hydrogen weapons and their elimination. . . ." Soviet delegate Gromyko took the line that the Soviet Union was proposing a "different approach" to the disarmament problem since the linking of conventional and atomic disarmament "has been a serious trouble on the way to agreement."[7]

This generally conciliatory Soviet public posture on disarmament questions continued when Gromyko, on July 12, 1956, appeared to accept the ceilings proposed by the Western powers in March 1956 of 2,500,000 men for Soviet and U.S. forces and 750,000 men each for Britain and for France. Moscow said it was prepared to agree to these levels "as a first step," provided the West agreed to follow this in a second stage with reductions to the lower levels that Moscow had endorsed at the 1955 Summit. The Soviet "acceptance" was also made within the context of a larger program that included a ban on the testing and *use* of "atomic" and "hydrogen" weapons, a ban on the production of nuclear weapons, and the destruction of all nuclear stocks.[8]

After the Disarmament Commission adjourned on July 16, 1956, President Eisenhower and Premier Bulganin resumed their correspondence. Most of the letters concerned nuclear testing, the Soviet Union urging an immediate test ban without inspection, which it held to be superfluous.[9]

On November 17, 1956 Moscow sent Washington a declaration attacking alleged imperialist plots in Hungary and Egypt, which closed, however, by presenting a modified ver-

[6] *Documents on Disarmament, 1945–1959,* Vol. I, pp. 603–607. (Italics added.)

[7] U.N. Document DC/SC.1/PV.73 (United Nations, March 27, 1956), p. 11.

[8] *Documents on Disarmament, 1945–1959,* Vol. I, pp. 670–671.

[9] *Ibid.,* Documents Nos. 175, 176, 177, 178, 182, and 184.

sion of the May 10, 1955 proposal. Thus the Soviet Government returned to its advocacy of nuclear as well as conventional disarmament. This document would later serve as the basis for the Soviets' opening position when the DCSC met again in 1957. The declaration defined for the first time the territorial limits within which Moscow would permit aerial photography — a zone eight hundred kilometers to the east and west of the line where NATO confronted Warsaw Pact forces in Europe — but failed to indicate when this variant of "Open Skies" might come into effect.[10]

In the disarmament discussions of 1956, however, neither side addressed itself directly to the other. Dual and even quadruple monologues were the result. "Interim sparring" is Bechhoefer's apt term for the disarmament proceedings in the latter half of 1955 and throughout 1956, as both sides groped toward the positions adopted during the "intensified effort" begun in 1957.[11] Certainly until the United States completed in mid-November 1956 its announced reappraisal of policy, the many exchanges of views could hardly have been more than "debates, even among our allies, and not true negotiations."[12]

Propaganda

Not quite in lock-step but rather with some cultural or technical lag, Moscow's manner of manipulating the disarmament issue outside the negotiating forum came to parallel the shift in the content of Soviet disarmament proposals.

[10] *Ibid.*, Vol. I, pp. 721–729. In October 1955 Molotov had stated that aerial photography could be considered during the final stage of a comprehensive disarmament program.

[11] Bernhard G. Bechhoefer, *Postwar Negotiations for Arms Control* (Washington: The Brookings Institution, 1961), pp. 313 and 326.

[12] *Ibid.*, p. 325. One point of historic interest concerning the reference in the March 27 Soviet proposal to ban "thermonuclear" tests is worth mention. It was probably aimed at inhibiting Britain's first H-bomb test, although this was also a time when the United States was highly interested in testing tactical atomic weapons. In any event, by July 12, 1956 Moscow was explicitly proposing a ban over nuclear as well as thermonuclear tests.

The necessity and, indeed, the alleged achievement of a significant relaxation of East-West tensions emerged as the dominant themes in Soviet propaganda in 1955.

These themes evolved, however, with some uncertainty. Soviet propaganda did little toward the end of 1954 and during the first months of 1955 to reinforce the conciliatory impression made by Vyshinsky on September 30 at the United Nations in his agreement to negotiate on the basis of the Anglo-French disarmament memorandum. Rather, Soviet communications adhered to a recriminating line directed against both the London-Paris accords to rearm West Germany and the December decision of the NATO Council to equip NATO forces with tactical nuclear weapons. A characteristic Soviet comment ran: "He who wants disarmament cannot rearm West German militarism."[13]

Stalinist proclivities were evident in January 1955 when the World Peace Council launched the Vienna Appeal signature campaign aimed to expose Western "preparation for nuclear war" — a move that prefigured the stance Soviet negotiators would take at the DCSC from February 25 until March 8, 1955. The month of January also saw Moscow charge the United States before the U.N. Security Council with "aggression" in the Formosan crisis.

From mid-March 1955, however, as Soviet diplomacy began to display flexibility in dealing with Yugoslavia and Austria, as well as with the disarmament issue, the Soviet propaganda line began to change. A World Peace Assembly scheduled for May was postponed until June, apparently to permit the formulation of a position more in accord with the May 10 proposals and the mounting Soviet campaign for *détente*. Moscow's new gradualist approach to controlled prohibition of nuclear weapons based on progress in conventional reductions and confidence-building measures was quite out of keeping with the World Peace Council's tradition, reiterated in the Vienna Appeal, of demanding the outright prohibition

[13] Editorial, "Atomic Weapons Must be Destroyed," *International Affairs*, No. 3 (March 1955).

of all weapons of mass destruction. Certainly the May 10 recognition of the problem of clandestine production and storing of nuclear weapons was entirely counterproductive for agitation on the need to "ban" nuclear weapons.

But while the relative complexity of the May 10 proposals did not translate readily into self-evident propaganda propositions with which to rally mass support, the note of accommodation in Soviet disarmament proposals allowed the peace fronts perhaps greater influence by stressing that the positions of East and West had drawn so close that agreement was now "only a matter of good will." Although the reservation that Harold Stassen placed on all U.S. "pre-Summit" positions in September 1955 was sharply criticized by the Soviet diplomats, there was a long silence where a propaganda line publicly "exposing" the United States might normally have been expected.[14] Khrushchev himself did not make a public comment on the American reservation until the Twentieth Party Congress in February 1956.

Apparently undeterred by the cool response to Moscow's new line among Western governments, the Khrushchev-Bulganin team continued its peace offensive, illustrating another of its facets as they toured Asia late in 1955. Bulganin meanwhile kept up his correspondence with Eisenhower, and visits were arranged for "K and B" to London and Paris.

The new orientation in Soviet policy was given doctrinal justification in February 1956 when Khrushchev announced that war was no longer fatalistically inevitable and that in some instances a peaceful transition to socialism was possible.[15]

[14] Even in the official organ of the Cominform the Stassen "reservation" was hardly noted, and then only toward the end of the year. See *For a Lasting Peace, For a People's Democracy* (Bucharest: Organ of the Information Bureau of the Communist and Workers' Parties), November 25 and December 30, 1955. Cf. *Pravda*, December 7, 1955.

[15] Leo Gruliow, ed., *Current Soviet Policies II: A Documentary Record of the 20th Communist Party Congress and Its Aftermath* (New York: Frederick A. Praeger, 1957), pp. 36–38.

2

Strategic Factors in Soviet Policy

It is likely that Soviet foreign policy in general and Soviet arms control policy in particular were powerfully influenced in this period by the military situation, including the strategic balance of 1955 between East and West, the weapons and space systems then in the planning stage, and the doctrines of Soviet military thinking that governed both strategic and tactical policies.

From 1953 through 1955, after prolonged debate among the military analysts, Soviet pronouncements came to acknowledge that the destructive power of nuclear weapons could inflict unacceptable damage on the Soviet Union. Painful experience in a half century of warfare made the Russian people and probably also their leaders especially sensitive to the possibility that the Soviet economy and society might be obliterated by the new weapons.

The Kremlin's policy response to the implications of nuclear weaponry in 1954–1956 was twofold. First, the foreign policy line summed up in Khrushchev's 1956 pronouncements at the Twentieth Party Congress on peaceful coexistence and the noninevitability of war reflected a desire to

33

advance Soviet interests in such a way as to reduce the possibility of military encounters with the West, and particularly with the United States. Second, the disarmament proposals of May 10, 1955 marked, for the first time in the postwar period, an apparent Soviet readiness to consider whether Soviet security might benefit directly from limited arms control agreements over and above any relaxation of East-West tensions or political settlements that might be achieved.

And yet, although this response to the advent of nuclear weapons was undoubtedly stimulated in part by the Soviets' awareness of their immediate strategic inferiority to the United States, Moscow also presumably recognized at some point in 1954–1956 that it had achieved substantial progress toward a credible minimum deterrent and thus toward genuine mutual deterrence. This new situation was most promising for external policies of controlled risk based on the significant improvements in Soviet strategic power to which Moscow began to look forward in this period. Thus, while new restraints in foreign policies and an incipient interest in partial measures of arms control followed from the new Soviet strategic outlook, a desire not to restrict Soviet freedom of action prematurely with limited arms control agreements may have reinforced Moscow's antipathy to agreements with the adversary. The Soviet reading of the military-strategic ledger in this period resulted, then, in contradictory influences on Soviet interests in arms control and disarmament. What were the facts?

Stated Military Doctrine

In the early months of 1955, as Bulganin and Khrushchev ascended to power, a broad restatement of military strategy was made in the Soviet press, in which the outmoded "basic operating factors" of the Stalin years were replaced by modern strategic doctrine based on nuclear weapons and new delivery systems.[1] There were probably three main reasons for the open publication of a revised military doctrine.

First, there can be no doubt that a revision had already occurred among higher levels of the Soviet military community, and there was a pressing need to educate the lower levels of the military establishment and, to some extent, the populace. In the second place, the Bulganin-Khrushchev faction, which apparently enjoyed strong military support, had successfully employed the issue of military preparedness in its attacks on Malenkov, charging in particular that the Malenkov faction had failed to make necessary investments in the defense industries and armed forces, leaving the Soviet Union open to surprise attack.[2] The new tendency in military writing to favor expressions of modernization probably reflected an increase in the prestige and influence of the armed forces as a result of the Malenkov ouster.

Finally, these published doctrinal revisions represented a long-overdue response to the military "new look" formulated in the United States during 1953 and 1954, with its substantially increased emphasis on strategic air power. It is essential to bear in mind that in the United States the President's budget message of January 1954, for fiscal year 1955, called for the "creation, maintenance, and full exploitation of modern air power." Of the total $29.3 billion proposed in that message for the three services, the Air Force was to receive $11.2 billion, or about 38 per cent, representing for the first time in the postwar years a definite departure from the relatively equal allotment of funds among the services.

[1] See Herbert S. Dinerstein, *The Soviet Military Posture as a Reflection of Soviet Strategy,* RAND Research Memorandum RM-2102 (Santa Monica, Calif., March 24, 1958); see also Dinerstein, *War and the Soviet Union* (Rev. ed.; New York: Frederick A. Praeger, 1962).

[2] See, for example, *Komsomol'skaia Pravda,* January 8, 1955; also, Dinerstein, *War and the Soviet Union, op. cit.;* and Raymond L. Garthoff, *Soviet Strategy in the Nuclear Age* (Rev. ed.; New York: Frederick A. Praeger, 1962).

Consequently the Strategic Air Command became in the first two years of the Eisenhower administration a primary instrument of U.S. military strategy and national policy.[3] It is against this background that the published Soviet strategic doctrinal revisions of 1955 must be considered.

However, the appearance of new Soviet strategic aircraft in 1954 and 1955 gave clear evidence that the Soviet military establishment had initiated major programs for the development of strategic nuclear-armed aviation as early as 1950. Therefore a revision in military strategy must actually have occurred at a high and secret level of the military establishment even under Stalin. The publication of changes in military doctrine in early 1955 thus corresponded with a number of important factors — fruition of production plans laid down several years earlier, the emergence of a freer climate for Soviet strategic analysis, and the announcement of a "new look" for U.S. forces.

Strategic Forces in Being

Figure 2.1 provides a comparison of the strategic forces actually operational in the year 1955. The United States held clear superiority in the capability to deliver nuclear weapons over great distances. The B-36 heavy bomber, a few hundred of which were still in the Strategic Air Command (SAC) inventory, was capable of carrying a 10,000-pound bomb load a distance of some 10,000 nautical miles. Supplementing the B-36 was the new B-47 medium bomber, then being delivered in substantial numbers to SAC (see Figure 2.1) and, in conjunction with forward bases and aerial refueling, representing a long-range, high-speed, and high-payload nuclear capability.

In contrast, the Soviet operational force in 1955 was still based mainly on the aging TU-4, a copy by the Tupolev de-

[3] Robert Hotz, "Air Force Takes Key Role in U.S. Policy," *Aviation Week,* Vol. LX, No. 11 (March 15, 1954).

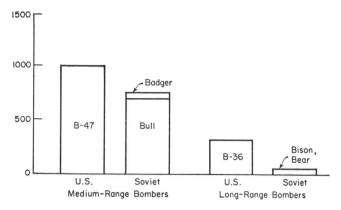

Figure 2.1. Strategic force levels, 1955.

Sources: *The Military Balance* [title varies] (London: Institute for Strategic Studies, 1959–1965); *United States Defense Policies in 1957* (House Document 436, 1958); *ibid. 1958* (House Document 227, 1959); *ibid. 1959* (House Document 432, 1960); *ibid. 1960* (House Document 207, 1961); *ibid. 1961* (House Document 502, 1962); *A Compilation of Material Relating to United States Defense Policies* (House Document 155, 1963); *Statement of Secretary of Defense Robert S. McNamara Before the House Armed Services Committee,* January 30, 1963; *Department of Defense Statement on U.S. Military Strength,* April 14, 1964 (release 308-64), *The New York Times,* April 16, 1964; Institute for Strategic Studies, *Disarmament and European Security* (London, August 1963); "Statement of Secretary McNamara to Democratic Platform Committee, August 17, 1964," *The New York Times,* August 18, 1964. See also Hanson W. Baldwin in *ibid.,* March 25, 1959; "Reds Boast of H-Missile," *The Christian Science Monitor,* November 18, 1959; "Gates Sees U.S. Safe," *ibid.,* January 19, 1960; "Secret Missile Report to Senate Revealed," *The New York Times,* February 5, 1960; "U.S. Downgrades Missile Gap," *The Christian Science Monitor,* March 16, 1960; *Aviation Week and Space Technology,* Vol. 78, No. 10 (March 11, 1963); Hanson W. Baldwin in *The New York Times,* February 14, 1964; "Interview with Robert S. McNamara," *U.S. News and World Report,* April 12, 1965, pp. 52–61; *Aviation Week and Space Technology,* Vol. 83, No. 16 (October 18, 1965), p. 24; *Flying Review International,* Vol. 21, No. 4 (December 1965), p. 209; *Air & Cosmos,* No. 132 (December 25, 1965), p. 35.

sign bureau of the B-29A, with performance characteristics similar to the original piston bomber. It was generally assumed that some seven hundred of these aircraft were still available to the Soviet Air Force in 1955. Although constituting a force that required a definite plan of counteraction, the low speed and low payloads of the TU-4 rendered it a comparatively low-grade threat.

In final development or early production, however, were three new high-performance strategic jet bombers: the Tupolev TU-95 long-range turboprop bomber, the Miasishchev M-4 turbojet heavy bomber, and the Tupolev TU-16 medium jet bomber. With the exception of a relatively few TU-16's in the Soviet Air Force inventory, none of these aircraft had reached true operational status. Through the skillful use of secrecy and deception, however, the Soviet government successfully created an illusion of an operational capability in strategic aviation that finally triggered the "bomber gap" debates of mid-1955 in Washington.[4]

On May 13, 1955 the U.S. Department of Defense issued the following official release:

> The Soviets have recently elected to expose some new aircraft developments in air parade formation over Moscow. These observations establish a new basis for our estimate of Soviet production of the heavy jet bomber (Type 37) Miasishchev M-4 and of the medium bomber (Type 39) Tupolev TU-16. There has also been an appearance of the turboprop bomber [Tupolev TU-95] and a new all-weather fighter has appeared, as expected. This knowledge is evidence of the modern technology of the Soviet aircraft industry and advances which are being made by them.[5]

In rehearsals over Moscow prior to May Day a flight of eight M-4 heavy bombers had been observed on one day, and a flight of ten on the following day. Numerous TU-16

[4] See, for example, Stewart Alsop in *The New York Herald Tribune,* May 16 and May 27, 1955.
[5] *The New York Times,* May 14, 1955.

medium jet bombers were also seen in the rehearsals as well as the new turboprop TU-16, which appeared in a single model. On May Day of the previous year (1954) one M-4, believed to be a prototype, had been observed. The sighting of a possible ten to eighteen aircraft apparently prompted the announced revision in estimates of Soviet bomber strength. (It should be noted that the degree of revision was not stated, leaving the way open for exaggerated conjectures.)

The appearance of these various aircraft on and around May Day 1955 was followed by several articles in the Soviet press by Defense Ministry officials, who warned in effect that the Soviet Union now had at its disposal the weapons systems necessary "to anticipate a surprise attack and to strike before the aggressor can take advantage of his own preparations for an initial strike."[6] Several of these statements were published on May 8, 1955, two days prior to submission of the first major Soviet disarmament proposals of the postwar period.

On July 3, 1955, just two weeks before the opening of the Summit Conference, the Soviets staged an elaborate air show at Tushino Airfield outside Moscow. For several weeks in advance of the show, flights of new military aircraft appeared daily over Moscow, apparently to convince foreign observers that a Soviet strategic nuclear capability was a reality. It seems likely in retrospect that every available aircraft of the three main types was put into the air for these displays. The appearance of even relatively small numbers of these aircraft at Tushino did in fact serve to convince many Western observers that the United States was in immediate danger of losing its air supremacy.[7] Consequently, by skillful deception the Soviets were able to approach the Summit Conference at Geneva with what appeared to be an intercontinental nuclear delivery capability.

[6] Marshal A. M. Vasilevskii in *Izvestiia*, May 8, 1955.
[7] See *Interavia*, Vol. X, No. 8 (August 1955).

Strategic Weapons in Development

In 1955 the new B-52 intercontinental jet bomber, the world's most advanced strategic weapon system, had completed its development cycle and was in full-scale series production, leading to initial deliveries to SAC late in the year. Throughout the remainder of the 1950's the SAC B-52 force was to remain the prime strategic deterrent to the Soviets.

In contrast with the highly competent management of its strategic manned-bomber program, the American missile and space efforts in 1955 were somewhat diffuse. The best efforts in ballistic missile development were being made by the Army Ballistic Missile Agency at Huntsville, Alabama, which, on the basis of V-2 technology, was to complete development of the reliable short-range Redstone ballistic missile. The Air Force, with primary responsibility for long-range strategic delivery, until 1955 had concentrated primarily on the development of air-breathing cruise missiles such as the Navaho supersonic ramjet and Snark subsonic turbojet. It seems likely that failure of the United States to concentrate on a unified ballistic missile program during the 1950–1955 period offered still another incentive to the Soviets to place increasing effort in this direction and so accomplish a technological breakthrough in the arms race.

In January 1955, shortly after a thermonuclear warhead of reduced weight had become available, a development contract was issued in the United States for the Atlas intercontinental ballistic missile (ICBM). In September 1955, at least partly in reaction to heightened U.S. awareness of new Soviet weapons programs, the Atlas program was placed on a priority basis.[8]

On the Soviet side, all three new strategic aircraft had undoubtedly completed their development cycles and were in series production. As force level estimates for 1963 indicate,

[8] *Jane's All the World's Aircraft, 1963–1964* (New York: McGraw-Hill, 1963), p. 398.

however, the two long-range aircraft, M-4 and TU-95, were apparently never mass produced, leading to a possible conclusion that the promise then apparent in the Soviet ballistic missile effort led the leadership to conserve its resources in order to concentrate as much manpower and industrial capacity as possible on strategic missile programs.

The various events of August to November 1957 indicate clearly that several different Soviet missile and space programs must have been established and in operation during 1955. The key events from which an estimate of this kind must be dated are the successful firing of the multistage ICBM in August 1957; the launching of Sputnik I on October 4, 1957; the launching of Sputnik II (with an 1,100-pound payload, indicating a substantial thrust capacity of Soviet vehicles) on November 3, 1957; and finally the showing of the medium-range ballistic missile (MRBM) Shyster (NATO designation) in Red Square on November 7, 1957. Although the Soviet rocket program as a whole had begun in earnest immediately following the surrender of Germany in 1945, it is likely that the most promising MRBM and ICBM programs were placed on a crash basis in 1955. The strongest evidence for this is the reallocation of scientific and technical manpower in 1955 noted by Korol.[9] It is apparent, then, that even in 1955 the Soviet ballistic missile program was achieving substantial success. By early 1956, for example, the Soviet leadership was openly claiming a nuclear missile capability. In a speech before the Twentieth Party Congress in February 1956, Marshal Zhukov said:

> Soviet armed forces, due to the constant attention of the party and government in securing the defense capability of the nation, have been completely reorganized. They now have diverse atomic and nuclear weapons, mighty guided missiles, among them long-range missiles. They are in possession of a first-class jet air force capable of solving any problem that

[9] Alexander G. Korol, *Soviet Research and Development: Its Organization, Personnel, and Funds* (Cambridge, Mass.: The M.I.T. Press, 1964), pp. 69 ff.

might arise in the event of aggressive attack. The Soviet Union does not threaten anybody and does not intend to attack anybody.[10]

While the total volume of the defense effort, measured in current rubles, remained roughly stable in the 1953–1956 period, its composition seems to have altered radically. (See Chapter 3 for further details of the Soviet economic situation in this period.) In 1952 the Soviet Union was arming to meet what was perceived to be an immediate military threat. Thus the maintenance of large ground forces, the procurement of conventional equipment, and the expansion of tactical air power accounted for a high proportion of the defense budget, although, to be sure, feverish efforts in the area of nuclear weapons technology and long-range aircraft were being made. But since the "threat" was immediate, much emphasis had to be placed on the available weapons systems. After 1953 the immediacy of the perceived threat to the Soviet Union declined appreciably, and the need to procure existing weapons systems was correspondingly reduced. At the same time, within a total defense effort that declined only marginally, expenditures on the development of advanced strategic delivery systems (mainly manned aircraft at this point) and nuclear weapons probably increased somewhat.

There is reason to believe that in 1955 or 1956 the Soviet Union intensified its development program of intermediate and intercontinental ballistic missile systems. Between July 1955 and December 1956 total employment in Soviet research and development institutions increased by a startling 23 per cent. Total defense expenditures did not reflect the crash effort in the missile field because military manpower costs and the procurement of conventional weapons seem to have been concurrently reduced. These efforts were visibly rewarded by 1957 when the Soviet Union began serial production of MRBM's and successfully tested an ICBM.

A decade of vigorous research in missile technology, ini-

[10] AP from TASS, February 20, 1956.

tiated by Stalin after the war, had opened the prospect of turning the strategic balance against the United States. If it were true (which proved not to be the case) that the Soviet Union was moving into a position of military parity with the West and would perhaps soon surpass the West in some respects, this development could have tremendous advantages as a backdrop for political and economic warfare. No less important to the Soviet perception of its own security requirements was the fact that the threat of force might also be needed as a last resort to maintain order within Eastern Europe and the Soviet Union.

Implications for Disarmament

The development of the Soviet strategic outlook in 1954–1956 that rested both on increasing Soviet recognition of mutual deterrence and on the expectation of a breakthrough in strategic nuclear weapons, had many implications for the Soviet position on arms control and disarmament.

The Anglo-French proposals of April 1954 — espoused by Washington, accepted by Moscow as a basis for discussion in September 1954, and then partially incorporated in the Soviet proposal of May 10, 1955 — envisioned extensive nuclear and conventional disarmament carried out in two stages, calling for but not spelling out the nature of a third stage of general disarmament. Stopping short of a third stage, the net effect of either the Western or the Soviet proposals would have been to transform the military balance so radically as to leave virtually insolvable the question of which side would profit the more strategically.

For example, the elimination of nuclear weapons, proposed for late 1957 in the Soviet plan, would eliminate the basis of Western deterrence policy, but would also strike at the key area in which Moscow may have expected to achieve superiority. At the same time, of course, the Soviets might have anticipated conventional superiority. Such uncertainties, combined with the as yet unresolved questions of inspection and control, the fixing of ratios, and Moscow's assessment of Western intentions, probably made comprehensive disarmament appear infeasible in 1954–1956, if not undesirable from the standpoint of military-political bargaining power — although, as pointed out earlier, Moscow's intentions were not fully probed. In any event, Moscow's intensive rocket development program and its willingness to export arms to the "third world" quite clearly assumed neither an early abatement of the arms race nor a reduction in the usefulness of military force. In addition, Soviet readiness to rely on limited numbers of prototype long-range bombers for security and bargaining purposes indicated an expectation that Western inspectors would not soon uncover Soviet military weaknesses.

On military-strategic grounds, then, it is dubious whether Moscow viewed its own proposals for comprehensive nuclear and conventional disarmament as constituting a net gain if accepted by the West. In any case, the Kremlin seems not to have deemed the chances of acceptance as sufficiently high to warrant caution in propounding the proposals. This is true not only of the Soviet proposals of May 10, 1955 but, a fortiori, of those of March and July 1956, after the Geneva spirit had lost its bloom.

Implications for Arms Control

The Soviet attitude to partial measures in this period was somewhat different, and it can even be argued that the several agreements reached in 1963–1964 had their origins in 1954–1956. What the Soviets term "partial measures of disarmament" and what some Westerners call "arms control" appeared then to receive serious consideration from the postwar Soviet leaders for the first time. The May 10, 1955 proposal included such measures as part of the comprehensive disarmament program that was put forward; and later in 1955 and

1956 Moscow showed an increased willingness to negotiate them separately. This new approach to partial measures seemed to dovetail with the Soviet strategic outlook, as indicated by the various partial measures of conventional and nuclear disarmament espoused by Soviet diplomats in 1954–1956.

In the first place, the military systems of both nations would have been profoundly altered by the reduction to 1.5 million men, as envisaged by both Western and Soviet proposals of April and May 1955. However, Moscow's ability to agree in principle to reduced ceilings for Soviet armed forces was aided by military moves in progress, which were to be accompanied by reductions in Soviet ground forces by some 2 million men in 1955–1956, while Western forces had already been drastically cut immediately following the Korean armistice. Although Soviet forces would have suffered a larger proportional cut than American forces, the 1.5 million ceiling would probably have compelled the United States to shut down many of its foreign bases (and of course the May 10 proposals explicitly called for liquidation of bases by the end of the second stage). The Soviet Union in contrast might more readily have kept its demobilized soldiers in reserve training, and moreover would remain geographically closer to probable areas of East-West conflict.

Reductions of British and French forces to the 650,000-man level proposed by the West and endorsed by Moscow would have entailed little sacrifice for London and Paris. But Bonn's proposed *Bundeswehr* of 500,000 men would, as indicated, have been seriously curtailed by Moscow's summit proposals to limit the forces of smaller powers to 150,-000–200,000 men.

Again, the liquidation of foreign bases, a common theme in postwar Soviet propaganda and policy, would have deprived the Western alliance of its major support deriving from U.S. conventional and strategic forces in Europe and around the Soviet periphery. Moscow already planned in

1955 to withdraw from Austria, Porkkala-Udd, and Port Arthur and claimed to have eliminated all its foreign bases, though many remained in East Central Europe. The West was thus challenged to reciprocate in full measure by abolishing its foreign bases.

Hints in 1955 by President Eisenhower and in the Eden Plan of Western interest in arms limitations, disengagement, and neutralization in both Germanies and neighboring (East European) states were well received by Moscow. If executed they could have resulted in American withdrawal from the continent, a strategic desideratum that could theoretically justify the withdrawal of Soviet troops from East Central Europe. Similarly, prevention of West German rearmament might have compensated for withdrawal of Soviet influence in East Germany, a vulnerable outpost difficult to control.

It is likely too that the installation of fixed control posts to inhibit surprise attack would have helped to allay Soviet anxieties about a first strike from the U.S. Strategic Air Command bases surrounding the Soviet Union, including those in the continental United States. Perhaps of even greater importance would be the inhibiting effect of such controls on a possible offensive initiated in the future by a rearmed West Germany. The sites proposed for these posts did not include missile launching stations from which future Soviet threats could be made, and the proposal was faulted by the West in part on this ground. Nevertheless, since at least significant factions in the Soviet debate on strategic theory discounted a missile attack without an accompanying build-up of conventional forces, there is no reason to assume on that ground alone that the proposal was not serious.

Any limitations on the stationing of nuclear forces would in practice have frustrated Western plans to emplace tactical nuclear weapons in Central Europe to offset Soviet conventional forces; they would have also rendered impossible the nuclear armament of West Germany under NATO. Moscow, for its part, could have retained on Soviet territory its bomber and, later, missile forces targeted on Western Europe.

Again, whether Moscow actually wanted a nuclear test ban would depend on the state of the nuclear weapons art in both East and West. In 1955 it probably seemed to be a question that could be resolved later, given the likelihood then that Washington would probably oppose a test ban until a control system could be devised and unless limitations were also placed on conventional forces. In any case the Soviet Union was rapidly catching up to, and in some respects surpassing, the United States in the testing of nuclear and thermonuclear weapons, and could look forward to the day when — from a position of parity if not superiority — it could afford to halt testing.

So long, however, as Moscow lagged behind the West in important areas of nuclear weapons procurement and deployment, a ban on nuclear weapons production was obviously unthinkable. Moscow's 1955 proposals staged the "cutoff" on nuclear weapons production slightly later in the disarmament process than in Western plans. In 1956 Bulganin rejected any such cutoff that was not part of a larger disarmament program since it would "legalize" existing nuclear weapons of which the West still had more than Moscow. And, as we have seen, Moscow went on record in May 1955 with the statement that the international confidence necessary for Moscow to admit foreign inspectors in the near future was wholly insufficient to support the degree of inspection required to ensure a ban on nuclear weapons production.

Limits to Partial Measures

The basic limitations on Soviet interest in these partial measures included those that interfered with Moscow's desire for East-West *détente* and those that adversely affected the material and ideological support required to keep Communist governments in power and to sustain the dynamism of anti-capitalist forces in the underdeveloped countries and in the West. In addition certain political and military conditions presumably would have had to be fulfilled before Moscow would enter into any partial measure. There could, for example, be no measures that weakened the Warsaw bloc more than NATO. This ruled out Eisenhower's proposal for mutual aerial photography of the Soviet Union and the United States, which would have provided the West with much more new intelligence than it did the East. Moreover, U.S. bases abroad were not included in Washington's proposal. There could be no inspection or controls in excess of the disarmament immediately planned. This condition also ruled out the "Open Skies" proposal, since the West portrayed it only as a "gateway" to disarmament. Similarly, French proposals for elaborate machinery to check "financial disarmament" probably struck Moscow as an intrusion not justified by the anticipated result. One could expect no staged disarmament without a defined timetable. The West should have no opportunity to stop midway in the disarmament process, for example, at some moment when its intelligence requirements had been satisfied. Nor could there be limitations on Chinese forces without Peking's participation. This at least was Moscow's position at the well-publicized Summit and Foreign Ministers' conferences. But on several occasions in the Disarmament Subcommittee, Soviet delegates proposed limiting Chinese forces to the same level suggested for U.S. and Soviet forces.

In surveying the evidence, it is apparent that certain asymmetries in the military balance, summarized in Table 2.1, exerted a very strong limiting influence on the range of measures that Moscow could regard as being both advantageous for the Soviet Union and acceptable to the West. From the military-strategic point of view only the most marginal of measures would seem to have offered Moscow any immediate interest or practical expectations. These, as we have suggested, may have included ground controls against surprise attack, limitations on the stationing of nuclear forces, measures to inhibit West German rearmament, and perhaps at some future point, a nuclear test ban.

TABLE 2.1. SOME MILITARY ASYMMETRIES IN 1955

The West	The Soviet Union
Expectations of gradual changes in the military environment	Expectations of sudden improvements in the Soviet position vis-à-vis the West
Reliance on SAC and nuclear weapons	Reliance on conventional forces with Europe as hostage
Strategic dependency on overseas bases	No strategic dependency on overseas bases
Relatively open society	Relatively closed society

Soviet appreciation of the possible advantages of such measures seems to have been a by-product of the new realism of the post-Stalin Soviet military-strategic outlook, enhanced by a doubtless worrisome sense of Soviet strategic inferiority to the West. But if present weakness could have prompted a Soviet interest in *détente* and possibly in arms control agreements, the expectation of strategic parity or even superiority probably set severe limits to sustained interest in such moves. Nonetheless, on the premise that the Soviets, like the West, prefer to negotiate from strength rather than from weakness, the prospect of ICBM's in its inventory could at least arguably have made Moscow more confident of its longer-range ability to negotiate with the West on favorable terms.

3

Economic Factors in Soviet Policy

What economic incentives may have reinforced the Kremlin's interest in lessening East-West tensions and in reducing military allocations of men and material? Were there arms control measures that would be economically as well as militarily advantageous?

We have found no evidence that there existed in 1955 economic pressures of a sort that would have provided Moscow with an urgent motive to pursue disarmament agreements with the West. What was present, however, was an economic situation in which significant relaxation of tensions would allow the Kremlin to divert resources to a concentration on weapons systems of possibly decisive future importance while saving on both funds and manpower required for present defenses.

The Economic Burden of Defense

As can be seen from Figure 3.1, the absolute level of Soviet arms spending in 1955 was approximately equal to that prevailing in 1952 at the height of the defense efforts during the Korean War. While arms spending was visibly lower in 1953, 1954, and 1956 than in 1952 and 1955, the rough stability of the volume of total possible arms spending over this period is probably the most significant feature of the data. In 1953 and 1954 the Malenkov leadership announced reductions in the planned level of the defense budget, as did Khrushchev in 1956. In terms of actual reported expenditures and total possible arms spending these reductions were less than dramatic. Soviet production data, however, suggest that in 1953 and 1954 the output of tanks, military transport, and artillery was cut in favor of the production of tractors and other civilian machinery. The use of defense plants for the production of consumer durables such as refrigerators suggests that airframe production for tactical craft may also have been reduced.

The 1956 budget cut made by Khrushchev, who only the previous year had chided Malenkov for neglecting defense, was larger in volume and percentage than the reductions of 1953 and 1954. These minor deviations in the defense line probably reflect more the convolutions of the post-Stalin struggle for power than thoroughgoing disagreements on basic policy. Both Malenkov and Khrushchev seem to have been interested in the stability and perhaps retrenchment of the defense budget.

In retrospect, Moscow probably expected that the costs of the defense effort would not rise beyond a tolerable level since increased outlays on advanced weapons procurement could be counterbalanced by expected growth of the Soviet economy and possibly also by cuts in military manpower (over 2 million men in 1955–1956) and conventional weapons procurement. In fact the Soviet Union was not forced to make significant sacrifices of other goals in order to maintain the defense effort at its prevailing level. Indeed, in the years 1954–1956 Soviet industry appears to have grown at the

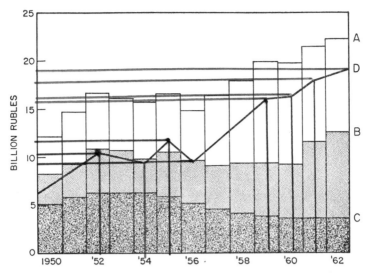

Figure 3.1. Estimated Soviet defense and space expenditures, 1950–1962.

Line A represents an estimate of possible total defense and space expenditures developed by J. G. Godaire, "The Claim of the Soviet Military Establishment," in U.S. Congress, Joint Economic Committee, *Dimensions of Soviet Economic Power* (Washington, 1962), *passim*, and pp. 39, 40. It is known that the official defense budget grossly understates actual Soviet outlays on defense inasmuch as it fails to encompass the bulk of military R & D, some advanced weapons procurement, and some installation costs. Godaire's estimate involves additions to the official defense budget of (1) official outlays on science, most of which are known to go for defense purposes, and (2) certain unexplained residuals in the Soviet budget, arbitrarily reduced to reasonable limits. As regards absolute magnitudes of the Soviet defense effort in given years, the accuracy of Godaire's estimates is highly problematical. His assessment of relative magnitudes, that is, the shape of the curve, appears to be closely suggestive of reality. In most years Godaire's estimates parallel the official defense budget; a sharp upward deviation after 1956 is confirmed by a sharp decline in the growth of civilian machinery output as a result of a presumed diversion of resources to defense. See Rush V. Greenslade and Phyllis Wallace, "Industrial Production in the USSR," in U.S. Congress, Joint Economic Committee, *Dimensions of Soviet Economic Power, op. cit.,* p. 120.

Line B depicts the official Soviet defense budget as realized and most rapid pace seen in the 1952–1962 decade.[1] And yet there probably remained some degree of competition for resources between defense, especially for conventional armaments, and agriculture.

[1] Professor Abram Bergson's studies of Soviet national income indicate that the proportion of GNP devoted to defense in 1955 was about the same as in 1950 before the Korean War rearmament got under way. (Bergson's figures were 10.9 per cent in 1950 and 10.3 per cent in 1955, but they appear to be based on the official budget, which is an understatement of total defense outlays.) The diversion of resources to current military production during 1950–1952 sharply retarded the growth of civilian machine production, which in turn cut into Soviet investment capabilities. The growth of civilian industry was thus retarded. After 1953, although the level of military research and development probably rose and the output of some advanced aircraft may have increased, much plant capacity and current material supply were diverted to the production of civilian machinery. The growth rate of civilian machinery output increased from about 7.5 per cent per year in the years 1951–1953 to about 16 per cent in 1954–1956, and aggregate civilian industry from slightly over 9 per cent to slightly over 11 per cent per year in the same periods. Owing to an increased capacity to emplace new equipment in industry, industrial labor productivity (output per employee), a cherished indicator of progress to Soviet planners, increased in 1954 and 1955 at about twice the rate of the previous three years. See Abram Bergson, *The Real National Income of Soviet Russia Since 1928* (Cambridge, Mass.: Harvard University Press, 1961).

announced at the end of the fiscal year coextensive with the given calendar year. As a rule, the official published annual defense budget is slightly lower than the official planned budget announced at the beginning of the fiscal year. Official realized defense expenditures are from Godaire, *op. cit.*, p. 37. These figures are available also in *Narodnoe khoziaistvo SSSR*, under "Finansy i kredit." Planned expenditures for any year are available in the published budget, which usually appears in December or January.

Line C represents the estimated costs of Soviet military manpower (pay and subsistence) and is a product of military man-years, from Godaire, *op. cit.*, p. 43, times an estimate of the average cost per man (1,090 new rubles), derived by Abraham S. Becker, *Soviet National Income and Product: The Goals of the Seven-Year Plan*, RAND Memorandum RM-3520-PR (Santa Monica, Calif., 1963), p. 139.

Line D represents possible total "weapons and space systems development and procurement" outlays and is derived by subtracting the cost of military manpower (Line C) from possible total defense and space expenditures (Line A).

It is also possible that Soviet leaders underestimated the costs of defense in the missile age that was soon to begin. The Kremlin may have failed to appreciate the extent of the cost differential between developing prototype long-range bombers (and later, ICBM's) and procuring them in large numbers. Or it may have planned to rely largely on prototypes, the exact number of which would be shrouded in secrecy, rather than on mass production of these fearful and expensive weapons. The consequences for the economy of the large-scale transfer of scientific manpower to the defense industry, which began during 1955 and 1956, were probably not yet apparent. But even given the ability of the economy to bear the new costs of defense with relative ease, the Soviet leaders could not have been unaware of the opportunities forgone in the development of the civilian sector.

Stalin's successors inherited an agricultural situation marked by virtual stagnation. Owing to increased attention to incentives and especially to the supply of greater amounts of capital to agriculture, the leadership in 1955 could expect marked improvements in the near future, if not exactly at the present. The hopes of the regime centered principally in the Virgin Lands Program, under which large areas of marginal farm land in Siberia and Central Asia were being brought under the plow in order to raise total grain output. The program depended on massive inputs of machinery that were made possible only by the reduction of conventional weapons production after 1953, although it required less capital investment than other approaches to agricultural development.

Substantial improvements were being made in civilian living standards largely owing to Malenkov's "new course," which, although it did not proceed to the point of altering the basic predominance of heavy industry, had infused sufficient new investment into the consumer industries to produce impressive relative increases in the output of consumer durables and food. A significant role in raising living standards was played by the release of inventories of consumer goods in 1953 and 1954.

Thus Khrushchev sought to make the best of two possible worlds in 1955 by temporarily raising the defense budget — a source of gratification to his military constituents, conservative elements in the party, and some plant managers and scientists — and by promising more food as well. The still rapid Soviet growth rate permitted living standards to increase absolutely even while heavy industry and defense retained or even increased their share of the economic pie.

The tone and content of the Twentieth Party Congress early in 1956 indicated that the Soviet leadership was highly pleased with the current growth record of the Soviet economy, relatively confident that growth would continue to be rapid, and highly sensitive to the manifold implications of Soviet economic performance for the achievement of its international goals. The future military potential of the Soviet Union, its prestige in the eyes of neutrals, and the respect it received from opponents were seen to hinge very greatly on economic growth; peaceful economic competition with capitalism was becoming the most active front of the cold war. At the same time Soviet leaders may have appreciated that broad secular trends were acting slowly to retard the growth rate of the economy, as evidenced by the relatively conservative goals of the Sixth Five-Year Plan relative to those of the Fifth. They would therefore have been concerned to keep the claims of defense on the resources of the economy from increasing significantly.

Implications for Policy

We can now inquire whether there were in fact any economic reasons why the Soviet Union chose to demonstrate a serious interest in disarmament and arms control measures in 1955. Two alternative explanations are plausible. They hinge not so much on the general level of arms spending and the condition of the economy as on the point in time at which the Soviet leadership decided that a missile breakthrough was distinctly possible and that they should proceed in its pursuit. If the decision to proceed with missile development on a crash basis were taken late in 1954 or early in 1955, it could be argued that the Soviet Union would have been interested in disarmament discussions aimed primarily at promoting *détente* with the West, on the theory that relaxation of tensions would allow the Soviet Union to concentrate its arms effort on systems that would come to fruition only after several years.

By avoiding the necessity of procuring existing weapons systems, the possession of which even in large numbers might not alter the current strategic balance significantly, the Soviet Union could develop advanced systems without detracting from economic growth. Certain kinds of arms control and disarmament agreements would not endanger this objective since rocket development could eventually continue under the rubric of space exploration. Agreements to limit possession or testing of nuclear missiles were, however, extremely remote in 1956, as will be seen in considering the political context of the period.

But if it is assumed that the Soviet leadership did not decide until late in 1955 or early in 1956 to exploit the revolutionary implications of the missile technology under development (an assumption supported by the previously described dramatic increase in R & D employment between July 1955 and December 1956), another explanation of Soviet behavior at the negotiating table may be advanced. Until the missile breakthrough became a reasonable certainty the chances for the success of Soviet strategy may have appeared uncertain, though hopeful, since the absolute superiority of the United States in intercontinental aircraft was large and growing despite talk of a "bomber gap." To overtake the United States on this front would have been not only expensive but less than fruitful strategically since the developing air defense systems in the West were tending to increase the number of bombers required to inflict even marginal damage, and it was probably not considered economic to step up production of bombers, particularly in the light of promising missile developments. While the Soviet Union was the vastly inferior competitor in the bomber race, an arms control agreement — or period of *détente* — that reduced the margin of American superiority was economically as well as militarily attractive because it would buy an increased measure of security without increased sacrifice in agriculture and the civilian economy generally. Similarly, a *détente,* and the adoption of a more conciliatory arms control posture to that end, would mitigate the risk of a full-scale arms race, which in 1955 might have seemed to pass the threshhold of both economics and strategy.

Two additional economic advantages of *détente,* although marginal in importance, should be noted. First, the long-term credits to finance the import of Western machinery would be much easier to obtain in an atmosphere of relaxed East-West tensions. Such trade, the Soviet Marxist view suggests, would also be useful in building a material base for peaceful co-existence. Second, the still prevalent view among Soviet economic spokesmen was that the capitalist economies might collapse without defense spending or, short of that eventuality, that the latter would benefit less from defense savings than would a planned socialist economy.

Combinations and variations of the various alternative explanations of Soviet behavior may be suggested. Soviet leaders may have perceived the implications of missile technology early in 1955 but may have been hesitant to proceed with its development on a crash basis because they were not sanguine about the costs involved. Given the unlikely assumption that the political prerequisites of agreement were present, this economic reasoning would have militated for a final strenuous attempt to achieve a favorable disarmament agreement and would have appeared a reasonable course. Conceivably they may also have felt that any agreement could be structured so as to preserve their nascent missile lead while diminishing U.S. superiority in manned aircraft.

What we have called manifest Soviet arms control and disarmament policies in 1954–1956 were, we believe, intimately connected to the strategic posture, present and planned, of the Soviet Union. This connection we see as part of a more broadly orchestrated political and diplomatic offensive growing out of the changing perceptions of Soviet leaders as to the best way to protect the security of the nation and at the same time to advance its international objectives. In this sense, while the over-all allocation of economic and human resources was an integral part of the strategic outlook, economic factors in the narrower sense were probably not of vital importance in conditioning Soviet policy on arms control and disarmament in 195

4

External and Internal Political Factors

What did Moscow expect to achieve with its shifts in foreign policy manifested in the *détente* of 1955 and in the new line adopted at the Twentieth Party Congress? In adopting a more conciliatory foreign policy toward the West and in taking a more "reasonable" approach to disarmament and arms control, was Moscow seeking merely to attenuate the struggle with the Western powers, and thereby to set tacit limits to the arms race and lower the danger of war? Did Moscow now perceive an additional interest in cultivating those in Western governments who were more favorably disposed to agreements with the Soviet Union? These are some of the questions that arise in considering the political factors that influenced Soviet conduct in these formative years of a new approach to the West.

Structural Changes in Foreign Policy

The developments in 1954–1956 in both the Soviets' negotiating position and their political use of the disarmament issue were part of a more pervasive but not unprecedented shift from a relatively antagonistic to a somewhat more re-

59

laxed and manipulative line in Soviet foreign relations generally. During the first postwar years Stalin had chosen to emphasize foreign policies based on a view of the world characterized by the struggle of two irreconcilably opposed camps. Realization of the counterproductive consequences of such a posture led to some moderation of harsher policies in 1949, and to official recognition in 1952 that "contradictions" within the non-Communist camp could be exploited profitably by such devices as the Communist-led peace movements.[1] Nonetheless, up to the time of Stalin's death in the spring of 1953 the Kremlin's official view tended to portray the world in terms of a simple dichotomy: the world of socialism versus the world of imperialism. Intermediate political forces and opinions were not openly recognized to any great extent between or within these two camps. There were no significant neutralist tendencies in Western Europe to warrant Soviet policy change. Western "ruling circles" were seen as uniformly antagonistic to the Soviet Union and committed to a relentless struggle to reimpose the capitalist order. Nehru and those like him were essentially the "agents of imperialism," as was Tito. Such was the basically unworkable view from Moscow when Stalin died.

Significant alterations had taken place in this world view by the Twentieth Party Congress in 1956. Recognition of diversity within the non-Communist world (and to some extent within the Communist world as well) was at the heart of the new Soviet efforts to manipulate and persuade rather than coerce, to accumulate indirect influence rather than struggle for direct control. The 1954–1956 period marked the first major phase of this change. In 1955 the Summit Conference and the pronounced *détente* that accompanied it symbolized the first series of Soviet moves to attenuate the basic two-camp struggle of Stalin's years and to promote the develop-

[1] See Marshall D. Shulman, *Stalin's Foreign Policy Reappraised* (Cambridge, Mass.: Harvard University Press, 1963).

ment of what Palmiro Togliatti in April 1954 characterized as exploitable "intermediate" forces.

International moves by Moscow in this period almost uniformly reflected the changed orientation. The signing of the Austrian State Treaty on May 14, 1955 was entirely consistent with an intensified and, as it turned out, long-lasting desire to exploit neutralist and anti-American sentiment in Western Europe. Khrushchev's pilgrimage to Belgrade in May–June 1955 suggested a new sense of sophistication about the hitherto anathematized diversity within international communism (and may well have sharpened latent Sino-Soviet antagonisms). At this time also Moscow and the Western European Communist parties were seeking to tap new sources of mass sympathy and support within Western societies, as later evidenced in Khrushchev's Twentieth Congress pronouncement on the "peaceful transition" to socialism and in the new prominence assigned to Communist-guided peace movements in Soviet strategy. As we shall see, the striking disarmament move of May 10, 1955 was also conditioned by the new Soviet recognition of diversity in the non-Communist world.

Finally, the relaxation of frontal pressure on Western Europe that accompanied the *détente* of 1955 and the pursuit of indirect advances in relations with the West generally was accompanied by the initiation of the drive for influence in the economically underdeveloped world. The start of this campaign was signaled by Nehru's visit to Moscow in June–July 1955. Simultaneously there was an intensification of the tendency of the Communist parties in the "third world" to enter into collaboration with the "national bourgeoisie" they had so long treated with enmity. Moscow's new focus on the emerging nations was also reflected in the Czech arms shipments to Cairo, initially negotiated in the summer of 1955, and in the Khrushchev-Bulganin Asian tour later that year. While the Soviet leaders continued to emphasize the importance of the "Spirit of Geneva" to Asian audiences, the Soviet Union became the first power to detonate a hydrogen bomb from an aircraft — a fact whose significance could not be lost on the leaders of either the West or the "third world." Thus, as Soviet policy toward the West adopted a more cautious and complex mixture of blandishments and threats, Soviet political expectations centered increasingly on the erosion of Western influence in the new states and the expansion of an anti-Western "zone of peace" that would lay the basis for new additions to the Soviet camp.

In short, the pendulum movement long observable in Tsarist and Soviet foreign policy was occurring once more. In 1955, for the first time since 1919, Moscow seriously entertained the expectation that the socialist camp would in fact become the leader of mankind in the near future.[2] The path to victory, as in the 1920's, was expected to lead through the East and only from there to the West. Little noticed in 1954–1955, however, the changes in Soviet strategy toward the West and the "third world" were helping to create a long-term danger to Soviet interests in a politically hostile and, ultimately, a militarily threatening China. Certainly the Kremlin still hoped in 1955 to keep China within a Soviet-led Communist camp — a wish that helped to motivate the termination in 1954 of unfavorable economic relations that Stalin had imposed on Nationalist and subsequently on Communist China. However, the Sino-Soviet ideological differences that followed the Twentieth Party Congress in 1956 were probably in the air as early as 1955.[3] Although the nature of Peking's influence on Soviet policy in 1954–1956 is not clear, one can at least speculate that Moscow's desire to move effectively into the *tiers monde* was quickened by the realiza-

[2] See Alexander Dallin, *The Soviet Union at the United Nations* (New York: Frederick A. Praeger, 1962), p. 115.

[3] Walter C. Clemens, Jr., "Moscow and Arms Control: Evidence from the Sino-Soviet Dispute" (Cambridge, Mass.: Center for International Studies, M.I.T., 1965, mimeo.), pp. 3–6.

tion that Peking could also vie for leadership in Africa and
Asia, as was demonstrated at Bandung.

The View to the West

While the expansion of Soviet power and of international
communism was seen increasingly in terms of an extended
historical process, in the short term simultaneous collaboration and struggle with a heterogeneous adversary became
somewhat more possible. As we have seen, the broad foreign
policy trend of 1954–1956 to seek out and exploit differences
of interest and opinion — "intermediate forces" — in the
non-Communist world included a new Soviet political interest
in the disarmament and arms control issue to influence decision making in the West. This change in the Soviet approach
marked a significant step in the development of Moscow's
willingness to collaborate with its Western adversaries to deal
with the threat posed by contemporary armaments.

When the Soviet leaders looked to the West in these years,
they are likely to have seen opportunities to exploit in the
differences existing within the leadership of each major
Western country, including the United States, and between
the various NATO governments. To a lesser extent, new
advantage may also have been perceived in the exploitation
of differences between Western European governments and
their populations, especially in France and Italy. A hostile
and uncompromising foreign policy line toward the West
would diminish the various Western leadership divisions,
causing the divergent groups to rally around the flag in
defense against the Soviet threat — as must have been
brought home to Moscow by German entry into NATO on
May 9, 1955 via the Western European Union after long
years of the cold war. On the other hand, a less antagonistic
foreign policy line might well exacerbate Western elite differences, lower the military and political pressures from the

West, and facilitate local Communist advances in Western Europe.

The Soviet press gave an indication, albeit in flamboyant language, of the Kremlin's view of differences within the "ruling circles" in Washington.[4] On the one hand there were the "madmen" who backed "positions of strength" — Dulles, Nixon, Senators McCarthy and Knowland, Admiral Radford, General Gruenther, and the Pentagon as a whole.[5] Opposed to these "aggressive" forces were influential men who took a more "sober" approach to foreign policy — such as Adlai Stevenson[6] and Senators George and Mansfield.[7] President

[4] See William Z. Foster, "Usilenie fashistskikh techenii v SShA," *Kommunist*, No. 1 (January 1955); editorial, "The U.S. 'Policy of Strength' — Its Miscalculations and Failures," *International Affairs*, No. 2 (February 1955); N. Sergeyeva, "The Sentiment of the Ordinary American," *New Times*, No. 14 (April 2, 1955); E. Korovin, "The A-Weapons vs. International Law," *International Affairs*, No. 5 (May 1955); M. Krementsov and G. Starko, "Military Bases in Foreign Territories," *New Times*, No. 21 (May 21, 1955); editorial, "End the 'Cold War'!" *International Affairs*, No. 6 (June 1955); Y. Lebedev, "Adlai Stevenson on U.S. Foreign Policy," *New Times*, No. 27 (July 1, 1955); and editorial, "On the Eve of the Four-Power Conference," *International Affairs*, No. 7 (July 1955). All references to *International Affairs* refer to the journal published in Moscow (not London) unless otherwise specified.

[5] See A. Trianin and G. Morozov, "Podgotovka i propaganda atomnoi voiny — tiagchaishee prestuplenie protiv cheloveshestva," *Kommunist*, No. 8 (May 1955); Iu. Arbatov, "Imperialisticheskaia propaganda SShA — ugroza miru narodov," *Kommunist*, No. 7 (May 1955); "Dalles vastaivaet na gonke vooruzhenii . . . ," *Pravda*, May 27, 1955; A. Alexayev, "The U.S.S.R. Disarmament Proposals — A Major Contribution to Peace," *International Affairs*, No. 7 (July 1955); and editorial, "On the Eve of the Four-Power Conference," *International Affairs*, No. 7 (July 1955).

[6] Sh. Sanakoyev, "New Type of International Relations," *International Affairs*, No. 1 (January 1955); M. Slavyanov, "Firm Foundation of European and Universal Security: The Warsaw Conference," *International Affairs*, No. 6 (June 1955); Y. Lebedev, "Adlai Stevenson on U.S. Foreign Policy," *New Times*, No. 27 (July 1, 1955); editorial, "On the Eve of the Four-Power Conference," *International Affairs*, No. 7 (July 1955).

[7] "Zaiavlenie senatora Dzhorzha," *Pravda*, May 19, 1955; "Amerikanskii senator o soveshchanii," *Pravda*, June 18, 1955.

Eisenhower, although he received some criticism, was not linked among the "madmen" or the "healthy forces." Later in 1955 Moscow characterized Eisenhower's "Open Skies" proposal as well intentioned and "sincere" but subject to abuse by those around the President. The appointment in March 1955 of Harold Stassen as Special Assistant to the President for Disarmament Affairs was termed a maneuver to divert public attention from the U.S. government's policy of conducting a frenzied arms drive.[8]

In addition to opportunities for political use of the disarmament-arms control issue in relations with the U.S. leadership, Moscow also perceived important exploitable differences between Europe and the United States, among the NATO governments generally, and within European societies.[9] Many of these differences Moscow attributed to "farsighted" European tendencies toward independence from Washington. The Kremlin probably hoped for an even greater impact of its soft line in Europe than in the United States because of Europe's keener interest in disarmament and an end to the cold war, in the Austrian settlement, in independence from American policies, and in trade with the East; and also because of organized pro-Soviet peace fronts and Communist parties, especially in France and Italy. Even after ratification of the London-Paris accords, strong voices in France and the Federal Republic opposed West German rearmament.

Thus Soviet media pointed to "irreconcilable contradictions, overt and covert [that] are growing both inside each capitalist country and between them [and that] undermine the

[8] For a Lasting Peace, For a People's Democracy, April 1, 1955, and "The Friends and Foes of Disarmament," New Times, No. 13 (March 26, 1955).

[9] Editorial, "Mezhdunarodnaia solidarnost' trudiashchikhsia," Kommunist, No. 6 (April 1955); M. Slavyanov, "Firm Foundation of European and Universal Security: The Warsaw Conference," International Affairs, No. 6 (June 1955); editorial, "Za urkeplenie druzhby sovetskogo i iugoslavskogo narodov," Kommunist, No. 9 (June 1955); and N. Inozemtsev, "Amerikanskaia politika s pozitsii sily i Zapadnaia Evropa," Kommunist, No. 9 (June 1955).

military and political agreements of capitalist states from within."[10] Manipulation of these conflicts, Moscow may have hoped, would throw uncertainty into the NATO alliance and maximize the pursuit of policies independently of U.S. direction, which in turn would limit the policy alternatives open to Washington.[11]

General Implications for Policy

In place of the traditional Soviet efforts to expose Western "hypocrisy" in the disarmament negotiations and to provoke mass opposition to Western foreign policies with simplistic slogans to ban the bomb, the Soviet leadership showed an increasing interest in directly manipulating elite opinion in Western countries. Soviet political exploitation of the disarmament issue in 1954–1956, in conjunction with other moves for a relaxation of East-West tensions, assumed a more sophisticated form, seeking to obscure East-West antagonisms and to encourage the development of moderate opinion in and around the Western governments, especially in the United States. It must be borne in mind, however, that the disarmament concessions and other conciliatory gestures of the period were consistently reinforced by displays of Soviet military power. As we have noted, the 1955 May Day parade featured repeated overflights of prototype intercontinental bombers, the appearance of which had profound repercussions in American military circles. Similarly, the Soviet answer to Germany's entry into NATO was to cancel the wartime treaties of friendship with London and Paris and to form the

[10] M. Slavyanov, "Firm Foundation of European and Universal Security: The Warsaw Conference," *International Affairs,* No. 6 (June 1955). See E. Menzhinsky, "French-American Contradictions in the World Capitalist Market," *International Affairs,* No. 8 (August 1955).

[11] See Y. Zhukov's 1965 retrospect in "The Problems of European Peace and Security," *International Affairs,* No. 6 (June 1965), pp. 3–9.

Warsaw Pact a week later. These seemingly contradictory moves suggested a strategy aimed at building an atmosphere in the NATO countries inimical to the continuation of harshly anti-Soviet policies. The saliency of Soviet military power would give pause to whatever "aggressive forces" in the West might be weighing an attack on Soviet territory. More to the point, it would increase dissatisfaction with the policies of men like Secretary of State Dulles and German Chancellor Adenauer, who operated on the assumption of unremitting struggle between the two sides. The military consequences of such antagonism, the Kremlin made clear, should cause anxiety in America as well as in Europe. If, on the other hand, the West steered a more moderate course, the Soviet government pledged reciprocation. In Bulganin's words, Moscow would "support those . . . elements which show a desire to ease international tension and maintain peace."[12]

In this way Moscow evidently hoped to influence Western decision making to favor a number of interrelated Soviet policy objectives: to deprive the more antagonistic aspects of the Western policy line toward the Soviet Union of their justification; to dissolve the social and political basis of Western willingness to use nuclear weapons; to destabilize and demobilize Western military alliances, and specifically to undermine the position of American foreign bases; to neutralize the ability of the United States to make political use of its military force in keeping NATO together and threatening the Soviet Union; to discourage Western commitment to an all-out arms race; and to inhibit and prevent West German acquisition of nuclear weapons. Thus, Moscow could hope to influence the moral and physical base of Western military power by unilateral action not involving the political costs of agreement between adversaries.

[12] *New Times,* No. 21 (May 21, 1955). For a reassessment of Soviet proposals for European security, 1954–1958, and of the Eden Plan, see Y. Zhukov, "The Problems of European Security," *International Affairs,* No. 6 (June 1965), pp. 5–7.

That the May 10, 1955 and subsequent Soviet disarmament moves were aimed at influencing Western decision making at a high level was strongly suggested by Soviet propaganda restraint in the following months. Instead of focusing attention on the fact that the United States was re-evaluating its previous stand, even following the "reservation" of September 1955, Soviet propaganda was confined to stressing the positive prospects for *détente* and the desirability, if not immediate possibility, of disarmament. A poignant note was sounded at the Helsinki Assembly convened by the World Peace Council in June 1955, when "many speakers expressed regret that the new Soviet proposals were still not sufficiently known in the West."[13] As it was, this gathering had unexpectedly been postponed in April, apparently to take into account the new Soviet line to the West. Soviet propaganda's relative restraint was presumably based on the assumption that a hostile tone of exposure would have had the effect of neutralizing any tendency in the Western leadership to seek some accommodation with Moscow during the period of maximum *détente*. At the same time the Kremlin may also have been curious to see what policy line was forthcoming from the West, rather than foreclose possibly favorable developments in arms control or other areas by antagonistic action.

Implications for Disarmament

As indicated, the major comprehensive plan put forward by Moscow in 1954–1956 was that of May 10, 1955, which was reiterated at the Summit. While such a sweeping measure might seem suitable only for mass agitation, the fact that it seemed to accept some major elements in the West's negotiating position made the May 10 draft more useful for an appeal by the Soviet leadership to influential opinion in the West. Out of the complex staging of the May 10 proposal

---

[13] *New Times* (July 1, 1955).

Soviet propaganda usually seized on the issue of conventional force reductions, stressing Moscow's willingness to accept precisely those levels called for by the West. In the Soviet view, propagation of comprehensive disarmament, and eventually of what came to be styled "General and Complete Disarmament" (GCD), in the East-West negotiations and at the United Nations would also serve to condition the international political atmosphere, identifying the Soviet Union with the cause of peace in the "third world" and promoting public awareness of the disarmament problem, if not pacifist attitudes, in the NATO countries. In addition, Moscow could pursue the "fight for peace" involving the mobilization of peace fronts under the slogan of disarmament, while under this cover it could slowly begin to explore the possibility of measures to control the military environment with the United States. At the same time, the Soviet leadership might hope to promote public attitudes in the West that in its view would contribute to the social changes ultimately required for disarmament.

Implications for Partial Measures

While the partial measures that Moscow advocated in 1954–1956 could communicate directly to Western leaders at least some degree of interest in coming to terms on certain arms controls, Soviet proposals generally seemed designed to aggravate differences within NATO, especially in connection with the rearmament and full participation of Germany in the Western alliance.

The Soviet proposal of ground control posts to prevent surprise attack lacked ready mass appeal, and the main Soviet interest here was probably to encourage Western governments to recognize tacitly a mutual interest in avoiding the outbreak of war, if not yet in entering into joint measures to this end. This proposal may also have represented an attempt to lower the apparent Soviet military threat to the West by indicating a desire to stabilize the military environment. We may also speculate that in addition to the military-strategic desirability of having observers at SAC bases around the Soviet perimeter, the implementation of the ground control proposal would have reflected a Soviet political interest in reassuring the West against conventional attack in Europe, since Moscow certainly did not need such an agreement to learn of mobilization in the open societies of the West.

In addition Moscow may have hoped for a certain disruptive impact upon NATO. With West Germany a member of the alliance as of the day before the Soviet proposals of May 10, 1955, Moscow had a new interest in finding and exploiting points of difference between Washington and Bonn. Relatively feasible arms control measures affecting the European region offered a means to this end. The ground control post proposal might have some appeal to the U.S. leadership for military reasons, and would become more relevant in future years. But it would remain disadvantageous to the West German government, owing both to the hardening effect of such measures on the *status quo* in Central Europe, and to the limitations they would place on Bonn's freedom of action in the military and political spheres.[14]

Discussion of the disengagement issue with the West also offered Moscow certain political advantages. Coupled with the Soviet political use of intercontinental air power and the increasing deployment of Soviet MRBM's against Western Europe, indications of Soviet interest in disengagement helped to undermine U.S. influence in Europe. From the point of view of popular propaganda, Moscow's support for disengagement offered a means of mobilizing against NATO anti-American, anti-German, and neutralist sentiment in Western Europe and Britain. In particular, disengagement

[14] Several former U.S. negotiators interviewed during this research confirmed our impression that Moscow was willing in 1955 and after to pay a high political price in Central Europe to halt West German rearmament.

seemed to present a reasonable alternative to West German rearmament and to NATO plans (announced in December 1954) to deploy tactical nuclear weapons in Western Europe.

A less feasible measure, however, was the Soviet proposal of an all-European security pact to replace the military alliances of East and West. From the Soviet point of view, propagation of this measure clearly followed from the Kremlin's rising interest in obscuring the "two-camp" struggle between East and West. Like Soviet fraternization at the Summit with the leaders of the adversary states, and the new affability of the Soviet leaders at diplomatic receptions in Moscow, the proposal to dissolve the opposing military alliances reflected the new Soviet interest in moderating the East-West confrontation, in allowing somewhat less anti-Soviet opinion to gain influence in the West, and in reducing the external pressures that helped to maintain the unity of the North Atlantic alliance.

An issue on which Moscow could appeal both to influential opinion in the West and to mass sentiment throughout the world was the problem of nuclear testing. A number of events in 1954–1955 had dramatized the problem — the "Lucky Dragon" incident of March 1954, the February 1955 announcement of the U.S. Atomic Energy Commission on the unexpected contamination from strontium-90 as a result of nuclear testing, and the April 1955 opposition of the Bandung Conference to nuclear testing. Moscow sought to capitalize on this popular sentiment and in 1955–1956 began to put itself forward as the chief exponent of a test ban. In this the Soviet Government clearly sought to enhance its international image, and to stigmatize and inhibit Western testing. Perhaps the most clearly directed pressure was aimed at the British hydrogen bomb program, especially against the first British thermonuclear test early in 1956, when Soviet proposals called for the prohibition of thermonuclear rather than nuclear testing. Although the test ban problem had acquired leadership interest in both East and West by 1957, on the whole it remained politically somewhat novel in this earlier period and was more energetically exploited by Moscow as an agitational issue.

Having considered Moscow's view of the West and its political interests in proposing certain arms controls to Western governments, we may surmise that Western conduct in the months following the May 10, 1955 proposal resolved any doubt that Moscow might have entertained about the readiness of the "moderate" forces in Western governments to enter into meaningful disarmament measures with the Communist states. Nonetheless, it is conceivable that the Soviet leaders also perceived in the revision of U.S. positions in 1955–1956 an indication of a somewhat more serious approach to the whole problem of arms control and disarmament. Khrushchev's experiences at the Summit probably sharpened his awareness that Western leaders, above all Eisenhower, also recognized the suicidal nature of nuclear war and would probably do all they could to avoid such war. At the same time, even though the *pax atomica* was expensive and dangerous to maintain, it precluded Western efforts to "roll back" the Iron Curtain and would deter Western attempts to interdict the Soviet entry into the "third world." In this perspective there is no prima-facie reason to assume, as some have done, that the Soviets necessarily drew from the growing nuclear stalemate the conclusion that disarmament agreements were essential or possible. What *is* likely, given the shifting tides of strategy and outlook, is that a more reasonable negotiating position on control of armaments was put forward, much as it had been increasingly in the West, out of a new sense of urgency and of the seriousness of the problem but without great expectations for agreement.

The Internal Political Situation

A key factor in determining the shifts in the Soviet approach to arms control and disarmament was of course the arrival of new leadership in the Kremlin. In certain respects, the military-strategic, external political, and economic factors just enumerated were present, albeit to a lesser extent, in Stalin's day. What had changed most was the Soviet decision makers' perception of those factors and their reactions to them. Molotov, Stalin's close associate, continued to advance Stalinist views on foreign policy in 1955, deriving contrary conclusions to those drawn by Khrushchev in observing the same situation.

The zigzag in Moscow's external relations from September 1954 through May 1955, particularly on the disarmament issue, seemed to correspond with the changing power positions of Malenkov, Molotov, and Khrushchev. The intraparty struggle apparently proceeded in three stages. First, from Stalin's death to Malenkov's removal in February 1955, Khrushchev, Bulganin, Molotov, and others attacked and defeated the Malenkov-Mikoyan line featuring the "new course" in domestic economic policy, involving possible limitation of investment in defense and heavy industry together with tendencies to compromise in external relations. In the fall of 1954 there had been signs of a Malenkov-Khrushchev alliance against Molotov on foreign policy issues, including relations with Tito and possibly the disarmament move of September 30, 1954 and the settlement on Trieste in October 1954. However, a sharpening of the Soviet foreign policy line took place between November 1954 and February 1955 that strongly suggested a *rapprochement* of Khrushchev and Molotov with others for the purpose of ousting Malenkov. As a consequence, in February 1955 Moscow seemed to retract its negotiating offer of September 1954.

Second, after Malenkov's removal a grouping composed of Khrushchev, Mikoyan, Bulganin, and conceivably Malenkov seems to have been formed, as Khrushchev evidently led an attack against Molotov in February–April 1955. In this period the Soviet position on disarmament returned to the more conciliatory position of September 1954. By the end of

April 1955, following Soviet moves toward an Austrian settlement, the publication of Tito's criticism of Molotov in the Soviet central press on March 9, the promotion of eleven top military men, and the progressive change of the Soviet position in the disarmament negotiations on March 12, it seemed that Molotov's resistance had been broken. Late in April 1955 a decision was apparently taken by the Presidium to discuss Molotov's attitude at the forthcoming July plenum of the Central Committee of the Soviet Communist Party (CPSU). At the same time, however, *Pravda* and *Kommunist* reminded Khrushchev (not by name) that the Central Committee Secretary was chosen to execute the decisions of the Central Committee, suggesting that an alliance had coalesced to check further direct advance by Khrushchev.

Nonetheless, in the following weeks until the July plenum and the Summit Conference, the third period of the intraparty struggle, Khrushchev apparently preserved sufficient latitude to make a powerful attack on Molotov's position. By proposing foreign policy concessions Khrushchev may have been able to provoke debate and decisions within the Presidium that had the effect of isolating Molotov. By May 1955 the point had evidently been reached where the new foreign policy line could go ahead on all fronts, in effect locking Molotov out. This was formally confirmed at the July plenum when, with the new foreign policy line at its peak, the decision was taken to convene the Twentieth Party Congress. The shock of "de-Stalinization" that was to meet the delegates there had in fact been preceded by significant progress in the "de-Stalinization" of postwar Soviet foreign policy. It was doubtless no accident that one effect of the new foreign policy moves to strengthen "moderate" trends and weaken the "aggressive circles" within Western elites was to isolate and weaken Molotov and the more inflexible proponents of a "two-camp" struggle within the Soviet elite.

In addition to these domestic political uses of disarmament and arms control, Stalin's heirs had a more general interest in a breathing space in which to conduct the succession struggle and to stabilize a new rule. This meant that the proffered *détente* had to be persuasive to the West, which for years had demanded "deeds" of Moscow. And yet, domestic political considerations also placed a limit on Soviet policies that exceeded tacit understanding with the adversary. The Khrushchev-Bulganin regime is likely to have been insufficiently stable in the summer of 1955 to have carried out substantial agreements with the adversary, especially when the full extent of "de-Stalinization" and the political bargaining power necessary had yet to be determined. Although the modernization of Soviet society — the result of industrialization, urbanization, and education — created new pressures for freedom and welfare once Stalin had died, no mechanism existed by which these pressures could directly affect the Kremlin's policy. Although Stalin's successors stressed their devotion to the domestic and external issues most salient to the Soviet public — prosperity and peace — public opinion could still be molded and disregarded. Nonetheless, the pervasive modernizing tendencies in Soviet life should be counted among the forces that militated for a liberalization in Soviet foreign policy, and for the adoption of a more realistic approach to the problem of controlling the modern means of war.[15]

Ultimately, however, the basic question remained whether the Soviet regime and the international Communist movement could withstand the psychological-political impact of a long-term disarmament treaty, or of *détente,* and whether negotiated disarmament or an East-West entente might not vitiate the *élan* and the very *raison d'être* of communism. Even if we assume that Khrushchev and his associates faced up to this question, we can only conclude that the repercussions of a

[15] The most thorough discussion has been in Alexander Dallin *et al., The Soviet Union and Disarmament: An Appraisal of Soviet Attitudes and Intentions* (New York: Frederick A. Praeger, 1965), pp. 73–81.

possible disarmament treaty may have seemed far too hypothetical and remote in 1955. If they were actually faced, they probably made disarmament all the more inappropriate in view of Khrushchev's rising optimism about the future of Soviet communism. This optimism, as perceived by the new leadership, was a function of all the factors mentioned: military equality or superiority vis-à-vis the West, policy differences within and between the capitals of the West, opportunities in Asia and Africa, and expectations of Soviet economic growth and capitalist economic decline.

5

The Rise and Decline of the "Spirit of Geneva"

Despite the apparent narrowing of differences on disarmament in May 1955, and despite the rising "spirit of Geneva," it was clear halfway through the 1955 Geneva Summit Conference that both sides were still in fact taking opposite stands on basic questions. The reservation placed in September 1955 on all U.S. pre-Summit Conference disarmament positions made the differences explicit; at the rancorous Foreign Ministers' meeting in October the dwindling *détente* received a *coup de grâce*. Before bringing together the various strands into a picture of Soviet interests in the period, it may be useful to consider the factors pro and con that worked to promote and then subvert the movement toward *détente* and disarmament.

Factors Favoring Agreement

First, the virtual impossibility of achieving invulnerability to nuclear attack, the desirability of curbing nuclear production and proliferation, the fear that the opponent might make a technological breakthrough — all these expressions of a revolution in military strategy imparted a greater urgency to progress toward stabilizing the military environment. The desire in Moscow and Washington to avoid a nuclear holocaust was reinforced by increasing demands from the emerging nations of Asia and Africa to resolve East-West differences, halt the arms race, and stop nuclear testing.

Within the two alliance structures, proponents of West German participation in NATO delayed East-West summit talks until ratification of the London-Paris accords in April–May 1955, perhaps on the grounds that talks could then proceed from strength and without the danger of the debacle that befell the European Defense Community project. On their side, Soviet negotiators were presumably confident that Communist unity would not suffer from East-West negotiations. The ferment that was to be stirred by the February 1956 CPSU Congress had not yet weakened Moscow's influence in Peking and Eastern Europe. Soviet optimism about the growth of the socialist camp and the forces of "anti-imperialism" in general tended to outweigh cautions concerning the possible repercussions of *détente*. The Warsaw Pact, formalized in mid-May, offered "parity" in negotiations with NATO.

Finally, the "spirit of Geneva" was in large part a function of the new leadership in both Moscow and Washington. Khrushchev and Bulganin in Moscow, Eisenhower and Eden in the West were new men in those offices; they brought a new spirit of conciliation to East-West relations.

Negative Factors

On the negative side, the same factors that implied the desirability of curbing the arms race made it extremely difficult to do so. Nuclear production had already reached a point where hidden caches of atomic weapons could evade inspec-

tion. The fear that the adversary might achieve a technological breakthrough was accompanied, especially in Moscow, by hope that one's own scientists might overturn an
unfavorable balance of power. While the West hoped to improve its position in Europe via the new *Bundeswehr,* this
development produced increased anxieties in what soon was
formalized as the Warsaw Pact. And aside from these dynamic factors, the existing military situation in 1955 embodied many asymmetries that made it hard to find equivalent
strengths to trade off in disarmament agreements.

These factors, in combination with the uncertainties of
future technological development, meant that an extremely
complicated formula would be needed to persuade both sides
that their security could be enhanced by some package of
arms limitation or reduction. Comprehensive disarmament, it
is true, could erase the unique strengths of each side, but the
political prerequisites for such extensive measures were lack-
ing. The superpowers were not entirely ready for partial
measures such as a test ban or surprise-attack controls because of technological and political uncertainties as yet unresolved.

Ideological conflict, suspicions reinforced by historical experience, and continuing political disputes all conspired to
undermine and impede East-West *détente.* The range of
conflict appeared in the issues that one side proposed and the
other rejected for discussion at the Summit Conference:
liberation of Eastern Europe and an end of international
Communist subversion, suggested by the West; the seating of
Peking in the United Nations and the return of Taiwan to
Communist China, advocated by Moscow.

Although Moscow and the West agreed to side-step these
issues at the Summit Conference, the problem on which most
debate concentrated was (and remains) the most immediate
source of Soviet-Western conflict: Germany and European
security. Western insistence on "allowing" West Germany —
or a reunified Germany — to join NATO was diametrically

opposed to Soviet demands that Germany be neutralized as the price for possible reunification. The ill feeling resulting from this encounter vitiated whatever impetus toward disarmament or formal arms controls seemed to flow from the "spirit of Geneva."

The formal unity on both sides was to some degree in doubt. In the West it rested on persuasion and compromise of diverse interests; in the East it sprang from the fact of Communist rule in each country. Washington's flexibility in dealing with Moscow was sharply circumscribed by the objective of obtaining West German rearmament; as this goal became more an accomplished fact, it also became a basic factor in hardening lines between the alliances. And finally, the new heads of government, while more flexible than their predecessors, had by no means altered the fundamental objectives of their countries. Moreover, both had to contend with powerful conservative forces within their own societies.

Positive Aspects of the Proposals

As to the proposals themselves, they were characterized by greater realism and feasibility on both sides. Comprehensive proposals struck a more reasonable balance then ever before in the staging of conventional and nuclear disarmament. Although both Soviet and Western proposals in 1955 envisioned the complete destruction of nuclear weapons prior to complete disarmament, mutual recognition that their elimination should follow drastic conventional cuts foreshadowed the positions endorsed by both sides in 1962 and 1963 on the need for a nuclear umbrella throughout the disarming process. Both Western and Soviet comprehensive proposals in 1955 focused on the rough equivalent of what appeared as Stage II in the later general and complete disarmament plans — an aim that now appears more feasible than Stage III.[1]

---

[1] See, for example, Lincoln P. Bloomfield *et al.*, *International Military Forces: The Problems of Peacekeeping in an Armed and Disarming World* (Boston: Little, Brown, 1964), pp. 60–63.

Partial measures proposed in 1955 also reflected a greater sophistication, and foreshadowed an increasing East-West concern to inhibit surprise attack, halt nuclear testing, prevent frictions along the frontiers in Central Europe, and maintain high-level communications, particularly in times of international tension. Increasing awareness of the dangers of the spread of nuclear weapons, and of the complexities as well as the importance of international inspection, was now shown by Moscow.

In short, the new realism shown in manifest Soviet arms control policies correlated positively with the new acknowledgment in Soviet strategic thinking of the importance of surprise nuclear attack.

Negative Aspects of the Proposals

On the negative side, neither side had really done its homework. The U.S. negotiators in March and April 1955 made proposals beyond their probable capacity to deliver, given the review of American disarmament policy begun only in March 1955 and not completed until mid-November 1956. Basic research and analysis of inspection procedures to control a nuclear test ban, budgetary limitations, and other disarmament measures were seriously deficient — a fact repeatedly stressed by Western representatives in the latter half of 1955. The major Western response to the May 10 *démarche* turned out to be the "Open Skies" proposal, but Eisenhower's decision to present it was not taken until after the Summit Conference had begun and Bulganin had offered a more feasible variant of the May 10 program.[2]

Soviet disarmament positions seemed no better prepared

[2] Dwight D. Eisenhower, *Mandate for Change* (Garden City, N.Y.: Doubleday & Co., Inc., 1963), pp. 519–520; see also Robert J. Donovan, *Eisenhower, the Inside Story* (New York: Harper & Bros., 1956), pp. 345 ff. Details of the Donovan account have been contradicted by others close to the scene. But reports converge in relating that U.S. planners did not expect the Soviets to accept the "Open Skies" proposal but still believed it useful to put forward.

than Western ones. When examined, the proposal of May 10, 1955, for example, revealed an inner inconsistency in that it called for comprehensive disarmament by 1958, while at the same time emphasizing that sufficient confidence did not exist to permit agreement on the inspection of nuclear disarmament. A further indication of Soviet uncertainty in this period occurred earlier in 1955, when *Pravda* and *Izvestiia* on March 16 and 20 defended the uncompromising Soviet proposal of February 25, apparently oblivious to the more conciliatory position adopted by Gromyko in negotiations on March 11 and 18. Lack of realism and a portent of future difficulties were reflected by the absence of a major power, Communist China, at the negotiating table; Peking's participation, Moscow warned, was essential to any large-scale agreement.

What becomes clear about 1955 is that although it revealed the first glimmer of hope that the ideal of international agreement to reduce and limit arms represented a national policy instead of a purely utopian dream, nonetheless the conditions were insufficient either to generate a spirit of urgency about it or, more importantly, to overcome the negative weight of past conflicts, continued hostility, unresolved disputes, mistrust of intentions, and the general inertia that characterize a traditional mode of response. Thus the turning point was at best a partial and inconclusive one.

The Basis for Détente

It has been suggested that certain features of the Soviet May 10, 1955 proposal, notably its practical concern over surprise attack and its belated public recognition of the facts of life about nuclear stockpiles, could be construed as reflecting "sincerity" — always being careful to define "sincerity" as a serious intent to negotiate on a measure, and not necessarily a repudiation of international ambitions or an intention to negotiate a genuine political settlement. By these standards it is possible to conclude provisionally that in 1955 the new

Soviet leadership probably wished to "do something" about the arms problem to a degree that it had not previously.

But it must be emphasized again that Soviet disarmament diplomacy in this period — as always — was subordinate to the larger Soviet overview of the place of the Communist movement in history, the prospects for advancing its fortunes, and the choice of optional strategies for so doing. Soviet disarmament policy cannot be viewed, as disarmament sometimes is in the West, as autonomous, representing an imperative, whether strategic or moral, before which all other goals and strategies pale. The interplay between disarmament and security — or politics — remained crucial for both sides.

The apparent preference of Soviet leaders in 1954 and 1955 for a *détente* in East-West relations grew at least in part out of new calculations about the unacceptability of general nuclear war.[3] The specific disarmament and arms control measures proposed by Moscow were governed in turn by the basic decision to seek *détente*. But if *détente* was possible without surrendering on sensitive and vital points regarding inspection (that is, penetration and intrusion), the Soviets were not about to jeopardize their system for an abstract concept of arms control. On the other hand, if some arms control steps would create or reinforce a relaxation in the West, their price might be acceptable, and in any event virtue could be made of necessity by advancing a conciliatory position that "disarmed" the West politically and figuratively, if not militarily and literally. A "reasonable" position toward disarmament, even if spurned by the NATO allies, would tend in the long run to strengthen the moderates who wanted to soften the West's stance vis-à-vis the Communist camp. Demonstrations of Soviet military strength (bomber flights and H-bomb tests) mixed with assurances of peaceful intent would foster such "sober" thinking in the West.

In terms of feasibility the Kremlin seemed to assume that

[3] Some participants in the Geneva Summit meeting have concluded that one of its real achievements was the frank discussion, both public and private, of the consequences of all-out war.

while *détente* was both possible and desirable, disarmament, though desirable in some forms, was not so readily attainable. Soviet proposals for partial measures in 1955 and 1956 probably seemed more feasible and certainly less risky to Moscow than the more sweeping disarmament proposals. Some of these measures were probably in the interest of both sides; others were obviously of unilateral advantage. Demilitarized zones and control posts, for example, were advocated or endorsed by the West as well as Moscow. Although a source of potential political dangers, they could work to Soviet strategic advantage by reducing any assumed possibility of surprise attack from forward U.S. air bases. If the West had agreed to such measures, Moscow perhaps would have stood behind its proposals. Other Soviet proposals such as an all-European security system or the prohibition of nuclear weapons on German soil, while advantageous to Moscow, were clearly unacceptable to the West and therefore had potential only as propaganda. Soviet appeals to reduce troop levels proportionately and to liquidate foreign bases accorded with Moscow's military planning, but were infeasible then for the West. The major U.S. proposal — the "Open Skies" plan — was rejected by Moscow on the ground that it constituted "inspection without disarmament" and would pinpoint targets for SAC.

Perhaps the most significant factor underlying the change in Soviet strategy in this period was the military. If the uniquely destructive nature of nuclear weapons acted as a brake on Moscow's willingness to go all the way in war or in an arms race, the future prospects of potent, strategic nuclear weapons delivery systems must have had a contrary effect. Communists may be conditioned not to succumb to temptation, but temptation took the form in 1955 of an ICBM capability only a few years away, and the strategic outlook must have looked dynamic enough to make Soviet leaders hesitate to foreclose the possibility of a new trump card of this sort. But the prospect of improvement in the strategic balance may also have contributed to Moscow's hope that it could later negotiate from strength — including negotiations on arms control measures.

A series of complementary conditions can thus be assumed to have stimulated the shift in Soviet foreign policy and especially in policies toward arms control, which in practice interacted to produce a common orientation. The prime determinant was Moscow's acknowledgment of the policy consequences of the possibility of a surprise attack and nuclear holocaust. This consideration was reinforced by the desiderata for checking or neutralizing Western strengths (manifested by the ring of SAC bases, West German rearmament, and plans to employ tactical nuclear weapons in Europe), while maximizing present and expected Soviet advantages (in the form of medium and intercontinental missiles). These combined strategic reasons for avoiding direct conflict with the West were paralleled and buttressed by the political judgment that the harsh two-camp struggle of the late Stalin era had only strengthened Western unity and foreclosed opportunities to exploit differences within and between NATO governments and between the West and the emerging nations. The gains from the new Soviet strategy were expected to outweigh the political dangers to the *élan* and the unity of the Communist movement.

Of course there is no way to determine with assurance the outcome that Moscow anticipated would follow from its 1955 proposals. The very complexity and far-reaching nature of the May 10 comprehensive program (not to speak of the expected Western response) must have made the consequences of its implementation seem rather hypothetical. It remains entirely speculative whether, if confronted with Western acceptance in principle of the May 10 package, Khrushchev would have been prepared to make reasonable compromises that were necessary for agreement. It may be that the Soviet leaders themselves could not estimate the probable consequences of their proposals, but were willing on balance to gamble on political and economic victories as preferable in the long run to a policy geared to increasingly heavy — and dangerous — military emphasis. In this qualified sense we can conclude that Khrushchev and his associates were probably willing to live with their own proposals.

The strength of the many factors in the Soviet and international picture favorable to *détente* and arms control in 1955 proved to be surprisingly long lasting, persisting through bouts of cold war, and enjoying at least partial fruition in 1963. For Moscow and the West the 1955 negotiations laid the groundwork for technical improvement in disarmament proposals, both comprehensive and partial. More important, they helped to cultivate the frame of mind in which adversaries could collaborate in containing their potential for military conflict, looking forward to a day when a more profound consensus might exist between the parties.

PART II

FROM SPUTNIK TO CUBA: 1957–1962

A number of rather optimistic assumptions about the future of Soviet and Communist power had, we have speculated, a significant relationship to changes in the Soviet approach to arms control in 1954–1956. In the years 1956–1962, however, these calculations were shown to be faulty one after another, obliging Moscow eventually to reappraise and reformulate Soviet policy to accord with new realities.[1] In part the world continued to change; in part Soviet perceptions of the world became more realistic. In time Soviet policies were impelled toward still more radical adjustments than were apparent in the period from late 1956 to mid-1962.

During these years Moscow's public position on disarmament conformed to or amplified many of the innovations that had emerged in 1954–1956. In addition, certain tacit East-West controls were strengthened. Experts' talks on purely technical aspects of arms control were inaugurated, and produced some agreements. Joint agreement on the principles of a balanced and controlled program of compre-

[1] Richard Lowenthal, "The End of An Illusion," in *Problems of Communism*, Vol. XII, No. 1 (January-February 1963), pp. 1-10.

*hensive disarmament was achieved. A regional arms control
agreement was signed for Antarctica.*

*Again, only speculation is possible in seeking to disen-
tangle interests in arms control agreements from a possibly
transitory desire to lessen international tension. Furthermore,
while the manifest policies of each side often seemed to move
toward major agreement, as on a nuclear test ban, the curves
of apparent interest never completely intersected, and the
question always remained whether either side was ready to
make the concessions necessary for a compromise agreement.*

*The years from 1957 until the Cuban affair and its after-
math are significant for the refinement that took place in
Soviet thinking on the technical and political implications
of arms control; for the growing awareness in Moscow that
international politics may be seen as a "nonzero-sum" game
in which collaboration as well as competition can be advantageous to the adversaries; and for the profound changes
that came increasingly to militate for changes in Moscow's
approach to maintaining both its security and ideological
interests.*

*The 1954–1956 period can readily be viewed as a "round"
in which Moscow and the West sought to reduce tensions
and the danger of war. The years 1963 and 1964 may be
similarly regarded, as both sides stepped back from the brink
that they approached late in 1962. The years from 1957 to
1962 are much more difficult to categorize, for several reasons: one is the longer time span under review; another is
that the intensive moves of one side toward détente rarely
coincided with comparable movements from the opposite
side. More basically, whatever soft notes there might be were
often drowned out by hard notes in the policies of each side,
making it almost impossible to determine which theme, if
any, predominated.*

*Several ways of looking at Soviet policy during the 1957–
1962 period can be hypothesized, and each can find some val-*

idation in the record. First, Moscow's policy can be depicted as a linear, if zigzagging, curve leading continually toward détente and arms control. Second, this course can be regarded as a march, with occasional retreats, toward the overpowering of the West from a position of strength. Third, using the notion of "rounds," Moscow's policy can be viewed as an alternating hard and soft line, reflecting a possible ambivalence about whether to seek to dominate or collaborate with the West. Fourth, Soviet policy can be viewed as pursuing a hard and soft line simultaneously, using each one opportunistically to deal with the exigencies of time and place.

Such an analysis is the more difficult because, as Marshall D. Shulman has pointed out, both the left and the right syndromes of Soviet behavior may be used for offensive or defensive purposes.[2] A militant direct line could serve as a mode of revolutionary advance or as a way of imposing constraints on the adversary. A manipulative, more flexible style could be employed (as in 1955) to undermine the unity of the opposition while promoting an advance by other means.

Our perspective on the years from 1957 to 1962 is probably too short to determine whether the Kremlin's policy was moving determinedly toward détente with the West or toward a hoped-for power position from which it could dictate to the West. Both were probably true. Soviet policy, particularly on arms control, manifested both hard and soft tendencies. At moments, one or the other mode of behavior seemed to predominate; but usually both could be found. This simultaneity of apparent opposites may have reflected uncertainty in the outlook of the Kremlin leadership, divisions among the leadership, a dialectical response to a complex international and domestic situation — or a combination of these.

[2] Marshall D. Shulman, *Stalin's Foreign Policy Reappraised* (Cambridge, Mass.: Harvard University Press, 1963), pp. 4–13.

6

Strategic Doctrine and the Status of Forces

Continued evolution, in the years 1957–1962, in Moscow's view of the strategic situation and its implications for Soviet policy had the effect of furthering some of the developments in the Soviet approach to arms control noted in 1954–1956. But there were constants as well that may go far toward explaining the persistency of some features of Soviet arms control policy.

In the 1957–1962 period Moscow seemed neither to have feared a surprise attack from the West nor to have planned one itself, despite comments from both sides about pre-emption. The Soviet leadership evidently continued to calculate that an atmosphere of *détente* would help to lower the danger of a nuclear strike from the West. Since general war was not a prominent short-term expectation, medium-range planning could emphasize the political effects of the Soviet military posture rather than actual fighting capacity. Prototype rather than mass-produced weapons systems might to some extent be relied on, and a minimum deterrent could suffice.

But this strategy also meant that Soviet military secrecy would have to be maintained against the foreign observation sought by the West as the price of arms control agreements. For the long term, Moscow seems increasingly to have feared the spread of nuclear weapons, war by accident, a last-ditch capitalist reflex action, or catalytic war by a "revanchist" Germany (or an ambitious China). These considerations militated for agreements on certain forms of arms control.

Within this framework of continuity of outlook three stages may be noted: from 1955 to 1957 Moscow expected that the general military balance would soon turn to favor the East; from late 1957 to 1960–1961 the Kremlin showed confidence that, at least for "world opinion," the Soviet Union was regarded as the equal or better of the West militarily; from 1961 to 1962, Soviet confidence seemed to wane as the Kennedy administration dismissed in theory and in fact the possibility of a "missile gap" favoring Moscow. Underlying these perceptions were important concrete developments in Soviet strategic thought and in the East-West military balance.

Political Versus Military Factors

Throughout the 1957–1962 period Soviet military thought generally took account of traditional power factors as well as the facts of the nuclear age that had been officially acknowledged in 1954–1956. If questions of arms control policy had been left to military men alone, they might have decided that the Soviet Union should not reduce or limit either nuclear or conventional forces. But important differences of emphasis emerged between and within Soviet political and military elites.[1] Khrushchev sought to rely on nuclear-rocket

[1] The following analysis derives from a number of sources including Raymond L. Garthoff, *Soviet Strategy in the Nuclear Age* (Rev. ed.; New York: Frederick A. Praeger, 1962); Garthoff's introduction to *Military Strategy*, V. D. Sokolovsky, ed. (New York: Freder-

forces and reduce conventional forces, including the air force and navy. A secret session of the Central Committee in December 1959 (shortly after Khrushchev's return from Camp David and Peking) approved a one-third cut in the total number of Soviet forces. The proposed reduction set off another round of strategic debate at two levels: one was the economy-minded politicians versus the marshals; the other, the "conservative" marshals versus the "radical" ones. Defense Minister Malinovsky managed to hold a middle position, but inclined to the conservative viewpoint.

The practical outcome of the debate in 1960 was that the troop reduction favored by Khrushchev was begun, only to be halted in midstream by East-West tensions in the summer of 1961. Khrushchev's preferences were also manifested in the creation in May 1960 of a fifth branch of the Soviet armed forces — the strategic rocket forces. However, Khrushchev's suggestion to transfer demobilized soldiers into a territorial militia was not carried out, perhaps because the marshals feared it would serve to justify further cuts of military personnel.

The strategic debate continued after 1960 and was partially reconciled in the publication in 1962 of *Military Strategy,* the first over-all treatment of Soviet strategy since 1926. The basic orientation of the 1962 treatise followed the thrust of Defense Minister Malinovsky's address to the Twenty-Second Party Congress.[2] The book's editor, Marshal Sokolovsky, had been retired in 1960, perhaps because of opposition to Khrushchev's radical confidence in wonder weapons. The

---

ick A. Praeger, 1963); the introduction to the same book by Herbert S. Dinerstein, Leon Gouré, and Thomas W. Wolfe in the RAND Corporation's translation entitled *Soviet Military Strategy* (Englewood Cliffs, N.J.: Prentice-Hall, 1963); the Sokolovsky volume itself; and materials analyzed in Walter C. Clemens, Jr., "Soviet Disarmament Proposals and the Cadre-Territorial Army," *Orbis,* Vol. VII, No. 4 (Winter 1964), p. 778–799; and "The Soviet Militia in the Missile Age," *Orbis,* Vol. VIII, No. 1 (Spring 1964), pp. 84–105.

[2] *Izvestiia,* October 25, 1961.

articles collected in the book reflect a compromise between the radical and conservative schools but lean toward the latter. In Garthoff's words,

> The "Khrushchev doctrine," with its stress on *deterrence,* has been modified to meet more fully the requirements seen by the military for *waging* nuclear war should one occur. The compounding of these divergent professional views has required both ready forces to meet the contingency of a relatively short and largely intercontinental war (envisaged by the 'radicals') and forces to meet a protracted general war with extensive land theater campaigns (expected by the 'conservative' majority).[3]

Many conclusions of the Sokolovsky treatise had direct implications for Soviet arms control and disarmament positions, which will be considered in the following section. But it should be remembered that while the book may have reflected the views of the Kremlin's military advisors, this was not necessarily the outlook of the political leadership. The book was not a complete guide even to the military's thinking, since its impact on foreign audiences had to be considered.

East-West Balance[4]

The facts of the military balance in strategic weapons, as they can now be reconstructed, are sketched in Figures 6.1 through 6.4. Throughout the 1957–1962 period the West enjoyed a commanding lead in numbers of medium- and long-range bombers. In 1957 and 1958 the Soviet Union

[3] Introduction to *Military Strategy, op. cit.,* p. ix.

[4] This section is based largely on comparisons of Soviet and Western forces made by John H. Hoagland and presented graphically in the tables and figures in Chapter 6. The work is derived entirely from unclassified estimates in recent years. Heaviest reliance has been placed on the many estimates recently made public by the U.S. Department of Defense. The method used here in making these comparisons has been to consider only the number of vehicles in operational status. This approach is believed to provide a reliable if only approximate index of the strengths of both sides.

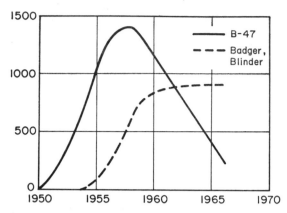

Figure 6.1.   Medium-range bombers.
Sources: see notes to Figure 2.1.

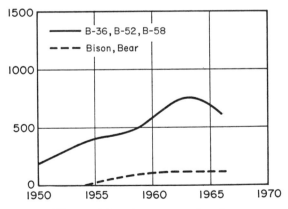

Figure 6.2.   Long-range bombers.
Sources: see notes to Figure 2.1.

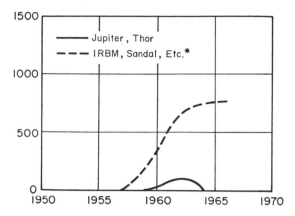

Figure 6.3.   Land-based MRBM/IRBM forces.

* West German sources place the total at 950 in 1965, 700 of which are targeted on Europe.

Sources: see notes to Figure 2.1.

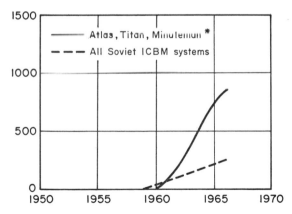

Figure 6.4.   ICBM forces.

* Totals exclude 544 U.S. and 120 Soviet submarine-launched ballistic missiles.

Sources: see notes to Figure 2.1.

began serial production of MRBM's. Comparable American Jupiters and Thors were not produced in such numbers because the U.S. deterrent was to be based more on long-range bomber and missile forces. Despite talk of a "missile gap," the only moment when the Soviet Union may have had more ICBM's on launchers than the United States was in late 1959 and early 1960. Even at that time, the Strategic Air Command delivery capability far outweighed the total Soviet capacity to strike North America.

By early 1961 it probably became possible for both sides to estimate that U.S. productive capacity would in the near future provide a vastly superior ICBM force and eliminate the deep-seated Western fears that had characterized 1959 and 1960. This turnabout was made possible mainly by the accelerated production of Minuteman, representing a new technology that finally emerged from the difficult post-Sputnik U.S. military development effort. The first Minuteman test launching occurred on February 1, 1961, and the first two Minuteman flights totaling twenty missiles were declared operational in December 1962. The Minuteman force grew very rapidly, as Figure 6.4 indicates. This rapid mobilization, coupled with broader public dissemination by the United States of its comparative force level estimates, probably helped precipitate the Cuban missile adventure. Possibly the Soviet leadership tolerated a knowledge of actual Soviet force levels held secretly within the U.S. defense community, but this was more difficult when these levels were also published before a world audience.

Throughout the entire period from Stalin's death until the Cuban missile crisis, America's strategic capability to attack the Soviet Union exceeded Moscow's ability to strike the United States. Since the mid-1950's and especially since 1959, however, the Soviet Union has possessed a minimum deterrent capable of inflicting great and perhaps "unacceptable" damage on the United States. And if the West chose to exaggerate the extent of Soviet power, Moscow did not object and seemed even to encourage such estimates.[5] Soviet secrecy, however, proved to be somewhat counterproductive to the extent that it goaded the U.S. effort to overcome non-existent bomber and then missile gaps.

Soviet R & D programs concentrated not only on the perfection of long-range delivery systems capable of lifting heavy payloads but on the development of high-yield warheads, culminating in the 1961 test of an H-bomb of over 50 megatons. By 1962 Moscow claimed to possess nuclear weapons of 100-megaton yield.[6] Khrushchev as well as Western analysts publicly doubted the military utility of such warheads,[7] but their sobering effect on the minds of men may have had great political utility in the Soviet view. Quite to the point, "deterrence" is rendered in Soviet Russian as "terrorization [*ustrashenie*]."

The one area in which Soviet military might has been unquestioned — its ability since the mid- to late-fifties to attack Western Europe with large numbers of medium-range bombers and (later) missiles — has also had heavy psychological overtones. At low cost to the Soviet Union, Europe has served as insurance against American pressure.[8] The Cuban episode clearly showed Moscow's interest in acquiring

[5] See, for example, Marshal Zhukov's boast of "diverse atomic and nuclear weapons, mighty guided missiles, among them long-range missiles," at the Twentieth Party Congress in February 1956, and the Sokolovsky claim of Soviet superiority in nuclear weapons: TASS, February 20, 1956, and *Soviet Military Strategy, op. cit.*, pp. 296–297.

[6] *Soviet Military Strategy, op. cit.*, p. 354. For a fuller documentation of Moscow's exaggerated claims during the period studied, see the introduction to *ibid.*, pp. 24–27.

[7] Khrushchev, speaking to the Socialist Unity Party (SED) in East Germany, declared that 100-megaton bombs were too large to be employed safely in Europe and that this yield represented the militarily useful limit of such weapons. (*Pravda*, January 17, 1963.)

[8] Reporting on an interview with Khrushchev, C. L. Sulzberger of *The New York Times* wrote in 1961: "Quite blandly he asserts that these countries [Britain, France, Italy] are figuratively hostages to the U.S.S.R. and a guarantee against war." Cited in the introduction to *Soviet Military Strategy, op. cit.*, p. 26.

a military posture important for its psychological effect along with its military utility.

Why Russia chose not to mass produce its ICBM's is a key question about which we can only speculate.[9] Did the decision reflect economic pressures? Faith in the adequacy of a minimum deterrent? Technological difficulties in producing more refined systems? The expectation of a quick-fix, such as Cuba or 50-megaton warheads seemed to offer, to "even" the East-West balance? A preoccupation with Europe? Or was it a combination of these and other factors?

Whatever the reason for the relatively low number of ICBM's Moscow actually produced, the distribution of these weapons between East and West clearly made it in Moscow's interest to propose in September 1962 that both sides reduce to "an agreed, strictly limited number" of nuclear delivery systems — the Gromyko "nuclear umbrella" proposal — during the process of general disarmament.

In regard to Soviet ground forces in this period, their role was highly valued by Soviet strategists, as the Sokolovsky volume made clear, especially in the "broken-back" aftermath of a nuclear exchange. They have nevertheless borne a large share of the reductions in over-all manpower of Soviet armed forces since 1955, as indicated in Table 6.1. During the 1950's, however, the Soviets carried out a complete modernization of their ground forces. Yet they continued to lack in most forms of strategic long-range mobility. Consequently their ground forces were tied to the Eurasian land mass.

Actual force levels are difficult to determine. Numbers or sizes are only relative indicators of absolute military strength. The size of the ground forces seems to have been fairly constant at between 2.2 and 2.5 million during the period 1957–1963. Available information does not indicate any

9 For additional discussion see the introduction to Herbert S. Dinerstein, *War and the Soviet Union* (Rev. ed.; New York: Frederick A. Praeger, 1962), pp. xv–xix.

significant down trend in ground forces in spite of the announced cuts in military force levels in 1955, 1956, and 1960. The 1956 cut was apparently executed; the 1960 cut, on the other hand, appears to have been started but then halted in 1961; the conclusion is that while in 1955 and 1956 the Soviets did reduce their ground forces, since then the level has remained fairly constant except for a brief reduction in 1960.

The total size of Soviet armed forces throughout the 1955–1962 period, however, exceeded by far the level that Moscow proposed for the initial stage of GCD. Thus, Soviet forces in 1955 totaled over 5.7 million and were reduced to their lowest point in mid-1961 — 3 million men. (The level that Moscow endorsed for the first stage of GCD varied between 2.1 and 1.7 million men.)

Table 6.1 also suggests the withdrawal and reduction of Soviet forces from Eastern Europe since 1957, an important point in analyzing the feasibility of various disengagement schemes for the Soviet Union. The great majority of Soviet forces in East Central Europe have been concentrated in East Germany.

Implications for Arms Control Policy.

Soviet military doctrine, taken with the changing balance of power, probably suggested to Moscow the desirability of two kinds of arms controls: those that would reduce the danger of surprise attack, accidental or catalytic war, or escalation; and those that would reduce certain Western advantages toward parity with Soviet strength. These desiderata, however, were probably to some extent vitiated by the expectation and then the achievement of a generalized assumption of over-all Soviet military superiority vis-à-vis the West. Following this, from 1960 to 1962, Moscow's waning military posture in relation to the West seemed to dictate

TABLE 6.1. SOVIET GROUND FORCES

	Men				Divisions						
Year	Ground Forces	Total Armed Forces	Announced Soviet Reductions of Total Forces	Total Airborne, Armored, Motorized, Rifle, Infantry, Artillery	Germany	Poland	Hungary	Rumania	European Russia	Central Russia	Far East
1945		11,365,000									
1948		2,874,000									
1955	3,200,000	5,763,000	640,000	175	22–31	?	?	?		(About 130 divisions west of Urals)	
1956											
1957	2,500,000		1,200,000	175	33 total						
1958	2,500,000	3,623,000	300,000								
1959	2.35 –2,500,000	3,623,000		175 (Many at reduced strength)*	22	2	4–7	?			
1960	2.24 –2,500,000	3,000,000 (July)	1,200,000	150	20	2	4	2			
1961	2.2 –2,500,000	3,800,000									
1962	2.2 –2,500,000	3,600,000		20	20	2	4	2	75		
1963	2.0 –2,200,000	3,300,000		140	20	2	4		75	32	17
1964	2.0 –2,200,000	3,300,000			20	2	4		75	22	17
1965	2,000,000	3,150,000*		140	20	2	4		75	22	17

STRATEGIC DOCTRINE: STATUS OF FORCES 101

Sources: *The Military Balance* [title varies] (London: Institute for Strategic Studies, 1959–1965); B. H. Liddell Hart, *The Red Army* (New York: Harcourt Brace, 1956); N. Galay, "The New Reduction in Soviet Armed Forces," Bulletin, Institute for Study of the USSR (July 1956); Lt. Col. J. B. White, "The Army of Communism," *Army Combat Forces Journal* (March 1954) Walter C. Clemens, Jr., "Soviet Disarmament Proposals and the Cadre-Territorial Army," *Orbis*, Vol. VII, No. 4 (Winter 1964), p. 779; William W. Kaufmann, *The McNamara Strategy* (New York: Harper & Row, 1964), pp. 21, 84, 120; *Disarmament and European Security* (2 vols.; London: Institute for Strategic Studies, 1963), Vol. II, p. A-13 (ii).

* Differences between earlier and higher estimates prior to 1963 and those for subsequent years may be due in part to changes in Western intelligence methods and not only to reductions in Soviet armed forces. Marshal Sokolovsky's claim in February 1965 that total Soviet armed forces had been reduced to the level of 2,423,000 projected by Khrushchev in January 1960 is believed to exaggerate the reductions made. But the ISS estimate of 2,000,000 Soviet *ground* forces in 1965 includes ground elements of the Air Defense Command, and some estimates place actual ground fighting personnel as low as 1,300,000. In any case there are three degrees of combat-readiness in the Soviet army and probably less than one-half the 140 divisions are at or near full combat strength. Perhaps 35 divisions of the total would require major reinforcement.

desperate Soviet efforts to re-establish parity or superiority rather than serious efforts at *détente* or arms control agreements with the West.

Some general comments on the Soviet approach to arms control arising out of Soviet military doctrine are also in order. *If* the conclusions of the Sokolovsky treatise were fully shared by the Soviet political leadership, a number of conclusions followed for Soviet arms control policy.

First, the official compromise reached between the contending military factions in favor of balanced forces suggests that, if Moscow entered a disarmament program, the Kremlin would have preferred "balanced" reductions of both conventional and nuclear forces rather than trying to eliminate first one or the other.[10]

Second, without disarmament, huge expenditures would be needed to sustain balanced forces. Because of Russia's economic situation in recent years, this prospect was not a bright one to the political leadership even in 1962.

Third, the Sokolovsky treatise also suggested that the most likely scenario for the outbreak of global war was a surprise attack by the West. In view of the crucial role of surprise attack in the initial stage of a war, Soviet forces conceived of their mission as being to pre-empt any Western plans for aggression. Although at the same time political estimates minimized the possibility of an American strike, these considerations may have combined with the Kremlin's awareness of the consequences of modern war to prompt a desire for safeguards to prevent surprise attack, particularly since Moscow may have in actual fact not been capable of a successful pre-emption.

Fourth, escalation of limited wars was still regarded as likely, but for the first time in Soviet writing the Sokolovsky book stated that Soviet forces must prepare for such conflicts. "Soviet military strategy must study the methods of waging

[10] The Soviet GCD proposal of 1962 was more balanced in this respect than its 1959 or June 1960 predecessors.

such wars too, in order to prevent their expansion into a world war, and in order to achieve a rapid victory over the enemy."[11] While such a view did not imply specific disarmament measures, it pointed to an emerging philosophy of broad restraints and arms controls. The relative absence in Soviet strategic writing of discussions of "controlled response" strategies — except to assert their futility — probably reflected a gap in Russia's military capability rather than any preference for "massive retaliation."

Fifth, continuing a Khrushchev theme of 1960, the Sokolovsky volume argued that tactical and strategic bombers were being replaced by missiles, but added that their "replacement may take a long time." For the present they could be used side by side with missiles and even be armed with air-to-ground missiles.[12] Thus, if the "radicals" among the Soviet marshals were not immediately ready for a "bomber bonfire," the possibility was not excluded for the future.

Sixth, no naval authors contributed to the treatise, but the book conceded that in a war with the United States the Soviet navy would play a greater role than in the past. Its first task would be to destroy enemy carriers and then submarines, although the U.S. Polaris threat was specifically minimized.[13] In accordance with the logic of the Sokolovsky volume and, probably more important, with Soviet naval weakness vis-à-vis the United States,[14] Moscow's GCD plan of 1962 proposed immediate liquidation of all submarines (atomic-powered and otherwise) and all surface ships capable of carrying nuclear weapons.

Finally, the Sokolovsky volume recognized that the instruments of nuclear attack were superior to defenses against them, and that in addition to pre-emption there was need for the development of active air defense based mainly on anti-

---

[11] *Soviet Military Strategy, op. cit.,* p. 288.
[12] *Ibid.,* p. 54.
[13] *Ibid.,* p. 55.
[14] See Table 6.2.

TABLE 6.2. COMPARISON OF STRATEGIC NAVAL MISSILE FORCES

	United States	Soviet Union
1959		First reports of modified Z-class conventional long-range sub to carry 3 short-range, surface-launched missiles.
1960	April: First successful underwater Polaris launch. November: U.S.S. "George Washington" operational with 16 Polaris A-1 (1200 nm) missiles.	Approximately 15 Z-class missile subs in production or operation.
1961		Approximately 6 nuclear-powered subs in construction.
1962	9 Polaris subs operational with total of 144 missiles.	18 Z-class missile subs in operation. Approximately 10 nuclear-powered subs, "some" carrying short-range, surface-launched missiles.
1963		30 missile subs, conventional and nuclear.
1964	12 Polaris subs operational with total of 192 missiles. Subs 1–5, Polaris A-1, 1200 nm; subs 6–18, Polaris A-2, 1500 nm; subs 19–41, Polaris A-3, 2500 nm.	400 conventionally-powered and 30 nuclear-powered subs. At least 40 can fire ballistic missiles and can carry an average of 3 such missiles.
1965	31 Polaris subs operational. About 500 fleet ballistic missiles.	370 conventionally-powered and 40 nuclear-powered subs.
Future	By late 1960's, 41 Polaris subs operational with total of over 650 missiles, range 1500–2500 nm. The Poseidon missile being developed will have nearly twice the payload of the A-3 missile and will replace the Polaris.	Continuing development and production of sub-launched ballistic missiles.

Sources: Same as Figure 2.1. See also Hanson W. Baldwin in *The New York Times*, December 11, 1960; and Frederick L. Oliver, "Soviet Navy Learns Value of Submarine," *The Christian Science Monitor*, January 23, 1961.

ballistic missile (ABM) complexes, and of civil defense.[15]
If Soviet theory did not yet appreciate the destabilizing influences that an ABM system could have on the total military
environment, the force of economic determinism may nevertheless have inhibited Moscow from attempting to develop an
effective defense against American missiles.

[15] *Soviet Military Strategy, op. cit.,* pp. 56–58.

7

The Economic Burden of the Arms Race

Moscow's interest in arms control, it was argued in Part I, derived little direct impetus from economic considerations between 1954 and 1956. The Kremlin seems rather to have made excessively rosy calculations about the future rate of Soviet economic growth and the savings possible through reliance on advanced military technology instead of conventional forces and massive inputs of personnel. From 1956 to 1962 the grounds of this optimism faded, one after another, presenting Moscow by 1961 or 1962 with strong economic incentives to reduce military spending, either directly by East-West agreement or indirectly as a by-product of international *détente*.

The decisive year marking a turning point in the Soviet economy's ability to sustain the arms race appears to have been 1958. From Stalin's death until 1958 the economic burden imposed by defense generally fell, as defense expenditures stabilized or declined and economic growth continued at a rapid rate. After 1956–1957, however, Soviet defense expenditures increased dramatically (see Figure 3.1, p. 52). But after 1958 the rate of Soviet industrial growth began to fall, thereby heightening the relative burden of defense spending. Further, by 1961 the political and military worth of an arms race with the West was itself becoming questionable, because the United States had begun to demonstrate that it could outspend and outproduce the Soviet Union in developing an arsenal capable of a "graduated response" to most forms of strategic and conventional warfare.

Thus, the economic incentive after 1958 to reduce defense spending was probably reinforced in 1961 by Moscow's recognition that it could not for the foreseeable future achieve any decisive gains in an arms race with the West. Moreover the burden of defense spending was impeding Soviet advance in what Khrushchev designated in 1959 as the main arena of East-West competition: economic growth. The lag in Soviet growth was preventing Moscow from fulfilling its promises of consumer affluence, from becoming the model for other countries to emulate, and — of lesser importance — from using foreign aid freely to influence the developing countries. The reasons for the decline in Soviet growth, to be sure, included many factors in addition to military expenditures, but if that one item could be substantially reduced, an accelerating effect might result.

Defense Expenditures

Very critical developments for Soviet arms policy seem to have taken place in the period 1955–1957 in the realms of both technology and defense spending. In 1955 the Khrushchev-Bulganin leadership rather ostentatiously increased the defense budget, in part for political reasons. Thereafter the *official* military budget fell off until 1957, and remained stable until 1961. Both total possible defense spending and total possible weapons systems development and procurement indicate a trough in 1956. Yet this was the very period when the Soviet Union was undertaking the research and development that led to the missile achievements of 1957.

Thus the Soviet Union entered a revolutionary phase in the development of weapons technology, one that held out prospects for eventual strategic superiority over the United States, under the banner of budgetary conservatism. Whether sharply accelerated spending was anticipated for the immediate future is difficult to determine. But the conservative nature of the early phase of ICBM development suggests that the original concentration was purely on prototype development. It could be argued that the Soviet leadership was unwilling to commit resources to a program for the development of an operational system until concrete and, incidentally, politically valuable test achievements had been registered. In any case, the Kremlin was probably confident that an economic short cut to strategic superiority had been found, since missile technology rendered the manned intercontinental bomber obsolete.

In 1958 and 1959 total defense and space spending rose very steeply, mainly, it appears, as a result of allocations to advanced weapons development. At this point the principal objective was probably to translate prototype ICBM development into an operational capability, a task that may well have proved more costly and difficult than had been previously anticipated. At the same time, considerable resources were probably devoted to expanding IRBM forces already technically operational. While the Soviet Union succeeded in this period in covering European targets with intermediate-range missiles, intercontinental striking power grew more slowly than Moscow had hoped and more slowly than most Western observers thought to be the case at the time. Rapidly rising weapons development and procurement outlays outstripped the savings that were produced by cutbacks in conventional arms production and military manpower. In short, it became clear in 1958 and 1959 that missile technology was not a cheap road to strategic superiority, but the Soviet leadership probably continued to regard as bright the prospects of eventually achieving superiority. In the meantime, the Soviet Union was profiting around the world from the propaganda impact of the missile gap that was widely assumed to favor Moscow.

The planned reduction of Soviet armed forces by one-third, announced by Khrushchev in January 1960, was justified by the First Secretary on the ground that modern technology permitted Soviet firepower to be increased even while the number of men under arms decreased. He indicated, as Soviet spokesmen had when Soviet manpower was reduced in 1956, that the demobilized soldiers would be a valuable asset to the nation's productive capacity. He also made the suggestion (not backed by Soviet military leaders) that the demobilized men might be trained in a territorial militia. Such a force, if established, could, as in China, be useful for organizing labor for projects in the remote regions of the country.[1]

In 1961 the Soviet Union announced the first explicit increases in defense spending since 1955, ostensibly as a response to the accelerated strategic build-up launched by the Kennedy administration.[2] In relation to the previous official defense budget, the increases of 1961 and 1962 were quite impressive (see Figure 3.1, p. 52). On the "total-possible-spending" curve, however, they appear as little more than a continuation of the post-1956 trend. It is probable that more than the first Kennedy budget (fiscal year 1962) and tension over Berlin in 1961 was behind the continued increase of Soviet arms spending: Moscow probably realized that a missile gap was in fact being created the other way. The Kremlin probably also perceived sometime in 1960 or 1961

[1] Walter C. Clemens, Jr., "Soviet Disarmament Proposals and the Cadre-Territorial Army," *Orbis,* Vol. VII, No. 4 (Winter 1964), pp. 778–799; and "The Soviet Militia in the Missile Age," *Orbis,* Vol. VIII, No. 1 (Spring 1964), pp. 84–105.

[2] At the officially declared ruble exchange rate, the announced increase of 31.44 billion rubles corresponded closely to the increase of $3.5 billion in the U.S. defense budget. See Alexander Korol, *Soviet Research and Development* (Cambridge, Mass.: The M.I.T. Press, 1965), p. 302, note 13.

that the imperatives of missile technology would force the Soviet Union to abandon its initial ICBM programs in favor of more sophisticated, second-generation systems. All this worked for continued increases in arms spending; it might be accurate to say that the Kennedy budget provided the motivation for making these increases public.

Defense and Economic Growth

Ascertaining the weight of defense as a component of Soviet gross national product (GNP) is one of the more hazardous aspects of a study of the Soviet economy in terms of national income. As might be expected, estimates vary with the methodology employed. Most estimates are consistent, however, in ascribing a decreasing weight to defense as a component of Soviet GNP over the past decade. It is probably safe to say that while defense accounted for 15–18 per cent of Soviet GNP in 1952, the range in 1962 was closer to 10–12 per cent.

Most indicators point to a gradual deceleration in the growth rate of Soviet industry from the mid-fifties through 1962 and beyond. Soviet claims show an average annual growth rate of 13 per cent for the years 1950–1955, and of slightly less than 10 per cent for 1955–1962. A reliable Western index, published by Greenslade and Wallace, indicates an average annual growth rate of 10.1 per cent for the earlier period, and 8.7 per cent for the years 1955–1961. More specifically, the Greenslade-Wallace data show that the growth rate of Soviet industrial materials production fluctuated between 11.5 and 10 per cent from 1954 to 1958. In 1959 it was 9.9 per cent; then it declined in 1960, 1961, and 1962 to between 5.5 and 6.8 per cent per year.

Thus the very dramatic increases in the absolute magnitude of the defense effort that occurred between 1958 and 1962, owing to the rapid growth of the Soviet economy over the past decade, did not reverse but only temporarily arrested the prevailing trend for defense to decline as a component of GNP. If the economic burden of defense is simply defined as its percentage of GNP, this burden was unquestionably less in 1962 than it was in the early fifties.

In the sense it is employed in this discussion, however, "economic burden" has other less precise implications that denote the kind of defense effort that might motivate the Soviet leadership to pursue certain international policies. The question we are concerned with addresses itself to the subjective priorities of the regime: the burden of defense can only be gauged in relation to the urgency of competing claims upon available resources, and defense as a percentage of GNP does not convey these subjective connotations of the concept of burden.

Maintenance of a rapid rate of industrial growth was probably the Soviet government's most urgent economic priority in the period under review. The policy of concentrating resources on the growth-oriented branches of industry remained substantially intact through the past decade in spite of variations in emphasis on the "heavy-industry line." Examination of the industrial growth record with reference to the changing level of defense spending proves informative in two respects. First, the performance of industry, in a broad sense, conditioned the relative burden of alternative claims on resources such as defense, consumption, housing, and agriculture. If industrial growth slowed, the claims of other sectors became relatively more burdensome since industrial growth was an overriding priority. Second, the defense effort may have exercised a direct retarding effect on industrial growth by cutting into resources available for investment and by diverting current material supplies and skilled labor away from the civilian economy.

Some retardation in growth rate had been expected by Western economists because of objective economic factors. As the stock of capital expanded, the burden of depreciation added additional strain on the investment resources of the economy. The capital output ratio for the economy as a whole had been increasing as larger percentages of annual investment had to be allocated to such nonproductive targets as housing and administrative facilities. Sources of rapid increments to the urban working force were drying up, at least temporarily. While there were still large areas of Soviet industry where borrowed technology could fruitfully be applied, the possibilities for gaining sudden and rather effortless advances in productivity through technological borrowing became more restricted than in earlier stages of industrialization, and the burden of indigenous nonmilitary industrial research increased. Of no mean importance has been the progressive obsolescence of Soviet planning and administrative formulas for directing the further growth of an enormous and already advanced industrial economy. For these and other reasons, equal percentage increments to gross industrial output were not as easily achieved in the 1956–1962 period as formerly. Thus there was a secular trend toward a declining industrial growth rate independent of the defense burden. But this trend acted to increase the defense burden in a subjective sense insofar as the allocation of additional resources to industry would have spurred growth.

Moreover, there is a distinct possibility that the higher defense outlays of recent years, both in magnitude and the quality of resources they represented, had a direct retarding influence on the industrial growth rate, at least in the short run. In the periods 1951–1952 and 1958–1959, when sudden and sharp increases in defense spending were observed, the growth of civilian machinery output showed a distinct retardation, undoubtedly because current inputs were diverted to military production. In the same periods, the portion of investment going to equipment and instrumentation in the economy as a whole showed a distinct decline, contrary to the long-range trend in the Soviet and other industrial economies. The defense effort was certainly responsible in part for the deceleration of Soviet industrial investment in recent years and thus must be assigned some direct causal role in the over-all industrial slowdown. It must be noted, however, that the *direct* impact of the defense effort on industrial growth was limited to the years 1958–1960. Civilian machinery output increased markedly in 1961 and 1962, suggesting that the defense acceleration announced in 1961 was more a continuation of the post-1956 trend than another sudden spurt.

Consumer Goods Production

Despite the ideological approval of "goulash communism" in the post-Stalin period, levels of popular consumption were probably the least pressing issue among the several economic objectives constantly in the minds of Soviet decision makers in the period 1956–1962. The welfare implications of communism receive heavy stress in ideological prognoses; but the concrete policy of the present is to maintain the rapid growth of industry and to solve the agricultural problem, and thereby to assure an affluent future for the Soviet people. There had been frequent flurries of attention to consumer problems in the years since Stalin's death, and in 1957 the regime undertook a massive campaign to solve the housing problem, one of the sorriest aspects of the Soviet welfare record. While a great deal of housing construction was undertaken, the campaign fell far short of meeting Soviet minimum standards for urban housing, and seems to have expired by 1961.

In 1960, after Khrushchev's visit to the United States, there were indications that a consumer campaign reminiscent of Malenkov's "new course" was to be launched. Moscow promised rapidly to overtake the West both in industrial and consumer production, and in fact the years 1958–1960 saw a steadily rising percentage of total state investment going to consumer industries. In 1961, however, this percentage began to fall and the traditional emphasis on heavy industry appeared unimpaired, probably associated with decisions on a harder line in foreign policy from mid-1960 till the Cuban crisis. Between 1950 and 1955 the growth of personal consumption was about 7 per cent per year. After 1955 improvements were markedly slower, probably about 4 per cent in 1960, even less in later years as industrial growth was slowed and agricultural production stagnated.

While the welfare concern of Soviet leaders was doubtless genuine, resource scarcity and their ideological predilections and relative immunity from popular pressures tended to make improvements in the Soviet standard of living largely a function of progress in industry and agriculture, which remained the immediate, practical preoccupations of the regime.

Implications for Policy

Soviet optimism about the course of the arms race seems to have been deflated by 1961. The absolute costs of the defense effort were probably rising faster than had been expected, and its detrimental effects on the economy were now being felt. For example, the expansion of the petrochemical industry, upon which progress on the agricultural front depended heavily, was undoubtedly jeopardized by the diversion of quality materials and skilled manpower to defense production. Operational ICBM forces were coming on the scene at a somewhat slower pace than had been originally anticipated. Most important, the increased defense efforts of the United States had transformed the pursuit of superiority into a race merely to keep the strategic gap from widening. Moreover, the technology of modern weapons, with its long lead-time factor, was forcing Soviet planners to make allocations on the basis of increasingly uncertain future expectations.

The unpleasant reality seemed to be that even strenuous efforts could not in the foreseeable future purchase Soviet strategic superiority via technological development. Merely to acquire a viable posture of minimum deterrence would require great expense. It appears that both the multimegaton explosions of 1961 and the Cuban escapade in 1962 were conditioned by frustration on the missile-production front, and were intended partly to recapture the psychological advantages of the post-Sputnik period as well as to uncover the key to genuine strategic superiority. At the same time, however, the "economic burden" of defense also began to reinforce other factors militating for a slowdown in the arms race — either by arms control or by a *détente* that altered Western defense policies.

8

Toward a Two-Front Foreign Policy

A distinct correlation between the shift in Soviet arms control policy and a broader turn toward softer modalities in Soviet foreign policy as a whole could be observed in 1954–1956. From 1956 to 1962, however, the basic patterns of Soviet foreign policy were more complex and their impact on Soviet arms control policy more difficult to discern. Soviet foreign policy throughout these years was increasingly engaged in a two-front campaign. Its successes and failures on one front would naturally interact with and affect its policies on the other front. Soviet arms control policy — because of its far-reaching military, political, and other implications — was naturally caught up in this two-front struggle.

As we look at Soviet policy on these two main fronts we should bear in mind that the general picture was profoundly influenced by the strategic and economic problems facing the Soviet leadership. The foundations on which the Soviet government had believed itself able to negotiate from strength were rapidly being eroded in 1960 and 1961, thereby introducing a note of desperation into Soviet relations on both

116

fronts that was not seen during the immediate post-Sputnik years, or indeed during the 1955 period.

Looking West

Two interlocking assumptions characterized the Kremlin's world view in this period, especially after 1959. The first was an expanding awareness of diversity among the Western elites, of a growing Western interest in *détente,* associated with the new analyses of arms control, that allowed Moscow the possibility of more active collaboration with the West in the absence of viable policy alternatives. The second was a growing belief that in the existing circumstances "compromise" would not constitute betrayal to the Soviet cause, but was rather an appropriate way of promoting it. Both can be seen as having contributed importantly to Soviet policy on arms control and disarmament, as the Kremlin's image of the West came to be a weightier determinant of that policy in the period under review than it had been in 1955. In order to strive for *détente,* not to speak of arms controls, without appearing "weak," the Kremlin had to believe that the Western leadership would respond in kind to Soviet conciliation and restraint.

Viewing the role played by "hard-liners" close to the centers of power in the West, the Kremlin was probably doubtful about the possibilities of far-reaching disarmament measures with the West. But it remained hopeful that an East-West *détente* was feasible, and "manifest" Soviet disarmament policies were generally keyed to appeal to influential opinion in the West. The 1955 Summit Conference indicated to Moscow that Eisenhower was a man of peace, surrounded however by advisers who kept him from following his natural inclinations. Although the East European uprisings in 1956 soured Soviet relations with the West for a time, they also demonstrated that the United States would not act with force to "roll back" the Iron Curtain. Strikingly,

Moscow and Washington found themselves supporting the same side in the Suez crisis in 1956 and, later, favoring India against China, at least by 1962. Washington's response to the Lebanon crisis in 1958 and, later that year, to the Soviet pressure on Berlin indicated that the West intended to "hold fast," regardless of speculation about a missile gap.

By mid-1959 the Soviet government had intensified its apparent commitment to negotiation and compromise with the West. Behind this lay a number of probable factors — Mikoyan's personal observations while visiting the United States in January, the deepening rift between Moscow and Peking, the apparent self-confidence that underlay the new Seven-Year Plan adopted early in 1959, and a change in the balance of forces in Washington with the death of Secretary Dulles in May. Reflecting the new accent in Soviet foreign policy, Moscow intensified its effort for an East-West summit meeting that might produce symbolic as well as tangible results. On June 20, 1959, according to Chinese sources, Moscow flatly refused China nuclear weapons assistance.[1] On July 27 the first of a series of Lenin documents on cultivating the "pacifist" bourgeoisie were passed to the press.[2]

Khrushchev's visit to the United States in September 1959 seemed to reinforce the Soviet line that negotiations were possible with the West. On October 31, 1959 he told the Supreme Soviet: "To put it bluntly, under peaceful coexistence states must meet each other halfway in the interests of peace." Khrushchev supported his argument by pointing out that the West had made concessions in dealing with socialist states, even though Western governments were opposed to socialism.[3] Again, in announcing a unilateral reduction of

[1] See the later part of this chapter for fuller analysis of this report.

[2] *Leninskii Sbornik* (Moscow: Gospolitizdat, 1959), Vol. XXXVI, pp. 451–455. (This is a collection of Lenin's miscellaneous writings, and is available in Russian only.)

[3] *Current Digest of the Soviet Press (CDSP)*, No. 44 (1959), p. 3.

Soviet armed forces on January 14, 1960 Khrushchev stated before the Supreme Soviet:

> While in the U.S.A. we became convinced that the most far-sighted statesmen, businessmen, and representatives of the American intelligentsia . . . want not a continuation of the arms race and further exacerbation of nerves but tranquillity and peace.[4]

The distinction between "sober-minded" and militaristic forces in the U.S. "ruling circles" was painted even more vividly elsewhere in the Soviet press.[5]

In April 1960, on the ninetieth anniversary of Lenin's birth, CPSU Presidium member Otto Kuusinen affirmed the existence of both moderate and aggressive forces in the West. He declared that a variety of factors had caused differences of opinion to develop in Western "ruling circles":

> The dichotomy in influential bourgeois circles is unquestionably significant for the success of the struggle for peace. Even in his time, Lenin pointed out that it is not a matter of indifference to us whether we deal with representatives of the bourgeois camp who gravitate toward a military solution of the question or with those representatives of the bourgeois class who gravitate toward pacifism . . . .[6]

At this same time the Soviet publication *New Times* produced an article giving a partial presentation of the 1922 Lenin documents on the Soviet disarmament and peace program made at the Genoa Economic Conference, published the previous year, as noted, in a relatively obscure source.[7] Al-

---

[4] *Ibid.*, No. 2 (1960), p. 8. Khrushchev added: "Any sensible person in the West who is a stranger to aggressive aspirations will reason approximately thus: 'Why should we increase our armed forces when the Soviet Union is undertaking a drastic reduction of its armed forces?' "

[5] See K. Semyonov, "Obstruction Tactics Continue," *International Affairs*, No. 8 (1959), p. 13; editorial, "The Burning Problem of Today," *ibid.*, No. 2 (1960), pp. 3–4; and L. Gromov and V. Strigachov, "The Arms Race: Dangers and Consequences," *ibid.*, No. 12 (1960), p. 18.

[6] *Pravda*, April 23, 1960.

[7] *Leninskii Sbornik, op. cit.*

though some Communists were presumably aware that these documents envisaged a purely instrumental use of a conciliatory disarmament posture in order to split Western elites, the *New Times* article in 1960 took them as evidence of a traditional Soviet commitment to negotiated disarmament and coexistence.[8]

After going out on a limb regarding the potential of the Camp David spirit, there is evidence that Khrushchev was embarrassed by Eisenhower's acceptance of personal responsibility for the U-2 flight. Nonetheless, while Khrushchev chose to break up the Paris Summit meeting, he indicated that the Soviet Union was not rejecting all negotiations, and added that it would be desirable to hold negotiations in six or eight months when the international atmosphere had cleared and the United States had elected a new President.[9]

The Kremlin seems to have viewed Kennedy's advent to power with cautious optimism, probably preferring it to a Nixon victory.[10] The December 1960 Statement of 81 Communist parties[11] and the January 6, 1961 address by Khrush-

---

[8] A. Leonidov, "The Making of a New Diplomacy," *New Times,* No. 14 (April 1960).

[9] N. S. Khrushchev, statement, *CDSP,* No. 20 (1960), p. 5. In his speech in East Berlin after leaving Paris, Khrushchev was willing to state: "If we can't get a working agreement or the settlement of disputed international issues with the present leaders of the U.S.A. or with the president who takes over from Eisenhower, we'll wait until the president after that." *Ibid.,* No. 21 (1960), p. 4. See also editorial, "The People Demand: Curb the Aggressor and Ensure Lasting Peace," *World Marxist Review,* No. 6 (1960), p. 5; and editorial, "A Policy of Perfidy," *International Affairs,* No. 6 (1960), pp. 3–4.

[10] See B. Marushkin, "Post-Election Thoughts," *International Affairs,* No. 1 (January 1961), pp. 50–54; L. Gromov and V. Strigachov, "The Arms Race: Dangers and Consequences," *ibid.,* No. 12 (December 1960), pp. 14–18; Commentator, "After the Elections, the Selection," *Pravda,* November 10, 1960, in *CDSP,* No. 45 (1960), p. 22. A more pessimistic view is expressed in Joseph North, "On the Eve of the U.S. Elections," *International Affairs,* No. 11 (1960), pp. 35–40; D. Kraminov, "New Tactics, Old Policy," *Za rubezhom* (February 25, 1961), p. 13, in *CDSP,* No. 10 (1961), p. 29.

[11] For text see G. F. Hudson, Richard Lowenthal, and Roderick

chev explicitly included statements that peaceful coexistence was favored by a definite section of the Western bourgeoisie — a section that Khrushchev said must be "used."[12] These assertions, of course, probably had as much to do with the Sino-Soviet dispute as with the Kremlin's view of the West or of Kennedy in particular, but it is significant that Moscow continued to advance them in the months following the U-2 incident.

The year 1961 was not propitious for Soviet recognition of "moderate" tendencies in the West. The new Kennedy administration came out with an increased defense budget; backed a major Soviet defeat in the Congo; allowed an invasion of Cuba with U.S. support; gave little ground in the Vienna meeting with Khrushchev; and matched or exceeded Soviet shows of force in Berlin. At the same time Moscow's relations with Albania and Communist China grew more strained as their polemics intensified. All these events conspired to limit Soviet freedom of action in dealing with the West on problems of arms control, although as we have noted there was some conciliatory Soviet behavior on the Joint Statement of Agreed Principles in September 1961. Thus, Khrushchev told the Twenty-second Party Congress in October 1961 that it would be "the gravest of mistakes" to imagine that "the imperialists have been brought to their senses."[13] And yet, in lifting the December 31, 1961 deadline for a Berlin settlement, he conceded that the "Western powers" had shown a "certain understanding of the situation . . . and were disposed to seek a settlement."[14] Moreover, in antagonistic

---

MacFarquhar, *The Sino-Soviet Dispute* (New York: Frederick A. Praeger, 1961), p. 189.

[12] *CDSP*, No. 4 (1961), p. 11.

[13] "Report by Comrade N. S. Khrushchev, First Secretary of the Central Committee of the CPSU, October 17, 1961," *Pravda,* October 18, 1961 in *CDSP*, Vol. XIII, No. 41 (November 8, 1961).

[14] Report of the Central Committee, CPSU, given by Khrushchev, *Pravda* and *Izvestiia,* October 18, 1961, in *Current Soviet Policies* (New York: Columbia University Press, 1962), Vol. IV, pp. 50–51. Cf. Gromyko's address of October 25 to the Congress, *Pravda,* October 28, 1961.

language he emphasized his main theme that Western leaders were taking a more reasonable approach to foreign relations.[15]

The ambivalence in Khrushchev's remarks in October 1961 proved to be almost symbolic of the vacillation and drift already noted in Soviet foreign policy generally in 1962. Moscow seemed unsure whether to emphasize a militant or a conciliatory line in dealing with its adversaries to the East and to the West. This vacillation was reflected in disarmament talks, where Moscow accepted in principle and then rejected an agreement on its proposal to ban war propaganda. Similarly, Soviet media and spokesmen alternated in presenting an image of a homogeneous or a heterogeneous adversary in the West.

In March 1962 the CPSU turned again to publishing Lenin's views on manipulating elite differences in the West through the use of the disarmament issue. This move, it should be noted, paralleled the opening of the Eighteen Nation Disarmament Committee (ENDC).[16] *Kommunist* also came out in March 1962 with an article signed by A. Arzumanyan, which obliquely referred to the desirability of exploiting elite differences in the West.[17] And in April 1962 *Pravda* and *Izvestiia* also printed photographs of the 1959 documentation, and added new archival materials on the decision-making process for the Genoa conference in 1922. In May 1962 the Soviet line toward Yugoslavia warmed again, an indication of a possibly more manipulative and softer orientation in Soviet policy generally.[18] The months of June and July also saw U.S.-Soviet agreements on scientific cooperation in outer

[15] "Concluding remarks by Comrade N. S. Khrushchev, First Secretary of the Party Central Committee at the Twenty-Second Party Congress, October 27, 1961," *Pravda,* October 29, 1961, in *CDSP,* Vol. XIII, No. 40 (December 13, 1961).

[16] L. Bezymensky and N. Matkovsky, "The Peaceful Coexistence Policy — Early Beginnings," *New Times,* No. 11 (March 14, 1962).

[17] A. Arzumanyan, "Vernyi put' obespecheniia prochnogo mira mezhdu narodami," *Kommunist,* No. 4 (March 1962).

[18] See, for example, *Pravda,* May 17, 1962.

space and, more importantly, on Laos. They also saw an exceptionally clear statement, which appeared in the Soviet journal for the world communist movement, of the need to differentiate in dealing with Western elites.[19]

At the same time, however, Khrushchev's election speech of March 10, 1962 had threatened the United States with a new "global rocket" capable of evading American warning systems and "invulnerable" to antimissile missiles; the Berlin issue continued to be agitated by the Soviet press; and, as the decision was made in the summer of 1962 to place Soviet missiles in Cuba, the Soviet press stressed the existence of a war danger arising from U.S. provocations in the Caribbean. This ambivalence in the Kremlin's private and public image of the West was not to be resolved until after the Cuban missile crisis, when Moscow seemed to have concluded that the United States was militarily strong and politically resolute but also stood ready to cooperate in reciprocal actions to keep peace and minimize tensions, and, where possible, enter specific agreements of arms control.

Looking East[20]

There was little evidence that China played any significant role in the decisions that brought on the shift in Soviet arms control policy in 1954–1955. But as early as February 1956, and certainly by the second half of 1957, the state of Sino-Soviet relations became a key determinant of the twists and turns of Soviet foreign policy generally and toward arms control in particular. The period under study was one of steady deterioration of Sino-Soviet relations, precisely in those areas that would most affect arms control policy —

[19] Adam Rapacki, "Socialist Diplomacy of Peace in the World Arena," *World Marxist Review,* Vol. V, No. 6 (June 1962).

[20] Some of the following points are discussed at greater length in Walter C. Clemens, Jr., "The Test Ban in Sino-Soviet Relations" (Cambridge, Mass.: Harvard University Center for International Affairs, mimeo.), 1965.

most prominently in the steadily increasing Chinese opposition to Soviet interest in *détente* and arms control.

The inducements toward accommodation with the West resulting from the Chinese political and — in the long run — potential military threat seem on balance to have been much more decisive than the restraints that flowed from Moscow's interest in keeping its most powerful ally within the fold.

The Chinese date the downturn of Sino-Soviet relations from the Twentieth Party Congress in 1956, while Moscow dates it from the Chinese ideological attacks of April and June 1960. One Western analyst sees the dispute as virtually irreparable after the summer of 1959 (subject however to a shift of leadership).[21] In any event, Moscow appears after 1959 to have decided to run whatever risks might be involved in pursuing its own course toward the West regardless of Chinese opposition. Although there were moments of lessened hostility, divergent political interests, ideological differences, and personal frictions moved Sino-Soviet relations almost inexorably toward an open rift.

According to Peking, Moscow had been "correct" until 1956 in calling for the complete prohibition of nuclear weapons, and China supported this view. But at the Twentieth Congress Khrushchev had stated that Russia would stop testing if other nuclear powers followed suit, and stressed that implementation of "such measures could pave the way to agreement on other more intricate aspects of disarmament." In Chinese eyes Khrushchev "divorced the cessation of nuclear tests from the question of disarmament. Subsequently [the CPSU leaders] were wrong on certain issues and correct on others, and we supported them in all their correct views."[22] And while Chinese objections to the ideological revisionism of Khrushchev were probably more muted in 1956 than Peking

[21] William E. Griffith, *The Sino-Soviet Rift* (Cambridge, Mass.: The M.I.T. Press, 1964), pp. 18 and 29.
[22] Chinese statement of August 15, 1963, in *ibid.*, p. 352.

later suggested, there can be little doubt that the Chinese leadership was dismayed at the vigor of the Soviet Union's economic and political march into the third world, especially since it was literally at China's expense.

Despite this early evidence of a Soviet interest in stopping the spread of nuclear weapons, the Chinese leadership decided in 1956 to depend on a transitional military strategy that required heavy reliance on the Soviet Union. Chinese hopes for Soviet nuclear assistance may have been fanned by Moscow's 1955 plan for sharing Soviet experience in the peaceful uses of atomic energy with the Communist bloc. By mid-1957 ten Chinese scientists were engaged in research in high-energy physics at the Joint Institute in Dubna. A research reactor and cyclotron, which the Soviet Union promised China in 1955, began operation in mid-1958.[23]

The strengthening of Khrushchev's personal position and the intensified Soviet commitment to Khrushchev's peaceful coexistence line, which followed the removal of the "anti-party group" in 1957, took place at the same time that the Soviet Union demonstrated its new military might by the successful launching of an ICBM in August and Sputnik I in October 1957. These dramatic feats suggested to Peking that the time had come for a more forward political strategy by the Communist camp; it turned out that Peking drew more radical conclusions from these successes than Moscow. For Mao Tse-tung, the ICBM test meant that the balance of forces had shifted in favor of the Communist camp; the East wind was now prevailing over the West wind. Soviet statements on the other hand averred only that the balance had turned in favor of the Communist bloc. The evidence suggested that Peking, convinced that the over-all strength of socialism outweighed that of imperialism, "was not hesitant to

[23] Anne M. Jonas, "The Soviet Union and the Atom: Peaceful Sharing, 1954–1958" (Santa Monica, Calif.: RAND Corporation RM-2290, November 20, 1958), p. 88.

jump the gun on Moscow in an effort to exploit the full significance of these developments in order to further Chinese aspirations."[24]

At the same time, Peking may have been encouraged at least temporarily to exercise restraint in its relations with Moscow by a Soviet commitment that, Peking later implied, bound Moscow to help China develop nuclear weapons. The primary source is a Chinese statement of August 15, 1963:

> As far back as June 20, 1959, when there was not yet the slightest sign of a treaty on stopping nuclear tests, the Soviet government unilaterally tore up the agreement on new technology for national defense concluded between China and the Soviet Union on October 15, 1957, and refused to provide China with a sample of an atomic bomb and technical data concerning its manufacture. This was done as a presentation gift at the time the Soviet leader went to the United States for talks with Eisenhower in September.[25]

Although there was little sign from the Chinese-Soviet scientific and military negotiations of late 1957 and early 1958 that Moscow had agreed to assist the Chinese with a nuclear military capacity, we do know that a large delegation of Chinese scientists headed by the president of the Chinese Academy of Sciences was in the Soviet Union from October 18, 1957 (three days after the pact is supposed to have been signed) to January 18, 1958, and that during this period agreement was reached for joint Soviet-Chinese scientific research in 1958–1962 on 122 different items. Later reports indicated the key fields in this research would be physics and the peaceful uses of atomic energy.[26] A hint that military matters were also involved in these negotiations came on November 6, 1957, when a high-level Chinese mission left for Moscow without prior publicity. Mao Tse-tung was also in Moscow in November and conferred with Khrushchev. Al-

[24] Alice Langley Hsieh, *Communist China's Strategy in the Nuclear Age* (Englewood Cliffs, N.J.: Prentice-Hall, 1962) p. 85.

[25] Document in Griffith, *op. cit.,* p. 351.

[26] Hsieh, *op. cit.,* pp. 100–101.

though different emphases in speeches by P'eng Teh-huai and Malinovsky on November 27, 1957 suggested that Moscow had not yet committed itself to providing nuclear weapons to China,[27] the Chinese foreign minister in May 1958 gave the first public indication that his country planned to produce nuclear weapons. A possible Soviet aid commitment in late 1957 or early 1958 might have taken the form of initiating (or intensifying) Soviet scientific and technological assistance to the Chinese nuclear weapons program. Such a commitment might well have been ambiguous, qualified, and long in term; it might have been tied to the 122-point scientific cooperation program agreed on in January 1958.

Soviet reluctance to aid China's nuclear program was no doubt deepened by Peking's independent course in domestic and foreign policy — as dramatically manifested in August– September 1958 in the bombardment of Quemoy and the initiation of the "great leap forward." The date of June 20, 1959, assigned by China to Moscow's refusal to provide a sample bomb, is consonant with the Soviet stress at that time on nuclear-free zones to which Peking was responding coolly. The timing of the refusal is also consistent with the Soviet broadcast to North America on June 12 assailing the "Washington claim" that the test ban under negotiation could not be trusted because China would not be a signatory. The broadcast accused Washington of persisting in this refusal "in order to have an excuse for getting out of all kinds of international agreements."[28]

After the Sino-Indian border conflict of September 1959, and Khrushchev's visits to Camp David and Peking, the Chinese began increasingly to criticize Khrushchev's pursuit of East-West *détente* and disarmament. In February 1960 the magazine *China Youth* called disarmament an "impractical fantasy" since the imperialists would never disarm themselves. In April 1960 came the Chinese broadside en-

[27] *Ibid.,* p. 102.
[28] International Service, Moscow, June 14, 1959.

titled "Long Live Leninism!" Imperialism had not changed since Lenin's day, it was asserted, and to attempt to negotiate disarmament or a relaxation of tensions was to mislead the people.[29]

The U-2 incident seemed somewhat to vindicate the Chinese image of the West. But Moscow continued in the following months to uphold its view that some members of the Western "ruling circles" took a sober and reasonable approach to East-West relations. Khrushchev now recalled Soviet specialists from China, sharply reduced Soviet trade with China, and reportedly tried to overthrow the Albanian leadership.

Following the attempted settlement at the 81-party meeting in Moscow in November 1960 there was an apparent lull in Sino-Soviet relations in 1961. This was shattered, however, at the Twenty-second CPSU Congress in October when Khrushchev denounced Albania, later breaking off diplomatic relations with Tirana. From March to September 1962 another outward lull seemed to prevail — a period of curious ambivalence in Soviet policy, as we have noted.

In late August 1962, however, according to Chinese sources, Moscow informed Peking of a decision to inhibit the spread of nuclear weapons:

> On August 25, 1962, two days before the United States and Britain put forward their draft treaty on the partial halting of nuclear tests, the Soviet Government notified China that U.S. Secretary Rusk had proposed an agreement stipulating that, firstly, the nuclear powers should undertake to refrain from transferring nuclear weapons and technical information concerning their manufacture to non-nuclear countries, and that, secondly, the countries not in possession of nuclear weapons should undertake to refrain from manufacturing them, from seeking them from the nuclear powers or from accepting technical information concerning their manufacture. The Soviet Government gave an affirmative reply to this proposal of Rusk's.
>
> The Chinese Government sent three memoranda to the So-

[29] *The Sino-Soviet Dispute, op. cit.,* pp. 82–112.

viet Government, on September 3, 1962, October 20, 1962, and June 6, 1963, stating that it was a matter for the Soviet Government whether it committed itself to the United States to refrain from transferring nuclear weapons and technical information concerning their manufacture to China; but that the Chinese Government hoped the Soviet Government would not infringe on China's sovereign rights and act for China in assuming an obligation to refrain from manufacturing nuclear weapons. We solemnly stated that we would not tolerate the conclusion, in disregard of China's opposition, of any sort of treaty between the Soviet Government and the United States which aimed at depriving the Chinese people of their right to take steps to resist the nuclear threats of U.S. imperialism, and that we would issue statements to make our position known.[30]

As a kind of corroboration of Peking's assertions, *People's Daily* charged on September 12, 1962 that the United States was obstructing the progress of the ENDC by demanding on-site inspections. But the article went on to indicate a deeper concern. The U.S.-U.K. statement on testing, said *People's Daily,* declared that the "treaty would make it easier to prevent the spread of nuclear weapons to countries not now possessing them. . . . The reason U.S. ruling circles are so interested in preventing what they call nuclear proliferation is not secret. . . . Washington is anxious to tie China's hands in developing nuclear weapons." *People's Daily* went on to say that "only a complete ban on nuclear weapons and the unconditional destruction of all existing nuclear weapons can prevent a nuclear war. . . . The discontinuation of nuclear tests . . . should under no circumstances become a means by which the United States may achieve and maintain nuclear superiority."[31]

[30] Document of August 15, 1963, in Griffith, *op. cit.,* p. 351.
[31] New China News Agency, Peking, September 12, 1962. This policy statement crowned a series of declarations on disarmament in which nuclear test cessation was generally made dependent on the banning of nuclear weapons. See Ciro Elliott Zoppo, *The Test Ban: A Study in Arms Control Negotiation* (Columbia University, unpublished Ph.D. dissertation, 1963), p. 385.

Did Moscow — as Peking alleges — inform the Chinese leadership on August 25, 1962 that it would sign a nonproliferation agreement with the United States? The Soviet rejection of the comprehensive and partial treaty alternatives proposed by Washington on August 27, 1962 gave no such clue. But, as we shall see, the Soviet negotiating position did shift slightly on August 29 and September 3, 1962, and Moscow's subsequent advocacy of the "black box" idea and the return to the three on-site inspections quota in the winter of 1962–1963 suggested that the Kremlin may have sought to move the test ban talks from a standstill.

On balance, one is left with the impression that the "nuclear war" problem and the "Chinese comrades" problem were proceeding for the Soviets on parallel tracks, and that what in fact was happening during this period was that the Soviets continued to give paramountcy to the "threat of war" problem but perhaps were becoming increasingly uneasy at the growing potential threat to the East. This took concrete form in adding to the urgency behind Moscow's interest in obtaining an end to nuclear testing and to nuclear spread. Consciously or not, the Kremlin's sense of common interest with the governments of the industrialized and *status quo* nations of the West was no doubt deepened as the *Weltanschauung* and strategy favored by Peking parted from that of Moscow. If a choice had to be made, it appeared increasingly that Moscow would prefer to alienate China than to forgo opportunities for policy successes in the West — especially if they helped to keep China from obtaining nuclear weapons or if they undermined the "dogmatist" position in the international Communist debate.

Disarmament as a Tool of Policy

The major objective of Soviet disarmament policy in the period 1956–1962 remained, as in the 1954–1956 period, the promotion of the Soviet Union's security interests with or without the enactment of East-West agreements on arms control. But there was this decisive difference: after 1956 the Soviet regime realized it was locked in a serious engagement on its eastern as well as on its western flank, and that a "hard" or "soft" move on one front would react and interact with events on the other. Before considering Moscow's political interest in specific measures we should consider the role that Soviet arms control policy could play in the over-all thrust of Soviet foreign policy in this period, first in dealing with the West and then in the international Communist movement.

Vis-à-vis the West. How did Moscow's disarmament policies tie in with the increased bargaining power accruing to the Kremlin from the alleged "missile gap?" While there was no simple "post-Sputnik offensive" pushing inexorably to force a Western retreat, there were soft and hard facets in Soviet policy, both of which sometimes served offensive and at other times defensive functions. Similarly Soviet arms control policy could function either in a basically soft, hard, or a combination of soft and hard policy for either an offensive or defensive objective. Examples may illustrate the diverse ways in which arms control proposals served Soviet purposes.

First, at times when Moscow employed primarily soft modalities to relax East-West tensions, arms control proposals served to strengthen the peace-loving image of the Soviet Union, to relax tensions, and to help persuade moderates in the West to move their governments toward *détente.* Such was generally the pattern from 1956 to mid-1960.

When Moscow reverted to a harsher line and to threats to obtain political objectives, Soviet disarmament proposals could provide a more conciliatory alternative, suggesting that acquiescence in Moscow's political demands would be rewarded by the strengthening of peace and improved control of dangerous situations. Thus pressure for a German peace treaty was accompanied in November 1958 by another version of the Rapacki Plan, which offered a reasonable-appearing arms control arrangement that could parallel a political settlement of the German problem.[32]

Third, a more conciliatory arms control posture could be used to thwart a tough Western response to tough Soviet foreign policies. Thus when Moscow was on the defensive over Hungary and engaged in a limited political offensive on Suez, the Soviet declaration of November 17, 1956 laid down a detailed disarmament program, presumably to recall Moscow's peaceful intent even while Soviet tanks roamed Budapest and Soviet volunteers were threatened in Egypt. Again, while the West endeavored to strengthen its defenses in Germany in the late summer and early fall of 1961, the Soviet government proposed a number of partial measures at the General Assembly to provide a reasonable solution to dangers in Central Europe. This stratagem differed from the parallel use in 1958 of Khrushchev's ultimatum and the Rapacki Plan in that by September 1961 there was no imminent prospect of a negotiated settlement, while in 1958 such a resolution was not foreclosed.

Similarly, Moscow's moves to resume nuclear test ban negotiations after the 1961 Soviet series of tests were obviously aimed at making it more difficult for Washington to resume testing. (The West also moved to resume test ban negotiations but eventually used the negotiations as a justification for more U.S. tests, since the Soviets turned down an effectively controlled ban.)

Fourth, arms control policy could contribute to a general program designed to intimidate the West and show Soviet displeasure over Western policies. Several instances suggest the point: breaking off DCSC negotiations in September 1957; resuming but quickly breaking off the Ten Nation talks in 1960 after the Paris Summit Conference; insisting in 1961 that the Soviet test ban proposal be accepted or that the test

[32] Warsaw announced a revised Rapacki Plan on November 4, 1958, while Khrushchev's demand for a "free city" of West Berlin came on November 10, 1958.

ban talks be submerged in GCD negotiations; refusing to approve a Soviet-sponsored ban on war propaganda in 1962 after U.S. troops moved into Thailand and after German Defense Minister Strauss wrote that the *Bundeswehr* should be armed with nuclear weapons.[33]

Fifth, the proposals themselves during 1956–1962 could also be interpreted as addressed to specific strategic threats. From 1956 through 1958 Soviet policy makers (with Polish assistance) worked hard to promote disengagement or other partial measures that would frustrate Western efforts to station nuclear weapons in Germany. In 1958 Moscow proposed an end to testing just after a Soviet test series had ended and Western tests were to resume. The nuclear-free-zone proposals of 1959 and 1960 were clearly aimed at frustrating U.S., French, and possibly Chinese plans to test or station nuclear weapons in the Balkans, the Baltic, the Far East, and Africa. The 1958 Surprise Attack Conference and subsequent negotiations provided an opportunity to publicize the dangers flowing from the ring of overseas U.S. air and (later) submarine bases. Throughout the 1956–1962 period vocal Soviet support for a nuclear test ban allowed Moscow to put pressure on the West to cease testing even while Moscow itself tested with an air of righteousness. And some of Moscow's most reasonable-appearing partial measures were put forward in September 1961 while the West was attempting to strengthen its defenses in Germany.

Sixth, "manifest" arms control policy was sometimes little affected by turns toward the left or right in over-all Soviet policy. Thus some progress continued to be recorded in test

---

[33] The Strauss article, however, had been written so long beforehand that it could only have been a pretext. Moscow's reneging on the war propaganda item may have been motivated in part by a desire to maintain a tense atmosphere that would help rationalize increases in Soviet food prices during the summer of 1962. The resultant embarrassment for the Soviet negotiator illustrated again how isolated disarmament affairs could be from the mainsprings of Kremlin policy.

ban negotiations following the 1960 Summit debacle, although GCD talks at the Ten Nation meeting were visibly affected. One explanation might be that Moscow wanted an agreement on nuclear testing and therefore decided to ignore all histrionics. It could also be that the Soviet Union had political reasons for keeping open this one line of East-West negotiations in which some hope for progress existed. Such progress might make a desired impression in Washington, Peking, and even in Moscow.

Finally, the diverse ways in which Soviet arms control proposals could serve the over-all thrust of Soviet policy to the West are suggested by the times and manner in which GCD was advocated: in September 1959, as a means toward *détente;* in June 1961, as a way to prevent further progress on test ban talks; in September 1961 (the McCloy-Zorin agreement), as a basis for further negotiations; and in 1962, as a device for promoting mass agitation at the World Disarmament Congress in Moscow, while other policy moves, both "hard" and "soft," were being weighed.

The most common function of "manifest" Soviet arms control policy, however, was to condition the political climate in which Moscow's strategic interests were to be promoted. This, on the whole, dictated an appearance of reasonableness and feasibility. This appearance was essential where Moscow's proposals aimed at East-West agreements or at a reduction of tensions that might achieve results similar to an agreement. In this spirit, the Soviet proposals most likely to strike the West as reasonable were partial measures on matters of mutual concern such as those involving surprise attack, nuclear testing, and, at least in London, the unsettled questions such as armaments in Central Europe.[34]

---

[34] A high-ranking French official explained in 1958 that his government's opposition to the Rapacki Plan was precisely that it might lead to the withdrawal of U.S. forces from Europe. In 1955 and later the Eisenhower administration showed interest in demilitarization of Central Europe, but could not obtain Adenauer's support.

Similarly, "restraint" rather than "exposure" was the usual way of dealing with Western disarmament positions. Moscow did often claim that Western intransigence was the main reason why disarmament negotiations had failed. But when compared with Soviet propaganda of the Stalin period or even with the treatment of other themes during the 1956–1962 period (such as Western policy toward the underdeveloped nations, or Western military strategy), Soviet criticism of Western arms control policy was relatively mild. This general picture must be modified, however, to take account of hardening in Soviet disarmament propaganda at various moments from 1956 to 1962 — usually in connection with some new manifestation of East-West tension. Such was the case in late 1956 and early 1957 (Hungary and Suez); in mid-1958 (Lebanon and Quemoy); mid-1960 (the U-2 and the Paris Summit); and 1961 (Berlin and related events).

Finally, a drastic innovation in Soviet propaganda to the West from 1956 to 1962 was a reversal of the traditional position on the economic consequences of disarmament for capitalist society.

Vis-à-vis the East. Arms control policy also functioned in this period as an instrument of limited value to Moscow vis-à-vis the Communist bloc and the international Communist movement. The relevant issues under this heading relate not so much to Moscow's long-range calculations about revolution in the West as to its more immediate problems of preserving Soviet influence in Eastern Europe, keeping the Chinese Communists within the Soviet fold (or, failing that, blunting their challenge to Moscow's leadership in the Communist movement), and promoting Soviet influence in the developing countries. The first and second tasks, moreover, relate not only to ideological desiderata but also to the safeguarding of Moscow's security from threats along its Western and Eastern frontiers. However, the long-term interests of Soviet state security and the existence of the regime in Moscow are deeply involved in the maintenance of Soviet influence in the international Communist movement and, presumably, in the movement's expansion.

The impact of Sino-Soviet relations exerted a decisive influence on Soviet arms control policy after 1956. Here we shall suggest only the political use to which Moscow put its arms control policy in dealing with the problems arising from its relations with Peking. The Soviet Union had an obvious interest in perpetuating China's military and political dependence upon Moscow. This was one reason why the Soviet Union might not want China to acquire nuclear weapons but also why it might offer limited aid to Peking in order to encourage Chinese reliance on Soviet assistance until 1959.

However, the problem of whether Moscow should aid China in acquiring nuclear weapons was obviously a delicate one for "fraternal" parties of such stature and with a long history of discord. Once the decision had been taken against nuclear cooperation, a test ban treaty between the existing nuclear powers offered a possibility of inhibiting the Chinese nuclear effort. Soviet proposals for a nuclear-free zone in the Far East also became a means of exerting pressure against China's nuclear program, and probably infuriated Peking. But at least to other members of the Communist bloc Moscow could claim that it was opposing nuclear proliferation to Germany.

Perhaps the main political use that disarmament policies served in Moscow's relations with Peking was to counter the Chinese challenge to Soviet ideological "revisionism." The Soviet approach to disarmament and arms control was increasingly a source of Chinese displeasure. But Moscow tried to turn the issue around and use it against Peking, arguing that it was incorrect to insist that Lenin's 1916 dicta on disarmament should guide Communist policy when capitalism no longer encircled socialism and when the means of warfare had been so greatly transformed (as, in Moscow's later phrase, the atomic bomb did not respect the class principle[35]).

[35] *Pravda*, July 14, 1963.

It was another matter whether the needs of Soviet state security and Moscow's role in the Communist movement could be upheld effectively against the Chinese threat by reliance on arms control and collaboration with the West. What arms controls would be effective — a test ban, a nonproliferation agreement, or GCD with a "nuclear umbrella" for the superpowers? The more attainable arms controls seemed also the less promising as ways of keeping China from membership in the nuclear club. Or should Moscow continue to fight a two-front struggle, hoping that Soviet military and economic prowess would deter the not-too-aggressive West and suffice for many years before the somewhat more aggressive Chinese became a great military power?

These were questions to which Moscow may not have given a firm answer in 1956–1962. But the evidence suggests that Chinese pressures goaded the Soviets increasingly toward attempts at arms controls and at disarmament propaganda that would impede if not check the Chinese military and ideological challenge.

9

The Soviet Interest in Comprehensive Disarmament Measures

Soviet Proposals 1957–1962[1]

In the period from 1957 until 1962 Moscow brought forward four different versions of comprehensive disarmament, all of which purported to deal with both nuclear and conventional weapons, and all of which spelled out the steps to be taken through a third and final stage of complete disarmament

[1] The U.N. Disarmament Commission Subcommittee (DCSC) was the main venue of negotiations in 1957, when, from March to August, its final session was held. In the aftermath of the Berlin crisis of 1961, the General Assembly endorsed a proposal of the three nuclear powers that an Eighteen Nation Disarmament Committee meet in Geneva early in 1962, composed of eight neutral states in addition to the five Communist and five Western states that made up the Ten Nation Committee on Disarmament in 1960. The Conference of the Eighteen Nation Disarmament Committee (ENDC) convened in Geneva in March 1962 without France, which consistently refused to take part up to 1966. The other members of the Committee included Brazil, Bulgaria, Burma, Canada, Czechoslovakia, Ethiopia, India, Italy, Mexico, Nigeria, Poland, Romania, the Soviet Union, Sweden, the U.A.R., U.K., and U.S.

down to the level of police forces needed for internal security and fulfillment of U.N. Charter obligations. The comprehensive proposals advocated by Moscow from late 1956 until late 1962 do not seem to have offered a promising basis for East-West agreement. The problems common to all of them were inadequate inspection procedures, in the view of the West, especially in the refusal to allow verification of declared levels of initial and retained armaments; an inflexible and probably unrealistic timetable of four to five years; provision for the elimination of overseas bases in the first or the second stage of disarmament; and U.N. peacekeeping forces subject to great power veto.

The Soviet proposals between late 1956 and August 1957 were particularly striking for the manner in which they backed off from the inspection procedures that Moscow had endorsed in 1955 and early 1956. The subsequent Soviet proposals of 1959–1962 had in common the structural defect that they would radically alter the balance of nuclear and conventional weapons one way or the other. Khrushchev's proposals to the United Nations in 1959 put off nuclear disarmament until Stage III. But the Soviet proposals of June 1960 and March 1962 would have reversed this priority and destroyed all nuclear delivery systems in Stage I and all nuclear weapons in Stage II. None therefore offered a promising basis for agreement, unlike those of May 1955 which had the merit of corresponding at least somewhat to earlier Western proposals.

Some narrowing of the differences between East and West resulted from shifts in Soviet policy in 1960–1962. Moscow displayed some awareness of the need for an international inspectorate to affirm that conditions were ready for the transition from one stage to another. Most important, perhaps, Moscow recognized in September 1962 the desirability for the nuclear powers to retain a limited number of nuclear contingents after the first stage of disarmament.[2] As the

[2] A revised version of the Soviet draft treaty that incorporated

1962 proposal, particularly as amended by September 1962, constituted the most feasible Soviet program for GCD in the period under review, it merits closer examination.

The 1962 Proposal

There were a number of ambiguities in the 1962 GCD proposal that indicated a lack of serious attention to its consequences. Some of the ambiguities would even redound to Western military advantage, as witness some possible effects of implementing Stage I:[3]

1. The over-all force ceiling proposed suggested that the reductions for NATO countries other than the United States would be of the same proportion as for the United States itself. The logic of this was that the forces of the Warsaw Pact countries would be reduced by the same percentage as applied to the Soviet Union. Since the percentage reduction of Soviet forces to a level of 1.7 or 1.9 million men would exceed that of the United States, the Soviet plan in effect discriminated against the entire Warsaw Pact.

2. The Soviet 1962 plan specified that the reduction to 1.7 or 1.9 million men should apply to civilian as well as military personnel in the armed forces. In that event U.S. forces should have been numbered at 3.6 and not 2.6 million men. Nevertheless, Mr. Zorin in the negotiations said that U.S. forces were to be reduced about 35 per cent, which would correspond to a reduction of the U.S. level exclusive of civilian employees.

---

this and most of the Soviet proposals since March was circulated by the U.N. Secretariat on September 24, 1962 as U.N. Document A/C.1/867. However, Soviet delegate Tsarapkin demanded that the West first agree in principle to the "nuclear umbrella" concept before discussions were begun on its details. See ENDC/PV.83, November 26, 1962, p. 22.

[3] The following analysis is based in large part on Institute for Strategic Studies, *Disarmament and European Security* (2 vols.; London, 1963), Vol. I, pp. 44 ff.

3. The plan proposed that *all* submarines — not just those that could fire missiles — should be classified as nuclear delivery vehicles and therefore be abolished in Stage I. This view stretches military facts to the point of naïveté in order to demand the abolition of the one class of naval weapons in which the Soviet Union is predominant in numbers, if not in quality.

4. Moscow's refusal to specify the number of strategic delivery vehicles in the "nuclear umbrella" also suggested a lack of clarity, deepened by the fact that Moscow's plan did not propose to abolish any nuclear explosives in Stage I. These could be delivered by commercial airliners, military transport planes, and interceptors, all of which were not restricted in the Soviet plan.

The three most basic issues raised by the Soviet GCD plan as amended in September 1962 were the implications of the nuclear umbrella scheme; the enhanced role of conventional forces; and the necessity of an international enforcement and peacekeeping machinery.

Soviet acceptance of the nuclear umbrella principle in September 1962, and extended in 1963, was an advance when measured against the position of June 1960 and March 1962 that all strategic delivery systems should be abolished in Stage I. It seems evident that any agreement to this principle would have to specify both numbers of vehicles and megatonnage to be permitted. Assuming such an agreement, the disadvantages of the principle for the West would have been the consequent need to rely on massive retaliation instead of graduated deterrence; the lowering of Western strategic forces more than the Soviet; encouragement of the development of ABM systems (since the permitted number of missiles might be sufficiently small to be intercepted); and increase in the role of conventional forces, in which the Warsaw Pact countries would, as discussed below, enjoy superiority in Europe.

The possible advantages of the nuclear umbrella for the West were that it might stabilize the arms race and encourage both sides to think of their relationship in other than competing strategic terms; limit the number of explosives that might be detonated in case of an all-out war; and imply a system by which other states would be kept from building up their nuclear missile capability.

The drastic reduction of strategic nuclear forces would have increased the importance of conventional forces in East-West relations. This, however, would have worked against the West, since the Soviet plan would have forced the withdrawal of American forces from all overseas bases. The Warsaw Pact would have been left in Stage I with a numerical superiority in Europe of about 500,000 men, and half the remaining NATO forces would have consisted of poorly armed Italian, Greek, and Turkish contingents. The U.S. troops would have been far removed from the danger zone of Central Europe, but Soviet troops would have remained relatively close. Communist countries could have trained their civilians in militia and other reserve units more effectively than the Western democracies. Finally, the withdrawal of American forces plus Western reliance on a U.S. "nuclear umbrella" stationed outside Europe might have seriously fragmented the NATO alliance.

The disadvantages for Moscow of the Soviet GCD plan were that it proposed a larger percentage cut for Soviet troops than for U.S. troops, and the withdrawal of foreign forces from foreign bases, which might weaken Soviet influence in Eastern Europe.

The impossibility in the American view of enforcing the abolition of nuclear weapons and the permanent fact of unorthodox delivery systems made nuclear disarmament possible (at least for Stages II and III), assuming only that an international force could deal with any remaining secret nuclear force. While the United States had not taken an explicit stand on nuclear arms for a U.N. force, Moscow explicitly refused to consider arming U.N. peacekeeping forces with nuclear weapons and, more important, insisted upon their being subject to great-power veto, even in Stage III.

In favor of the Soviet position were the arguments that under the "nuclear umbrella" the two superpowers could deter one another; and that an international peacekeeping force would be used mainly to regulate disputes between smaller states, thus saving the superpowers from head-on confrontations in marginal areas.

It can only be concluded that the Soviet position on GCD, even as amended in 1962, was primarily designed for its propaganda effect rather than for its negotiability.

Policy as Propaganda

Soviet propaganda for GCD has apparently aimed at creating a peace-loving image for the Soviet Union in the West, the developing countries, and perhaps domestically. The penchant for all-out disarmament may also have reflected a reaction to criticism from China as well as a diplomatic tradition going back to the 1920's, an ideological propensity for total solutions, some lack of sophistication about the skepticism with which such propaganda is viewed in the West, and may even have been prompted by the need to come up with a diplomatic sensation for Khrushchev's 1959 trip to the United Nations.

The Soviet regime may have sought the best of all possible worlds by what Bechhoefer has called a "two-pronged" approach — one prong seeking the political advantages of advocating an idealistic program of drastic disarmament, the other working toward partial measures that might be capable of immediate negotiation.[4] If so, however, the Kremlin seems in this period to have alienated many of those in the East as well as in the West whom it sought to impress. If the

---

[4] Bernhard G. Bechhoefer, *Postwar Negotiations for Arms Control* (Washington: The Brookings Institution, 1961), p. 324.

Soviet regime sought to use its GCD stand, with its implicit opportunities for a propaganda of exposure, to minimize Chinese criticism of Soviet *détente* policies, the Chinese response was to attack more virulently "illusions" about the "warless world" before the overthrow of capitalism. And if the Soviet government hoped to use its comprehensive proposals only as preliminary propaganda before proceeding to more manageable topics, the problematic nature of the Soviet GCD proposals could engender only skepticism among Western leaders endeavoring to discern Soviet intentions. While the grounds for this skepticism were partially removed by the McCloy-Zorin agreement in 1961 and, more important, by modifications in the Soviet program in 1962 including the nuclear umbrella principle, Moscow's reluctance to spell out the details of such principles still left Western observers with a most cautious attitude toward Moscow's policy on GCD.

The propaganda importance Moscow attached to its disarmament campaign is seen from the large number of changes in the Soviet line that were announced not in the negotiating chamber but in more public arenas. To give just a few examples, Moscow's acceptance in 1957 of the principle of inspection over a nuclear test ban was first stated by Khrushchev in Finland before Mr. Zorin reversed the Soviet stand in the DCSC. The Rapacki Plan was announced in the General Assembly in 1957 and modified in a press conference in 1958. Moscow's proposals for nuclear-free zones in 1959 were generally expounded far from any negotiating chamber. Khrushchev's GCD proposal was made to the General Assembly in 1959. The Supreme Soviet announcement in 1960 of a unilateral reduction in Soviet armed forces was communicated to all the parliaments of the world and to the Inter-Parliamentary Union, ostensibly to obtain reciprocal action in other states. The General Assembly was the forum for Gromyko's announcement in 1962 (and 1963) that Moscow endorsed a "nuclear umbrella" principle.

Perhaps the best audience for Moscow's GCD propaganda

was in the "third world," where the Kremlin could seek to offset competition from the West and from Peking by utilizing, *inter alia,* grandiose promises of the benefits that would result from great-power disarmament. Agreement on Soviet disarmament proposals would allegedly lead to the elimination of foreign bases and to the destruction of the qualitative advantage of military power by which the imperialists still resisted the quantitative strength of the oppressed peoples; and it would halt the nuclear testing that threatened their health. In addition, Moscow promised them what China could not — at least so plausibly — a huge transfer of its defense funds to the development programs of the new nations.

These protestations concerning the advantages of peaceful coexistence and disarmament were qualified by the Soviet position that the achievement of a disarmed world and the establishment of peacekeeping forces under the Security Council were in no way to impede the "struggle of peoples who are struggling for their independence and social progress."[5]

While at least perfunctory support of GCD is to be expected at all negotiations, heavy or exclusive emphasis on GCD has generally been a signal that Moscow is not ready for serious negotiations in areas of possible agreement. Such, we conclude, was the situation in 1961 when Moscow wanted to merge the test ban talks with GCD negotiations. And such was the situation in 1962 when Soviet policy drifted, momentarily uncertain as to the appropriate blend of antagonism and conciliation to be applied in relations with the West.

[5] Khrushchev, in part to protect the left flank against Peking, made clear on January 6, 1961 that wars of national liberation were still unavoidable because imperialism woud not give way voluntarily. Even Khrushchev's December 31, 1963 proposal to prohibit the use of force in territorial disputes suggested a possible escape clause for wars of national liberation, and for recovery by China and Indonesia of occupied territory by whatever means were needed.

10

Partial Measures: Promising Prospects

Khrushchev's address to the General Assembly in 1959, which contained the proposal for GCD, also advocated a number of more readily negotiable partial measures, and went on emphatically to reaffirm the relevance of the proposals of May 10, 1955. The Soviet government was still convinced, the Premier said, that the May 10 proposals "constitute a sound basis for agreement on this vitally important issue."[1]

A wide range of partial measures was espoused by Moscow from 1956 to 1962. Khrushchev's 1959 address to the United Nations mentioned five such measures that the Kremlin frequently endorsed in this period:

1. The establishment of a control and inspection zone, and the reduction of foreign troops in the territories of the Western European countries concerned.

---

[1] U.S. Department of State, *Documents on Disarmament, 1945–1959* (2 vols.; Washington: 1960), Vol. I, pp. 1459–1460. Hereafter cited as *Documents on Disarmament, 1945–1959*. Later editions, since 1961 published annually by the U.S. Arms Control and Disarmament Agency, are similarly cited.

2. The establishment of an "atom-free" zone in Central Europe.

3. The withdrawal of all foreign troops from the territories of European states and the abolition of military bases on the territories of foreign states.

4. The conclusion of a nonaggression pact between the member states of NATO and the member states of the Warsaw Treaty.

5. The conclusion of an agreement on the prevention of surprise attack by one state upon another.[2]

Here we shall single out two sorts of partial measures for special emphasis: regional arms controls and a nuclear test ban. These were the partial measures backed most consistently and with the most apparent interest by Moscow. By focusing on them we shall also be able to provide a framework for discussion of related matters — nuclear-free zones, and surprise-attack measures such as control posts.

Regional Arms Controls

As noted in Part I, Moscow responded warmly in 1954 and 1955 to the Eden Plan, and brought forward on March 27, 1956 a Soviet plan for the creation in Europe of a zone of limitation and inspection of armaments. A more radical formulation of these ideas was circulated in Soviet notes to the Western governments on November 17, 1956 — in the wake of the Hungarian uprising — specifying that all foreign bases should be eliminated in two years, but also accepting the principle of aerial inspection in Europe.

Variations of the March and November 1956 Soviet proposals were reintroduced by Soviet diplomats at the DCSC, and in notes to Western governments in the first half of 1957, in which Moscow again warned Bonn that arming the

[2] As quoted in *ibid.,* p. 1459.

Bundeswehr with atomic weapons would preclude German reunification.[3] Various East European governments also began to make disengagement proposals with the effect of reinforcing Soviet positions. A "Balkan zone of peace" without atomic weapons and joined in a mutual security pact was proposed by Romanian Prime Minister Chivu Stoica in September 1957.

The Romanian initiative was followed by a similar Polish move. Polish Foreign Minister Rapacki proposed his plan for a nuclear-free zone in Central Europe in a speech to the General Assembly on October 2, 1957. This first version of the Rapacki Plan suggested the creation of a nuclear-free zone to include Poland, Czechoslovakia, and the two Germanies. Nuclear weapons would be neither manufactured nor stockpiled in this zone; the use of nuclear weapons against the territory of this zone would be prohibited. The four great powers would guarantee these provisions by a "broad and effective control" comprising ground and aerial inspection. The plan did not propose merging NATO and the Warsaw Pact but argued that the "system of control established for the denuclearized zone could provide useful experience for the realization of a broader disarmament agreement." No provision was made for a reduction of troops in the zone.

A second version of the Rapacki Plan was brought forward by the Polish Foreign Minister at a press conference in Warsaw on November 4, 1958. Rapacki indicated that the revised plan was intended to meet the Western objections to his initial proposals.[4] A two-stage plan was now suggested: first, a freeze on existing nuclear weapons in the zone; second, a reduction of conventional forces and, simultaneously,

---

[3] The following analysis of Soviet bloc and Western proposals and commentary is based largely on documentation in Eugene Hinterhoff, *Disengagement* (London: Stevens and Sons, 1959). For a convenient summary and chronology of disengagement proposals, see his Appendix 10, pp. 414–442.

[4] For these objections see *Documents on Disarmament, 1945–1959,* Vol. II, pp. 936, 1023–1025; Hinterhoff, *op. cit.,* p. 229.

complete denuclearization of the zone. Both steps would be strictly controlled. The novelty of this revised Rapacki Plan has been exaggerated by some analysts: numerous Soviet statements backing the Rapacki Plan in late 1957 and early in 1958 had already advocated not only denuclearization but also withdrawal of foreign troops from the zone.[5]

The utility of ground control posts in Central Europe was stressed again by Soviet negotiators at the surprise-attack conference that met in Geneva from November 10 to December 18, 1958. Moscow made clear that these posts would be of little avail if not linked with other steps to reduce concentrations of forces in Central Europe. The Soviet government therefore proposed (a) a reduction in the foreign armies on the territories of European states and (b) not keeping modern types of weapons of mass destruction in either part of Germany.[6]

Another manifestation of Soviet policy toward Central Europe came on November 10, 1958 — the same day the surprise-attack conference opened — when Khrushchev announced that the occupation of Germany must be ended and West Berlin converted to a "free" city.

The reaction of the West to the Khrushchev stick and the Rapacki carrot was negative, however, and the Soviet response was to present still other proposals and to lift, temporarily at least, any semblance of an ultimatum on Berlin. From December 1958 to September 1959, variations on the Rapacki and free-city plans were put forward in talks by Khrushchev with Philip Noel-Baker, Carlo Schmid, Field Marshal Montgomery, and Hugh Gaitskell; in Mikoyan's press conference in the United States; in addresses to the Twenty-first Party Congress; and finally in the Soviet GCD proposal at the United Nations in September 1959.

[5] See, e.g., Bulganin's letter of December 10, 1957 to Eisenhower, *Documents on Disarmament, 1945–1959*, Vol. II, p. 924–926.

[6] U.N. Document A/4078, S/4145, Annex 8 (November 28, 1958), pp. 3–7.

Political Implications of Central European Disengagement

The Kremlin's strategic interests in Central European disengagement cannot be divorced from the political repercussions of such a measure. In the event the West accepted some version of the Rapacki Plan, U.S. and British forces would probably have to retire from the continent and the threat from German "revanchism" would be substantially reduced. For Moscow the threat of surprise attack, escalation, accidental or catalytic war — possibly involving tactical nuclear weapons — would be reduced. These strategic desiderata would probably have been judged by Moscow as justifying whatever loss of Soviet political influence occurred in Eastern Europe. After 1957 more than twenty Soviet divisions were concentrated in Eastern Germany but only two or three in Poland, Hungary, and Romania. The most serious loss of Soviet influence would be in East Germany, but that country was already an economic and political liability. The risk of its defection from the socialist camp did not necessarily outweigh the advantages of the neutralization of all Germany. The popularity of Communist institutions in other parts of Eastern Europe was increasingly staked on a kind of "new course." Soviet forces, in any event, would remain not far distant even if they withdrew from Poland, Hungary, and Romania, and disengagement would not affect the Soviet-based strategic forces that held Western Europe hostage against the United States.

If, on the other hand, the West refused disengagement, Moscow could still pose as the champion of peace; still tell Peking that it opposed nuclear proliferation to Germany and hence to China; and still sow dissension among and within the Western governments. Eastern Europe would still remain psychologically and militarily dependent on the Soviet Union against the threat from a revisionist West Germany, and, at the least, Communist propaganda for disengagement would tend to complicate Western efforts to station NATO forces in Germany and develop the *Bundeswehr*. The existence of divergent views on disengagement among the Western elites probably encouraged Moscow to continue its affirmations of support for various versions of the Rapacki Plan.

It is probably fair to say that Moscow has, at least since 1956, favored arms limitations in Central Europe, which, though potentially dangerous to Soviet political influence there, would admirably have promoted Soviet strategic interests. The revised Rapacki Plan of 1958 went far even toward accommodating Western complaints about the strategic imbalance that would result from merely denuclearizing the zone. Many strategists and political analysts in the West have argued the case pro and con, and the ultimate judgment on such matters would involve major assumptions about the role of Germany in NATO. What is clear is that by 1959 the governments in Washington, Bonn, and Paris had demonstrated an almost complete lack of interest in further discussion of disengagement in Central Europe. After 1959, therefore, even though Moscow might still have been willing to negotiate on regional arms control in Central Europe, its proposals could have only an indirect effect on the prospect for negotiations as a result of the limited propaganda effect of Soviet statements.

In the one contemporary example of formally agreed demilitarization of a significant territory, the Soviet Union, the United States, and ten other countries with interest in Antarctica signed an agreement on December 1, 1959 to use that territory "for peaceful purposes only." The parties obligated themselves not to build military bases there, carry out maneuvers, test weapons, or carry out nuclear explosions.

Toward a Nuclear Test Ban[7]

If disengagement represents an arms control problem that is predominantly political, the problem of halting nuclear

[7] The Geneva conference on the cessation of nuclear testing,

testing has been clearly complicated by intricate technological factors. But its political ramifications were global in scope both because of their relation to the nth-country problem, and because they reflected pressure from world public opinion.

At the outset, it is worth summarizing the involved story of the test ban negotiations as they influenced Soviet options. Here we can focus on the three major alternatives presented in terms of U.S. interest in effective controls and Soviet requirements for secrecy and military security: a comprehensive test ban; a partial ban with a moratorium on underground tests; a partial ban with no restriction on underground tests.

First, the several Western versions of a comprehensive treaty were unacceptable to Moscow because of the extensive control measures proposed. The Soviet versions were turned down by the West because they offered too little control. Western insistence on technical reliability was interpreted in Moscow as stalling or as a desire for espionage, while Soviet resistance to intrusion raised fears in the West that Moscow might cheat.

The second hope for a compromise agreement seemed to lie in a limited test ban accompanied by a moratorium on underground testing, during which control systems were expected to be improved so that seismic disturbances could be detected and identified with minimal or no intrusion. A number of obstacles prevented such a compromise.[8] First, the Soviet Union in 1956 and 1957 treated a test ban as a

which had well over three hundred meetings from its start in 1958, met for the last time in early 1962. Its members then gathered as a subcommittee of the ENDC, where the nuclear powers continued their deliberations on a test ban.

[8] Of course many other problems remained to be solved even if East-West differences were reconciled in the moratorium. As Eisenhower and Macmillan made clear on March 29, 1960, their agreement to a moratorium was conditional on progress in the negotiations concerning the composition of the international control organ, its voting procedures, and so forth.

separable measure but the West did not. Therefore the West turned down the Soviet proposal of June 1957 for a two- or three-year moratorium on all nuclear testing with international control posts on U.S., U.K., and Soviet territory. Second, after the West accepted the idea of a separate test ban in 1958 and a phased (that is, limited) test ban in 1959, the West tended to advocate a much shorter moratorium than was acceptable to Moscow. The Eisenhower-Macmillan statement of March 29, 1960 stated that the moratorium had to be of agreed duration. Moscow on May 3, 1960 proposed a limited ban with a four- or five-year moratorium, but the West on September 27, 1960 advocated a moratorium of twenty-seven months and on March 21, 1961 a moratorium of three years. Third, after Moscow resumed nuclear testing in 1961, the West turned down the very concept of a moratorium not formalized by treaty. Therefore the Soviet proposals of November 28, 1961 and August 29–September 3, 1962 for a limited test ban with moratoriums of indefinite length were summarily rejected. Fourth, when some momentum toward East-West agreement existed in the spring and summer of 1960, it was interrupted by political and military developments extraneous to the negotiations. Fifth, measures that one side would have found acceptable at one moment were proposed prematurely or too late. Thus the two- or three-year moratorium proposed by Moscow in 1957 corresponded with a position acceptable to the West only in 1960 and early 1961. And the four- to five-year moratorium advocated by Moscow in late 1961 and 1962 was not much longer than the three-year measure proposed by the West prior to the resumption of Soviet testing in 1961.

The third alternative was a limited test ban without any limitation on underground testing. This was offered to Moscow by the West on April 13, 1959, on February 17, 1960, on September 3, 1961, and on August 27, 1962, but it was not accepted until July 25, 1963.

A number of military considerations militated for Soviet

interest in a cessation of nuclear testing, if not in a formal treaty. One undoubtedly constant objective of Soviet policy was to prevent or impede the spread of nuclear weapons, whether the instrument of spread was U.S. bases on foreign soil or the acquisition or development of nuclear weapons by nth countries. Soviet propaganda and negotiating behavior endeavored to create a climate inimical to wider deployment and proliferation, even if no moratorium or treaty were signed.

Many examples may be cited. The early 1956 emphasis on banning thermonuclear tests was probably aimed at complicating Britain's plans to test a hydrogen bomb. A more serious Soviet concern has been to keep nuclear weapons out of Germany, and Soviet test ban proposals have usually been paralleled by additional plans for denuclearization programs. France's entry into the nuclear club seems to have been treated by Moscow as a foregone conclusion, but Soviet propaganda backed African protests against French plans to test in the Sahara. And by the establishment in Dubna in 1956 of a research center for peaceful uses of atomic energy Moscow may have hoped to sublimate, as it were, the aspirations of the Communist countries — especially China — for nuclear military power.

Soviet anxieties about nuclear proliferation to Germany were probably matched or surpassed by a desire to keep nuclear weapons from China, and the entire burden of Soviet propaganda against nuclear proliferation in the West could also be used to justify the Kremlin's denial of military assistance to Communist countries, above all to China, especially once it had been decided to deny China effective nuclear assistance. Early in 1959 Moscow agreed that the first article of a draft test ban treaty should allow all countries to accede, thereby dropping an earlier position that the test ban treaty should be limited to the three existing nuclear powers. Further, the differences in Soviet and Chinese statements during 1959 concerning the nature and desirability of a nuclear-free Far East suggest that Moscow was pushing Peking toward a commitment the latter sought to avoid. Finally, as we have observed, the Soviet government is reported to have notified China that it would enter into a nonproliferation agreement with the United States that had been proposed by Secretary of State Rusk.[9] (Press reports in 1964, however, indicated that Moscow had turned down a U.S. feeler in August 1963 concerning joint action to prevent the spread of nuclear weapons.)

The Soviet Union's unilateral test moratorium ran from March 31 until September 30, 1958, when Moscow began a test series that continued until November 3, 1958. Earlier that year, on August 22, the United States and the United Kingdom proposed a tripartite moratorium, which the Kremlin explicitly rejected on October 30. Nevertheless both Washington and London suspended all testing on October 31, and Moscow appeared to do the same after November 3, 1958. When the Geneva test ban negotiations recessed for six weeks on August 26, 1959, President Eisenhower directed that the U.S. suspension of testing be extended for the rest of the calendar year; Britain followed suit the next day. Then, on August 28, 1959, the Soviet Council of Ministers announced that "only in case of resumption by [the Western powers] will the Soviet Union be free from [its] pledge" not to resume atomic or hydrogen weapon testing. This commitment was renewed by Khrushchev on December 30, although Eisenhower warned on December 29, 1959 that the United States considered itself free to resume nuclear weapons testing, but would not do so without announcing its intention in advance.[10]

By 1961 another situation had developed. Although the

[9] See *Peking Review,* No. 33 (August 16, 1963).

[10] *Documents on Disarmament, 1945–1959,* Vol. II, Documents 252, 285, 308, 311, 317, 371, 372, 402; Moscow Radio, January 3, 1960. The Soviet Union later claimed that all the Western powers were profiting from France's nuclear tests in 1960–1961, but Khrushchev is said to have reassured a U.S. negotiator several months before the Soviet resumption of tests in September 1961 that Russia would never be the first to break the tripartite moratorium.

Soviet Union retained superiority in the ability to lift heavy payloads into space, the United States was producing far more nuclear delivery systems than Russia; this fact more than the Berlin crisis probably lay behind Moscow's decision to resume testing in 1961. After the 1961 Soviet tests in September and October, a panel of experts appointed by President Kennedy to evaluate Soviet progress agreed that "although the United States retained an overall lead in nuclear weaponry, the Soviet Union had made important cuts into the American leads and might have surpassed the United States in certain categories of weapons."[11] The evidence suggested that the 1961 tests had allowed the Soviets to reduce weight-to-yield ratios, increase the absolute yield of warheads, reduce the size of the fission trigger, and test new weapon designs under simulated combat conditions.[12] Nonetheless, following the U.S. and Soviet tests in 1962 Washington's appraisal was that the strategic balance still favored the West.

If Moscow's concern to halt nuclear testing was motivated partially by a desire not to pollute the atmosphere, this desideratum was clearly subordinate to military concerns. The Kremlin repeatedly rejected Western proposals that would have stopped atmospheric testing but either allowed underground testing to continue or to be prohibited, provided intensive inspection schemes were established. Although some observers doubted the utility of the large warheads exploded in 1961–1962, the Soviet Union appeared to achieve a kind of parity once more with the United States. The im-

[11] Robert Gilpin, *American Scientists and Nuclear Weapons Policy* (Princeton, N.J.: Princeton University Press, 1962), p. 254.

[12] *The New York Times,* December 8, 1961. (Publicly announced test totals at that time were: United States, 176; Britain, 21; France, 4 — for a Western total of 201 compared with 86 for the Soviet Union.) Ciro Elliott Zoppo, *The Test Ban: A Study in Arms Control Negotiation* (Columbia University, Unpublished Ph.D. dissertation, 1963), p. 471. However, President Kennedy stated on November 8, 1961 that the Soviet Union's total megatonnage tested was about 170, whereas the U.S.-U.K.-French total was about 126.

portance of the 1961 test series in Soviet eyes — either militarily or politically, or both — was reflected in a Soviet statement following the 1963 Moscow treaty to the effect that
neither side "gained" from the partial test ban, but that if
either party benefited, it was the Soviet Union, which possessed much larger warheads than the United States.

It is impossible to know with certainty whether or not
Moscow genuinely sought a test ban prior to 1963. The burden of available evidence suggests that the Kremlin sought
at least a *de facto* cessation of nuclear testing as early as
1957 and probably would have agreed to a comprehensive
test ban treaty then, provided intervention by international
inspection could be kept to a low level.[13] The 1957–1961
trend toward a narrowing of East-West differences was
spurred by concessions on both sides and by technological
improvements that facilitated control of a test ban with
minimal intrusion by inspectors in foreign territory. The
greatest stumbling block was the issue of underground testing, and the West had a greater interest than Moscow in
such testing and was more insistent on effective control. The
political price and loss of strategic secrecy decidedly created
major difficulties for Moscow.

In sum, disengagement may have been believed possible
until 1958 or 1959, by which time Washington, Bonn, and
even Paris came down firmly against it. A nuclear test ban
seemed to have strong support from Western officials beginning in 1958. But the high price that the West demanded
in terms of inspection, its condition that a ban should depend on progress on other matters, and the Western proclivity to introduce new scientific data into the negotiations,
may have cast doubt upon the West's ultimate intentions.

The greatest movement toward narrowing East-West differences came on the test ban issue. A general trend could
be observed toward greater understanding. Both sides began

---

[13] This assessment is shared by several U.S. negotiators interviewed by the authors.

to do their homework more effectively. Soviet writing began to show a greater familiarity with Western strategic thinking, especially after 1959. The Pugwash, Dartmouth, and other opportunities for informal discussions appeared to have some impact, generating both the "nuclear umbrella" principle and the "black box" system that Soviet diplomacy espoused in 1962. Each side seemed to believe that the test ban problem warranted concessions to the other's viewpoint. The West sought ways to reduce the amount of on-site inspection needed, and Moscow accepted specific inspection procedures — although acceptance was sometimes retracted. Technological improvements promised that national inspection systems could minimize or eliminate the need for international controls, perhaps even on underground tests. But although the two sides came tantalizingly close to agreeing on a moratorium on underground tests and a treaty banning all others, their respective interests never really coincided in the period.

Summary: Soviet Purposes Enhanced

Arms control policy was serving Soviet purposes in Eastern and Central Europe in a number of ways.[14] First, Moscow's disengagement proposals played on European fears of German "revanchism." The various modifications of the Rapacki Plan, especially in 1958, in ostensible response to Western objections, cultivated the impression that Moscow was quite willing to withdraw its forces from Eastern Europe if only the West would halt its plans for making the Bonn republic a forward base for another *Drang nach Osten*. Similarly, the Soviet proposal in 1959 to create a nuclear-free zone in the Balkans helped to reinforce a sense of political and

---

[14] The Soviet campaign to promote disarmament was generally popular in Eastern Europe, where economic hardship, dislike of Soviet occupation, and fear of renewed war combine to produce strong antimilitaristic tendencies among the population. Popular skepticism about Soviet motives, however, may have reinforced the need for plausibility in Soviet proposals.

military dependence upon Moscow to guard against any threat from NATO forces in Turkey or Greece.

Second, promotion of disengagement and denuclearized zones by Polish, Bulgarian, and Romanian leaders allowed the East Europeans some semblance of autonomy in the world arena. Polycentrism of course was increasing in spite of Moscow. But the Kremlin could probably have restrained the "people's democracies" from taking arms control initiatives had it wanted to. The fact was, however, that Soviet and East European interests seemed to coincide on regional arms control proposals, and it cost the Soviet Union little to allow Rapacki, Zhivkov, and others to act in concert with Soviet diplomacy. In fact a greater role for the bloc countries was needed to attain parity of Communist representation with the West, achieved when East European delegations took part in the 1958 technical talks, the 1960 Ten Nation Committee, and the ENDC in 1962.

The Soviet posture of favoring a test ban and nonproliferation of nuclear weapons to West Germany probably helped to justify Moscow's refusal to give the bloc countries nuclear weapons or technical assistance other than for peaceful uses. And, as suggested earlier, Soviet proposals for nuclear-free zones in the Far East, the Balkans, the Baltic, Africa, and other parts of the world offered a crude means of pressure to halt the spread of nuclear weapons as well as inhibit nuclear tests by China and the West.

The larger goals of halting nuclear proliferation and achieving a strategic balance favorable to the Soviet Union could be promoted by effective diplomatic and propaganda support for a test ban — whether or not an East-West agreement were reached. In this respect Soviet support of a ban on nuclear testing had greater potential appeal than the "ban the bomb" slogan of earlier years because the test ban issue could be portrayed in a manner that would appeal both to the "masses" and to the leaders in the West and the neutralist camp.

The test ban issue offered perhaps the best vehicle for continuing East-West negotiations on a topic of broad political interest. Such negotiations could promote *détente* and weaken Western advocates of an arms build-up and forward strategy. There was obviously much support for a test ban in the West, as the 1956 election campaign in the United States suggested and the 1958 moratorium on testing demonstrated. A conciliatory Soviet position on nuclear testing could thus offer a powerful instrument to intervene in the domestic political process in the West. This theoretical goal, as it turned out, was far from fulfilled because of the wide publicity given to Soviet recalcitrance on the issue of control and on-site inspection. Breaking the test moratorium in 1961 was especially damaging to Moscow's "peace-loving" image in the West. Even the 1961 Belgrade Conference of Nonaligned States offered a mild rebuke. And the 1961 General Assembly resolution against nuclear testing was implicitly addressed to Moscow as well as Washington.

Moscow's 1961 test series nevertheless helped to clarify the nature of Soviet propaganda objectives. Soviet peace propaganda was combined with the projection of a powerful and even terrifying image of Soviet military capacity, underscored by Moscow's announcement that it would explode a multimegaton weapon in October 1961. The Soviet Union may have felt compelled to demonstrate again that it was the military equal or superior of the United States, enabling Soviet peace propaganda, and, if desirable, Soviet policy, to proceed on the basis of negotiating "reasonably" from a position of great strength.

While Soviet propaganda for a test ban aimed to neutralize "aggressive elements" in the West it probably served to isolate opponents of *détente* in the Soviet leadership. Khrushchev and his supporters could cite technical data to argue that a test ban was in Moscow's strategic and economic interest. They could draw upon the prestige of Soviet scientists who stressed the health hazards of further testing. They could also point to the moratorium to which the West agreed in 1958 as proof of the possibility of limited collaboration with the adversary. Finally, Soviet negotiating behavior demonstrated to hard-liners in Moscow that the Khrushchev government was not going to agree to a test ban that permitted extensive or intensive intrusion on Soviet society or opened to the West important areas of military secrecy.

In addition to the military reasons we have mentioned, the resumption of nuclear testing by Moscow in 1961 probably offset criticism of Khrushchev's version of peaceful coexistence from his opponents in Peking and in Moscow. Such criticism had intensified after the U-2 affair, the Bay of Pigs, the first Kennedy military budget, and tension over Berlin in 1961. An incidental psychological benefit was of course the demonstration of Moscow's capacity to build and fire fifty-megaton bombs.

11

Khrushchev: Internal Challenge

The years from 1955 to 1962 were marked by several strong challenges to Khrushchev's leading position in the Kremlin power structure. In order to consider the kinds of internal pressures upon the First Secretary and (after 1958) Premier that may have shaped Soviet policy toward arms control and, more broadly, toward the Western world, a word should be said about the domestic interests that may condition Soviet moves toward agreements with the West.[1]

Contending Political Interests

The contending forces in Soviet society range across a broad spectrum but for purposes of a typology may be viewed in terms of (1) those forces most likely to favor disarmament and *détente,* and (2) those most likely to oppose it. Some of

[1] See also the discussion in Alexander Dallin *et al., The Soviet Union and Disarmament: An Appraisal of Soviet Attitudes and Intentions* (New York: Frederick A. Praeger, 1965), pp. 48–60, including the "note on Soviet policy-making on arms control and disarmament."

the elements in these groups may consciously collaborate, such as military and industrial leaders. Others, however, may act without coordination but for a similar goal, for example, the consumers and scientists in favor of cuts in the defense budget. During periods of international tension the demands of the consumers may be delayed. Thus Khrushchev explicitly blamed various East-West crises for the raising of food prices, the deferral of income tax reductions, and other inconveniences to the Soviet citizenry. In moments of international conflict the demands of the second group, already closer to the levers of power, would naturally carry more weight, and in crisis situations its support would be especially important for the party leader to maintain.[2] It appears likely that the elements in the second group exerted greatest pressure during times of high international tension but that Khrushchev most often preferred — for reasons of both internal and foreign policy — to damp such tension. If possible, he probably would have wished to help satisfy the demands of the consumers, assuming that the growth of heavy industry continued satisfactorily. With this structure in mind, let us turn to an analysis of the consolidation of Khrushchev's power in the period 1956–1962 and the challenges to it from within, the main ones coming in 1957, 1960, and possibly in 1962.

[2] An advisor on disarmament and other matters to three U.S. Presidents has written that there is "considerable evidence" the Kremlin finds inspection of disarmament unpalatable because of the pressure of a Soviet "military-industrial complex . . . that is, the Stalinist, militarist groups who distrust the United States, opposed Khrushchev's coexistence policy and generally advocate militant aggressive foreign policies." And "Russian officials and advocates of disarmament cite this opposition as *the main cause* of Soviet intransigence on the inspection issue." From *Where Science and Politics Meet* by Jerome B. Wiesner, pp. 170–171. Copyright © 1965 McGraw-Hill Book Company. Used by permission of McGraw-Hill Book Company. (Italics added.) That "advocates of disarmament" might exaggerate the role of conservative pressures is of course not excluded, perhaps even as a means of seeking further U.S. concessions. But its existence is reinforced by the abundant evidence of controversy between supporters of light and heavy industry and other opposing factions.

Although he was the most powerful figure in the Soviet Union by mid-1955, Khrushchev still had not secured complete dominance over the party Presidium. When revolution erupted in Poland and Hungary in the fall of 1956, in part as a result of his secret speech condemning Stalin, his position was greatly weakened. During the last months of 1956 and the first months of 1957 Khrushchev's power declined while the position of Malenkov and Molotov improved somewhat.[3]

During the first half of 1957 relations between the Soviet Union and the West were at a low ebb, but this had little to do with Khrushchev's weakened position and was mainly a consequence of events in Hungary and Egypt. In June 1957, Khrushchev's political opponents united in an attempt to remove him from power. That this was a "stop Khrushchev" movement and not a coalition united by agreement on either domestic or foreign policy can be seen by the fact that Malenkov and Molotov, despite their opposing policies, were able to join forces. Although outmaneuvered in the Presidium, Khrushchev was able to force his opponents to allow the Central Committee to make the final decision. Khrushchev had previously used his position as First Secretary to pack the Central Committee with his own supporters, and as a result five members of the opposition were removed from the Presidium (Malenkov, Molotov, Kaganovich, Saburov, and Shepilov) and one demoted to alternate status (Pervukhin). In their place nine full members were added, all of whom had close ties to Khrushchev.

Of special interest for Soviet policy toward the West, the ousted "antiparty group" was denounced for opposing the "party" policy of peaceful coexistence. However, no sharp impact could be noted on Soviet arms control policy. Shortly before the power struggle Khrushchev had agreed to the prin-

[3] Robert Conquest, *Power and Policy in the U.S.S.R.* (New York: St. Martin's Press, 1961), pp. 292–298; Merle Fainsod, *How Russia is Ruled* (Rev. ed.; Cambridge, Mass.: Harvard University Press, 1963), p. 169.

ciple of inspection of a test ban, and no radical alteration in arms control policy took place until late August when Moscow refused to negotiate further in the DCSC.

The defeat of Khrushchev's opposition and the latter's ouster from the Presidium marked the beginning of a new period in Soviet politics. Khrushchev's authority was bolstered still more by the removal of Zhukov in October 1957, Khrushchev's assumption of the post of Chairman of the Council of Ministers in March 1958, and Bulganin's removal from the Presidium in September of that year.

As Khrushchev consolidated his personal power and increasingly imposed his will on the Presidium, he relied less on the Central Committee. After 1957 and up to just before Khrushchev's own eclipse, the Central Committee declined just as it had earlier under Stalin. Agendas for the Central Committee came to be announced in advance, and sessions given widespread publicity like party congresses instead of being conducted in private as they were during a time of more "collective" leadership.[4]

At the same time, the policies of the Soviet Union, both foreign and domestic, often appeared vacillating and contradictory, indicating indecision at the highest levels. Some Western analysts expressed the opinion that these changes were due to the continued existence of strong limitations on Khrushchev's power.[5] Though Khrushchev greatly increased his personal power in 1957, realization of his preferences was never wholly assured. Other members of the Presidium apparently had a certain amount of independent power, which Khrushchev was forced to take into account when formulating policy.

[4] T. H. Rigby, "Khrushchev and the Resuscitation of the Central Committee," *Australian Outlook,* September 1959.

[5] Robert Conquest, "The Struggle Goes On," *Problems of Communism,* Vol. IX, No. 4 (July-August 1960); Carl Linden, "Khrushchev and the Party Battle," *ibid.,* Vol. XII, No. 5 (September-October 1963).

Military Influences[6]

At the time of the collapse of the 1960 Summit Conference, when many observers in the West speculated that Khrushchev was under strong pressure from a hostile opposition group, it was being suggested that Marshal Malinovsky was sent to Paris with Khrushchev in order to watch his moves. So far as can be ascertained, however, the high point in military influence was reached in the months immediately following the defeat of the "anti-party group" in June 1957. Zhukov threw his support to Khrushchev. But with the defeat of the "anti-party group" and the elevation of a number of his supporters to full Presidium membership, Khrushchev opted to oust the man upon whom he had depended, doing so in a series of moves in October–November 1957.

It appears in retrospect that Khrushchev cultivated the military from 1955 until 1957 by concessions that, it turned out, could easily be retracted — the raising of one officer to a high party post, a temporary increase in defense spending, a relaxation of party indoctrination procedures in the armed forces. Undoubtedly the military favored strong measures to repress the Hungarian uprising and, generally, to bolster the nation's defenses in every way. But there is no evidence that the military sought to alter Khrushchev's strategy of *détente* with the West, although it quite probably opposed the theory and practice of "collaboration" with the enemy. The five members of the "anti-party group" ousted in June 1957 were charged with opposing the peaceful coexistence line, but Zhukov's subsequent denunciation was on other grounds.

In the autumn of 1957 following the removal of Zhukov, a new period in party-military relations began. The new Defense Minister, Malinovsky, never attained membership in the party Presidium. The military lost much or most of the limited autonomy and influence over policy it had been able to gain in the period 1953–1957. As indicated earlier, obli-

---

[6] See also Dallin *et al., op. cit.,* pp. 82–103.

gatory political study for officers was reinstituted, the role of political officers was increased, party organizations in the armed forces were expanded in size, and military commanders were once again required to submit to criticism at party meetings.[7]

In this period from 1957 to 1962, party-military relations were marked by a divergence of opinion on two major issues. The first of these issues was the continuing conflict over party control of the armed forces. Party leaders tended to believe that the armed forces, like all else in Soviet society, must be under the close supervision of party officials. The military, on the other hand, sought greater autonomy in the everyday administration of the armed forces, and resented political controls as a slur on its ability and loyalty. Friction between party officials and military officers had existed since the first days of the Red Army, and there was no reason to expect that it would be resolved in the foreseeable future. But no matter how much the military resented party supervision, it was clear that after Zhukov's removal the military was able to do little to lessen it.

The second overt issue exacerbating party-military relations in this period was the conflict over the proper size of the armed forces. In January 1960, Khrushchev made a major speech on military strategy in which he outlined his views on atomic warfare and proposed to reduce the armed forces (which then stood at 3,700,000 men) by 1,200,000 over the next two years. It is hardly surprising that this was opposed by the military. The proposed reduction threatened the privileged positions of many officers. In addition, aside from considerations of self-interest many of the more conservative military leaders seemed to think that Khrushchev's radical reliance on military technology was endangering state security and therefore opposed the proposed reduction of ground forces. A kind of compromise resulted: the reductions were begun (only to be halted in midstream during the 1961 Berlin

7 Fainsod, *op. cit.,* pp. 485–486.

crisis), but Khrushchev's suggestion of transferring demobilized soldiers to a part-time militia never materialized. In any event it was rumored that opposition to the proposed force reductions hurtled two officers into temporary retirement: Konev from his post as commander of Warsaw Pact forces and Sokolovsky as Commander of the Soviet General Staff.[8] Both men, however, soon returned to responsible posts.

The role of the military generally and of Malinovsky at the Paris Summit in the determination of Khrushchev's foreign policy has been aptly summarized by Raymond Garthoff:

> On the whole, the military leaders, to the extent that their advice is solicited, continue to display the same degree of general conservatism as did Zhukov. This conservatism has meant an opposition to moves of accommodation or partial withdrawal (as in their favoring armed intervention to preserve the Hungarian base). It also has meant an opposition to "adventuristic" aggressiveness which threatens unnecessarily to risk a general war. Regrettably, Malinovsky personally is perhaps somewhat less of a moderating influence in this latter respect than was Zhukov (not as a humanitarian or friend of the West, but as a coldly calculating military planner).
>
> There are no indications of significant restiveness on the part of the professional military leaders, though there have been points of friction over various decisions of the political leadership directly limiting the armed forces.[9]

The reversal of the troop cuts begun in 1960 and the resumption of nuclear testing in 1961 were no doubt welcomed by many military leaders. But these were basically political decisions taken mainly in response to the changing international situation, and not necessarily in response to pressures from the military. While the military — even after Zhukov's ouster — probably exerted weight to retard or even reverse movements toward *détente,* its position was still sub-

[8] Matthew P. Gallagher, "Military Manpower: A Case Study," *Problems of Communism,* Vol. XIII, No. 3 (May-June 1964), p. 55.
[9] Raymond L. Garthoff, *Soviet Strategy in the Nuclear Age* (Rev. ed.; New York: Frederick A. Praeger, 1962), pp. 36–37.

ordinate to the party leadership, whose views it had to carry out, albeit reluctantly and with some dragging of feet.

Implications for Foreign Policy

We conclude that Khrushchev's position was probably less stable than its outward appearance. He had to act in some respects as a broker, trading off conflicting interests. Support for or opposition to his views from within the Party or the military constituted a marginal factor that, at moments such as the summer of 1960, could combine with other forces to throw Soviet policy one way or the other. While we doubt that he was actually "chained" at the Paris Summit Conference following the U-2 affair, it does seem likely that at least some of his demeanor was directed toward placating those who might have been saying "we warned you."

There is as yet no evidence that some of Khrushchev's domestic foes were allied with Peking, although their views may sometimes have gained weight by reference to Peking's. If such evidence comes to light, however, it would reinforce the contention that Khrushchev did have to cope with powerful critics whose views never came to public attention during his administration. And some new light on conflicts within the Kremlin may one day help to explain the Cuban adventure in 1962.

If the domestic political factor is weighed against the other determinants of arms control policy in the period, its role seems to have been quite marginal. Soviet foreign policy generally and arms control policy in particular were basically a response by the top Kremlin leadership to the international situation. Possible critics, whether of the "Stalinist" or liberal variety, could hardly organize any effective opposition, especially after 1957. Domestic pressures for peace and consumer prosperity could be catered to when conditions permitted or deferred on grounds of an international crisis. At the same time, no "external foe" was needed to legitimize the Khrushchev government as it had been in the case of Stalin; public opinion, such as it was, welcomed the relaxation of terror and promises of goulash communism. And while the Soviet people welcomed their government's ostensible campaign to ensure peace, a patriotic response could be counted on if the Kremlin warned of hostile machinations against the socialist fatherland. The ideological identification of peace, prosperity, and revolution as defined between 1956 and 1961 served to justify whatever twists and turns the Soviet leadership chose in pursuing its external relations.

12

From Optimism to Realism: A Summing Up

As suggested earlier, Soviet policies toward the West from 1957 to 1962 could be depicted in terms of four simplified models. Each of the four hypotheses could be partially, but probably not convincingly, supported by empirical evidence. First, there was no inexorable movement toward live-and-let-live, as demonstrated by the Cuban adventure if not by pressure on Berlin and elsewhere. Second, there was no unbroken "post-Sputnik offensive," because Moscow made serious moves toward improvement of East-West relations at many moments during these years but especially in 1958–1960. Third, there was no clear alternation of hard and soft modalities, because the two often operated simultaneously, most obviously, for example, when pressure began in late 1958 for a German Peace Treaty or again in 1962, when great ambivalence characterized Soviet policy. Fourth, it would be most plausible to argue that a hard and soft line generally functioned simultaneously, but this would beg important questions concerning the over-all thrust of Soviet policy. This

171

argument would offer a reminder of the tactical flexibility available to Moscow, but say little of its strategic objectives.

What emerges from a retrospective look at this "inter-Summit" period is a complicated picture with several basic ingredients: limited but significant evolution in Moscow's negotiating position on disarmament; more profound alteration in the ideological underpinnings of Soviet foreign policy generally; and qualitative transformations of some of the foundations upon which Soviet foreign policy rested, the implications of which were only hinted at prior to late 1962 and 1963. In looking at these five or six years we form the impression that the several peaks and valleys of apparent Soviet interest in arms control did not wholly reveal the variety of forces at work on Soviet strategy. Although some of these trends were significant in themselves, the salient fact about the years from 1956 through 1962 was that the "superstructure" of Soviet policy was not yet adjusting to deep-rooted changes in its base.

Changes in the Base of Policy

Perhaps the most significant development lay in the changes in the military and political determinants of Soviet policy toward arms control. Moscow's view of the East-West balance of military power, with the opportunities and limitations it implied for Soviet foreign policy, seemed to undergo dramatic alteration, moving toward and then away from high optimism. A similar but probably more marginal influence resulted from the rise and subsequent decline of the Soviet Union's economic prospects. The most significant new factor to enter into the Kremlin's view toward its relations with the West, and toward arms control as well, arose from the profound challenge — military as well as political — from Peking. Other elements at the base of Soviet arms control policy — Moscow's recognition of heterogeneity in the West and the Kremlin's confrontation with domestic political pressures —

continued to play an important role as they had in 1954–1956 but, despite fluctuations in their nature and weight, these two factors did not change so radically as the others.

What relative weighting ought we to assign to the factors? We begin with those that appear to have exercised a more decisive influence, turning then to those that exerted an important but more marginal role. In the first category we would rank Soviet calculations about the East-West military balance, the opportunities and problems in dealing with the West, and the prospects of Sino-Soviet relations. Among the secondary factors we would include the growing burden of defense upon the Soviet economy and the role played by the Russian opponents and supporters of Khrushchev's policies.

The Military Element in Policy

Of all the elements shaping Soviet arms control policy, military considerations appear to have been the most decisive in this period, both in moving Soviet policy toward arms control and in setting limits to the extent of such movement. This judgment does not contradict the argument that arms control was first and foremost a means of supporting Soviet foreign policy rather than Soviet military strategy, for its immediate purpose was to affect the political environment and in that way indirectly to regulate the strategic situation. But the motivation behind Moscow's concern to shape the political situation arose most urgently from the Kremlin's perception of certain military factors.

Soviet optimism in 1955 and 1956 regarding the strategic balance seemed justified in 1957 when the world had cause to talk of an incipient missile gap favoring the Soviet Union. Soviet confidence rode high until 1960–1961, when the United States reversed the alleged missile gap both in theory and practice. Moscow's propensity to negotiate on disarmament seemed to follow a "U" curve; from 1955 to 1959–1960, while self-confidence still reigned, the propensity to negotiate seriously was relatively high. From 1960 to 1961, while confidence waned — for military and other reasons — Moscow showed less interest in immediately feasible measures, although it did push GCD. In 1961 it tried to cash in on the last vestiges of the missile gap myth by renewed pressure on Berlin. It sought to counterbalance the mounting number of U.S. ICBM's by developing and testing giant nuclear warheads in September and October of 1961. Another desperate attempt to attain both the image and the reality of parity with the West came when missiles were shipped to Cuba in 1962. Only after that venture failed did Moscow seem to reconcile itself to a position of at least temporary strategic inferiority (braced, however, by a quite credible minimum deterrent), and accord high priority to arms control with the West.

While Moscow's view of the over-all strategic balance passed through these stages, the Soviet Union continued as in 1955 apparently to fear surprise attack, accidental war, catalytic war, and escalation — especially as a result of forward moves by Bonn or Peking. Similarly, the Soviet government became seriously concerned about nuclear proliferation to Germany and China. All these concerns underlay the mounting Soviet interest in regional arms control in Central Europe, ground control posts, and a ban on nuclear testing that might lead to preventing the spread of nuclear weapons and nuclear technology.

For these reasons it appears that the prime motivation behind Soviet interest in a nuclear test ban was strategic: to inhibit U.S. advances in the quality and quantity of long-range nuclear weapons; to halt the development of U.S. tactical weapons and their stationing in Central Europe; and to prevent before it was too late the acquisition of nuclear weapons by Bonn and Peking.

Military considerations also imposed key restraints on Soviet willingness to sign a test ban. The right moment had to be found when Soviet security vis-à-vis the West would best

be maintained by a freeze or an end to nuclear testing; and —
a more constant concern — a formula had to be found that
both prevented the United States from continuing underground tests and avoided the necessity of intensive foreign
inspection of Soviet nuclear and other military facilities. Even
after the revelations of U-2 reconnaissance, the Soviet Union
still prized the military security that kept its weak as well as
its strong points from enemy intelligence.

Another military restraint on arms control policy generally
was the apparent opposition of some Soviet marshals to cuts
in Soviet ground, naval, and air forces and their probable
opposition to steps that might alienate China and blur the
image of an evil capitalist adversary in the West. The role of
such opposition, while marginal in itself, could become decisive when combined with other pressures working against
East-West *détente* and accommodation in arms control.

Perceptions of the West

The second decisive influence on arms control policy
stemmed from Moscow's perceptions of the West. Khrushchev
assumed that there were elements in the Western leadership
that could be persuaded or coerced into accepting his version
of peaceful coexistence, even if it implied an expansion of the
socialist camp and contraction of the capitalist. The Soviet
government, as noted, worked out an elaborate justification,
quoting from newly resurrected scripture, for attempting to
collaborate and make compromises with the Western governments even while remaining ideologically hostile and "struggling" against them.

Did the Kremlin believe its own line about the malleability
of moderate forces in the West? It is difficult to correlate
precisely the Soviet emphasis on a heterogeneous adversary
with the emergence of a more conciliatory approach toward
Moscow in and around the American capital. It appears that
the Kremlin's expectations concerning a possible improve-

ment in East-West relations rose after Dulles' death in May 1959 until they were dashed by the U-2 incident a year later. A period of waiting set in to see which way the new administration in Washington would move, but the first Kennedy defense budget, the Bay of Pigs, the confrontation in Vienna, and the shows of force over Berlin probably indicated to Moscow that the new government intended to be firm. In general it appears that Soviet propaganda concerning the West's disposition to compromise persisted without undue regard for the hardening of American policy. Whether or not "moderate" tendencies dominated in the determination of Western policies, the Kremlin seems to have assumed that they were operative, that they could be strengthened, and that cooperation as well as competition was possible with the Western powers.

The Influence of China

The third decisive influence on arms control policy was China, which had played no visible role in the 1954–1956 shift in Soviet policy. From 1956, and especially after 1959, the state of Sino-Soviet relations grew steadily more strained. Peking, although it gave ostensible support to the Soviet Union's leading position in the Communist movement in 1956–1957, showed increasing disdain for the style and content of Soviet domestic and foreign policy. Disarmament was a particular grievance and represented the reverse side of another vexed issue — Moscow's refusal, made explicit in 1959, to give China a sample atomic bomb or additional technical data. The events of September 1959 at Camp David and in the General Assembly, followed by Khrushchev's subsequent words in Peking, eventually sparked an intense Chinese attack on the "illusions" of those who talked of a "warless world" and agreements with the "imperialists."

The Soviet Union seemed little restrained by China's criticism. Shortly after 1957, when Peking had claimed that the Soviet Union agreed to a pact on a new defense technology with China, Soviet diplomats made some of their most far-reaching concessions in the test ban negotiations. At the same time, concern over China seems to have spurred the Kremlin's attempts to halt nuclear testing and nuclear proliferation. Moscow's intensive propagation of nuclear-free zones in 1959 correlated positively with China's charges that Moscow refused in June of that year to provide her with a sample atomic bomb. The Kremlin endeavored to meet the Chinese ideological challenge in many ways, one of which was to argue more intensely the possibility and desirability of peaceful coexistence and disarmament not as a tactic but as a strategy.

Although the main thrust of the Chinese national interest drove Moscow into a more serious effort at accommodation with the West, on the interparty level the effect of Peking's ideological challenge to Khrushchev was probably to strengthen domestic opposition to a policy line of accommodation.

Thus a new element had to be weighed by the Kremlin. The optimism of 1955 seems to have made little allowance for the possibility that Moscow's most powerful ally would threaten the Soviet position in the international Communist movement and pose a long-term danger to Soviet security. The Kremlin's decision to respond to this threat not by appeasement but by efforts to curb Pcking's nuclear program, and to rebut its ideological challenge, exerted a decisive influence upon Moscow's arms control policy from 1956 to 1962. Nonetheless, there may have been some unwillingness in Moscow to alienate China totally, restraining the Soviet approach to arms control until the emergence of new circumstances by 1963 made a partial test ban treaty appropriate.

The Cost Factor

An influence that could not be crucial in itself, but which functioned to reinforce the trend of the more decisive considerations just listed, was the mounting cost of the defense effort relative to the over-all functioning of the Soviet economy. The Kremlin's calculations on both these counts seem to have been excessively optimistic in 1955 and even as late as 1959. The absolute expense of the defense effort soared after 1958, at the same time that general economic growth began to decline. The slowdown in the over-all growth rate was due to a number of factors, one of them being the increased burden imposed by the human and material resources devoted to defense. Even so, the Twenty-first Party Congress in 1959 proclaimed that socialism would triumph over capitalism in economic competition. But Soviet expectations were still too rosy. By 1961 and 1962 the rate of growth slowed still more. Moreover, it began to appear in 1960 and 1961 that the Soviet Union had no imminent prospect of surpassing the United States militarily, let alone in over-all industrial production, especially if Soviet resources continued to be allocated and used in their present pattern.

Khrushchev's marshals were arguing for a "balanced" military structure, which meant heavy outlays for all kinds of military forces. Expected savings from concentration on nuclear rocket forces would thus be precluded. But the effort to match the United States in the arms race was becoming an effort just to prevent the strategic balance from widening further to Moscow's disadvantage, and it was impeding progress toward making the Soviet Union a model of rapid industrial development and consumer affluence. When Soviet economists began to talk about the blessings that disarmament might bring to all economies of the world, they may well have had the Soviet Union uppermost in mind.

Had there been a prospect of radically increasing Moscow's bargaining power by greater investment in defense, or had there been an imminent military threat to Soviet security, the increased drag that military spending exerted on economic growth would not have been a serious influence on Soviet strategic planning. But coming at a time when other pressures militated increasingly for arms controls with the West, the promise of economic savings from curtailment of the arms race had increasing appeal to Soviet policy makers. At least by 1962, but probably several years earlier, the economic factor loomed much higher among the forces favoring a limitation of armaments than it had in 1955. Its effect was that of a multiplier buttressing the influence of the military and political considerations that made for a slackening of the arms race and a stabilization of the international military environment.

The Khrushchev Style

During this period Khrushchev's world view and his personal style were dominant factors in the determination of Soviet foreign and domestic policy. By comparison with Stalin, he relied much more on persuasion than coercion. The thaw and the fluidity that entered many aspects of Soviet society after Stalin's death made it virtually impossible for any one man or even any central elite to rule by fiat.

Whereas Lenin and Stalin left such matters to their foreign ministers, Khrushchev took great personal interest in propagating Moscow's disarmament policy. The main lines of Soviet disarmament policy probably followed his preferences, although the details may have been left to functionaries.

The extent to which Khrushchev's preferences could prevail depended, however, on his ability to cope with forces within Soviet society that opposed or favored greater moves toward *détente* and disarmament. He had to mobilize a certain amount of support for his views on measures such as arms control that could have far-reaching implications for every facet of Soviet society. He could generally count on a popular response from the Soviet public and much of the intelligentsia who wanted peace, prosperity, and political liberalization. Further, some plant managers and party leaders may have wanted to free resources from arms for investment in heavy or light industry and agriculture.

From other groups closer to the levers of power there was probably general resistance to any lessening of Soviet defense efforts and to more intimate relations with the capitalist foe. Many party leaders would oppose any extensive collaboration with the West, alienation of China, or political liberalization in the Soviet Union. Military leaders would oppose any weakening of defenses. Certain plant managers and scientists with a vested interest in defense production would likewise oppose a slackening of military investment. The influence of this "second" group would be combined and multiplied at moments when the West seemed recalcitrant (demonstrating the infeasibility of *détente* and disarmament); at moments when the military balance seemed to turn sharply in the Soviet Union's favor or in its disfavor; and at moments when Peking threatened to challenge Moscow's position.

Although no precise correlation can be determined between these domestic influences and fluctuations in arms control policy, it is probable that these marginal domestic influences on Kremlin policy, linked with the other four factors that have been enumerated, helped to bring on a somewhat tougher orientation in manifest Soviet foreign policy from the time of the U-2 incident in 1960 until the Cuban gambit in 1962. But even within the framework of this partial hardening of the Kremlin's line, as we have noted, some concessions in the disarmament negotiations continued to be made, and Khrushchev's ideologists deepened the Soviet commitment to the possibility and desirability of disarmament and compromises.

The combination of military, political, and economic forces shaping Soviet foreign policy in the period seemed, on balance, to militate strongly for a policy that would function either to gain a "quick fix," by which Soviet power could again try to match or surpass the West, or to enter a breathing space of relaxed tensions with the West that de-emphasized the military competition and political struggle. There was probably some stimulus from conservative elements in the

Soviet establishment for attempting the first of these alternatives. Perhaps some effort to satisfy their interests or to demonstrate that they could not be satisfied without great cost would have to be attempted before the second alternative could become a practical policy alternative. In any case, the success of a *détente* policy would depend also upon reciprocity in the West. Although Washington's intentions to resist Communist expansion were quite manifest in 1960–1961, the willingness of the Republican and Democratic leaderships to forgo a forward strategy was presumably not yet entirely clear to the Kremlin. For all these reasons the 1962 Cuban adventure would be decisive. Thus, the stage was set for new policy moves as the post-1955 synthesis of "struggle" and "cooperation" in Soviet conduct seemed to break down into a choice emphasizing one or the other.

PART III

THE SPIRIT OF MOSCOW: DÉTENTE AND LIMITED ARMS CONTROL AGREEMENTS 1962–1964

By mid-1961 the optimistic outlook that underlay the shift in Soviet arms control policy in 1954–1956 had been profoundly eroded. Despite Soviet advances in rocketry, the West had held fast and gone on to outstrip the Soviet Union in numbers of ICBM's. Despite the enticements and threats emanating from Moscow, the NATO alliance had shown considerable cohesion, even allowing for de Gaulle's independent course. By contrast, the one-time Soviet "bloc" had fallen into a state of severe disarray, with polycentrism in Eastern Europe and a profound rift in Asia. Despite Soviet blandishments, the emerging nations remained part of a "third" and not a Soviet world. Finally, fulfilling Western but not Soviet forecasts, the rate of Soviet economic growth began seriously to falter — in part because of the arms race — after 1958. Had the attempt to emplace Soviet missiles in Cuba succeeded, at least the military picture would have been more to Moscow's liking, and perhaps the other problems would also

183

have been favorably affected. The failure of the Cuban gambit, therefore, resulted in a serious narrowing of the foreign policy alternatives open to the Kremlin.

The same factors that induced a shift in Soviet arms control policy after Cuba also set limits on how far that policy might go: the problem of present Soviet strategic inferiority and the outlook for new technological or territorial breakthroughs; the presence of what Moscow termed "sober" and "aggressive" forces in the West; the unremitting pressure from Peking for a stiffer line toward "imperialism"; the extent to which the Soviet economy could sustain arms competition with the United States and benefit from a slackening of defense expenditures; and, finally, the balance of power and opinion among the Kremlin leadership.

13

The Negotiations: New Flexibility

Before and After Cuba

Shortly before the Cuban missile crisis erupted, the Soviet government adopted a more conciliatory negotiating posture on two important issues: the necessity for an uninspected moratorium to accompany a limited nuclear test ban, and the retention of the Soviet and American deterrents during the disarmament process. The incompatibility of these moves with the simultaneous preparations of the Cuban missile venture provides a striking illustration of the choice between conflict and collaboration that the erosion of alternatives appears to have forced upon the Soviet leadership.[1] The failure of the Cuban adventure left Moscow with little practical alternative but to soften the relationship with the United States by a further, although limited, show of flexibility in the Geneva negotiations and at other points of East-West contact.

On August 29 and September 3, 1962, after rejecting two alternative test ban proposals put forward by the United

[1] See Richard Lowenthal, "The End of an Illusion," *Problems of Communism,* Vol. XII, No. 1 (1963).

States on August 27, the Soviet delegate to the Eighteen Nation Disarmament Conference (ENDC) announced his government's willingness to sign a three-environment test ban with a moratorium on underground testing "while continuing negotiations on the final prohibitions of such explosions." A similar proposal had been made by Moscow on November 28, 1961, but with the provision that the underground test moratorium should continue until a control system for such tests was agreed upon as part of a comprehensive disarmament agreement. The Soviet position of August 29–September 3 seemed no longer to be contingent upon GCD — a minor but significant move in the light of Khrushchev's 1958 statement that the surest way to obstruct progress toward a test ban was to tie it to the issue of disarmament.[2] Although Soviet representative Kuznetsov clouded the issue on September 5 by reiterating Moscow's support for its stand of November 28, 1961, *Pravda* asserted that a new initiative had been taken, and Khrushchev declared that the Soviet Union sought a limited test ban with a moratorium subject to the negotiation of a comprehensive test ban.[3] In any event the Western delegates rejected the new Soviet overture on principle because — after the Soviet test resumption in 1961 — the West would no longer consent to an unpoliced moratorium.[4]

The other shift in Moscow's position prior to Cuba took place during the general debate of the Seventeenth General Assembly. Foreign Minister Gromyko announced on September 21, 1962:

Taking account of the stand of the Western Powers the

[2] *Pravda*, August 29, 1958. Also in U.S. Department of State, *Documents on Disarmament, 1945–1959* (Washington: U.S. Government Printing Office, 1960), Vol. II, p. 1116.

[3] *Pravda*, September 4 and October 2, 1962. See also *New Times*, No. 36 (September 8, 1962).

[4] Eighteen Nation Committee on Disarmament, verbatim records, ENDC/PV.76, August 29, 1962, pp. 14–23; ENDC/PV.79, September 3, 1962, pp. 72 and 78–80. See also verbatim records of September 5, 1962. See further on for corroboration of the significance of this Soviet initiative.

Soviet Government agrees that in the process of destroying vehicles for the delivery of nuclear weapons at the first stage exception be made for a strictly limited and agreed number of global intercontinental missiles, anti-missile missiles, and anti-aircraft missiles of the ground-to-air type which would remain at the disposal of the Union of Soviet Socialist Republics and the United States alone.[5]

This concession was characterized by Moscow as an effort to meet Western demands for retention of a "nuclear umbrella" during the early stages of the disarmament program. During the brief third session of the ENDC in November and December, Soviet spokesmen refused to clarify the Gromyko proposal until it was accepted "in principle" by the West.[6] Nonetheless, it seemed to imply that some real common interests might exist between Moscow and Washington on this issue.

The Cuban missile crisis of October 1962 was not followed by any immediate shift in the Soviet positions on the test ban, GCD, or collateral measures in either the U.N. General Assembly or the ENDC. At the General Assembly meeting in New York the Soviet government continued to attack Western proposals for a partial test ban or a comprehensive ban with on-site inspection. A more positive note was sounded on December 5, 1962, however, when the United States and the Soviet Union announced agreement on certain measures of cooperation in the peaceful uses of outer space.

The Soviet position on a nuclear test ban was formally modified for the first time since September when, on December 10, 1962, Moscow publicly espoused the idea of automatic seismic stations — "two or three" on Soviet territory — to control an underground test ban.[7] Delivery of the

[5] U.N. Document A/PV.1127, September 25, 1962, pp. 38–40.
[6] ENDC/PV.83, November 26, 1962, p. 22. However, on March 27, 1963 the Soviet delegate elucidated for the first time that Moscow would permit inspection of the missile launch pads as part of a comprehensive disarmament program. ENDC/PV.114, March 27, 1963, pp. 39–40.
[7] ENDC/PV.90, December 10, 1962, pp. 13–27. This idea had

sealed apparatus for periodic replacement in the Soviet Union would have to be carried out by Soviet personnel in Soviet aircraft, but Moscow would be prepared to agree to servicing by foreign personnel. A short time later, on December 19, Khrushchev announced Moscow would accept "two to three" on-site inspections per year for the control of a comprehensive test ban treaty,[8] thereby returning to a position first held in 1960. However, Washington insisted that the minimum number of inspections acceptable to the United States was between eight and ten.[9] The resulting impasse led Moscow to break off tripartite talks that had been held in New York from January 14 to 31, 1963. On April 1, 1963 the Western powers at the ENDC reduced their demand from eight–ten to seven on-site inspections,[10] but in the following month the debate degenerated to the point where the Soviet negotiator declared that it was "a sheer waste of time."[11]

While the test ban negotiations showed little prospect of success, the ENDC discussions on other arms control items in the spring of 1963 appeared equally inauspicious. The five Communist delegations attacked the Nassau agreement of December 1962, plans for U.S.-Canadian nuclear defense cooperation, the Franco-German treaty of cooperation of January 1963, and U.S. overseas bases — particularly those serving Polaris submarines. A number of Soviet proposals were aimed directly against these Western positions — a declaration "On Renunciation of Use of Foreign Territories

---

originated at the Tenth Conference on Science and World Affairs ("Pugwash") in London during September 1962. The Soviets subsequently made private approaches to the United States on this matter, in October and November, at the General Assembly and in Geneva. It was mentioned favorably by Radio Moscow on November 10 (Domestic Service, 0025 GMT) and by the Soviet negotiator at the ENDC on November 13, 1962.

[8] *Documents on Disarmament, 1962,* pp. 1239–1242.

[9] ENDC/74, January 31, 1963.

[10] ENDC/78, April 1, 1963, in U.N. Document DC/207, April 12, 1963.

[11] ENDC/PV.126, April 29, 1963, p. 24.

for Stationing Strategic Means of Delivering Nuclear Weapons,"[12] a draft nonaggression pact between the NATO and Warsaw Pact powers,[13] and a proposal for declaring the Mediterranean a nuclear-free zone.[14]

Limited Agreements

It was against this background of hostile negotiating behavior in the ENDC that Moscow was in fact negotiating a direct communications link with Washington, as well as a test ban agreement. Evidence of progress on the hot line was indicated on April 5, when the Soviet delegate declared that his government agreed to the U.S. proposal "immediately, without waiting for general and complete disarmament."[15] While the hot line agreement of June 20, 1963 was being prepared, private talks on a test ban treaty were proceeding among unofficial representatives of the United States, the Soviet Union, and Britain. The Western governments were able to announce on June 10 the scheduling of a "high-level" conference of the United States, the United Kingdom, and the Soviet Union in Moscow on July 15.[16]

Khrushchev announced on July 2 that in the forthcoming three-power talks in Moscow the Soviet government was interested in concluding a partial test ban agreement. Modifying the Soviet position of August 29–September 3, 1962, Khrushchev dropped the qualification of an (uninspected) moratorium on underground testing but now called for the simultaneous signing of an East-West nonaggression pact.[17]

[12] ENDC/PV.147, June 21, 1963, p. 49.
[13] ENDC/77, February 20, 1963, in U.N. Document DC/207, April 12, 1963.
[14] ENDC/PV. 139, May 31, 1963, pp. 21–22.
[15] ENDC/PV.118, April 5, 1963, p. 52.
[16] Great Britain, *Further Documents Relating to the Conference of the Eighteen-Nation Committee on Disarmament* (London: Her Majesty's Stationery Office, 1963), p. 7 (Cmd. paper 2184).
[17] ENDC/112, August 22, 1963, in U.N. Document DC/207, April 12, 1963.

While circumstantial evidence suggests that Khrushchev had opted for a test ban agreement even before his July 2 statement, and may have recognized that a partial ban held the greatest prospects of success on both sides,[18] it was not yet entirely clear that the nonaggression pact issue might not be used by the Soviet leadership to scuttle agreement at the last minute, especially as Sino-Soviet negotiations were also in progress in Moscow.[19] The three-power negotiations began in Moscow on July 15 as scheduled, and after the first day Moscow let the nonaggression pact issue drop to the background although it was clear that the final communiqué would have to make some mention of it. The negotiations thereafter were cordial and businesslike. The main problems arose in connection with a withdrawal clause and the question of depositories for the treaty. These were resolved with relatively little difficulty, strong Soviet resistance to the former being overcome by a circumlocution. On July 25 the treaty was initialed and on August 5, 1963 it was signed.[20]

The strong impression of *détente* generated by the limited test ban treaty pervaded the brief fifth session of the ENDC, which met through the month of August, but there were no basic changes of position on the part of either the Soviet Union or the West. Moscow continued to plead the case for a nonaggression pact and GCD. Soviet negotiators also advanced the various collateral measures proposed by Khrush-

[18] Moscow ceased jamming Voice of America broadcasts in May and June 1963 and signed the hot line agreement on June 20, 1963, as indicated above. Khrushchev publicly commended President Kennedy's American University speech of June 10 in *Pravda* of June 15, 1963; further, in June 1963, a Soviet publication singled out the fact that Secretary of State Rusk on May 29, 1963 had supported the proposal of a group of U.S. senators for a partial ban as being in the interest of both countries. *New Times,* No. 23 (1963), p. 32 (Russian edition, June 7, 1963).

[19] But while Khrushchev stressed on July 19 that the form of the nonaggression pact was negotiable, he did not make the pact a precondition for a test ban treaty. *Pravda* and *Izvestiia,* July 20, 1963.

[20] ENDC/100/Rev. 1, July 30, 1963, in U.N. Document DC/208, September 5, 1963.

chev in his speech of July 19, including a cut in military budgets, a reduction of forces in both Germanies, and measures to prevent surprise attack.[21]

New Soviet moves were, however, made at the Eighteenth General Assembly meeting in New York in the fall of 1963. On September 19, Mr. Gromyko further modified the Soviet position on a "nuclear umbrella," conceding that a limited number of nuclear missiles might be retained through to the end of the disarmament process. In addition, the Soviet government at the same time reversed the position it had taken on June 20, 1963 in the ENDC and assented to a joint Soviet-American agreement not to orbit nuclear weapons in space.[22] For reasons that will become clear, a formal treaty on this matter was not realized, and instead a U.S.-Soviet–sponsored statement was endorsed by the U.N. General Assembly on October 17, 1963, calling upon all states to refrain from orbiting nuclear weapons in space.[23]

Other signs of limited movement in Soviet positions on arms control in this period were evident as the year 1963 drew to a close. At the International Atomic Energy Agency Conference in Vienna the Soviet Union accepted some safeguards to ensure that fissionable fuel and reactors were not used for military purposes by aid recipients, and at the United Nations the Soviet Union joined the United States in an agreement on certain legal principles governing the exploration and use of outer space.[24]

The latter agreement, which was approved by the U.N. Committee on the Peaceful Uses of Outer Space on No-

[21] ENDC/PV.152, August 16, 1963, pp. 12 ff. On July 26, 1963 Khrushchev added the proposal of a Soviet-Western exchange of troop representatives between forces stationed in Germany. Moscow Domestic Service in Russian, July 26, 1963, 1400 GMT.

[22] *Pravda*, September 20, 1963.

[23] U.N. General Assembly Resolution 1884 (XVIII). See also *New Times*, No. 41 (1963), p. 32.

[24] Richard P. Stebbins, *The United States in World Affairs: 1963* (New York: Harper and Row, for the Council on Foreign Relations, 1964), p. 339.

vember 22, failed to contain several Soviet principles — such as the prohibition of nongovernmental activities in space — which had been objectionable to the United States. But the agreement was facilitated in no small part by an indication of Washington's willingness not to insist on on-site inspection of rocket launchers. This change in the U.S. position came well before the "Moscow Treaty," but Soviet representatives inquired subsequently if it remained the U.S. stand. On December 13, Khrushchev announced a unilateral reduction in the Soviet military budget and the possibility of a cutback in Soviet armed forces. And on December 31, 1963, he addressed a letter to all heads of state urging an agreement on the peaceful settlement of territorial disputes — a proposal aimed at least in part at China.[25]

Another limited East-West arms control was achieved on April 20, 1964, when — after an unpublicized plenum of the CPSU Central Committee in February — private negotiations between Washington, London, and Moscow led to simultaneous unilateral pledges by the three governments to cut back production of fissionable materials.

In the ENDC session that commenced on January 21, 1964 Soviet negotiators assumed a more antagonistic posture, vigorously rejecting the new U.S. proposals for a freeze on strategic delivery vehicles and for a reduction of Soviet and American strategic bomber forces. Instead, Moscow laid major emphasis on GCD (including its concession of September 1963 on the "nuclear umbrella"), the destruction of all bombers, reciprocal budgetary reductions, and a non-aggression pact. Moscow argued that the U.S. proposal on the nondissemination of nuclear weapons could not be taken seriously until the NATO multilateral force (MLF) project was abandoned; the Kremlin also refused to dissociate from other partial measures the proposal of ground control posts against surprise attack. By March 1, 1964 Mr. Gromyko was

[25] *Pravda*, January 4, 1964.

publicly charging the West with responsibility for the lack of progress at the ENDC,[26] and the note of recrimination continued to be evident in Soviet statements until the end of the session on April 28.

We might sum up the period from September 1962 to mid-1964 as one of extraordinary movement toward agreements on the fringes of the disarmament problem. But the Soviet approach reflected a notable duality between public and private negotiating postures. Soviet representatives in the negotiations continued to pursue lines of conduct that often seemed to undermine the possibility of agreement; privately, Moscow proceeded toward specific understandings with the United States.

[26] *Izvestiia,* March 2, 1964.

14

Propaganda: Antagonism Versus Compromise

Soviet propaganda treatment of the arms control and disarmament issue, in common with Soviet negotiating behavior
in the ENDC, displayed a degree of public hostility to the
West even when private talks between Moscow and Washington were proceeding favorably. The outstanding exceptions to
this rule arose in connection with the test ban and the understanding not to orbit nuclear weapons in space, when Moscow
exhibited definite propaganda restraint.

In the aftermath of the Cuban episode Soviet statements
pointed out the opportunities for U.S.-Soviet agreement on
the test ban and other arms control measures as a result of
Soviet concessions. Indeed, the same day Khrushchev announced that Russia's missiles were being withdrawn from
Cuba, Moscow asserted that the U.S. and Soviet positions on
a test ban were "close."[1] The Soviet proposals for "black
box" controls and, later, for three on-site inspections were
emphasized, as was the "nuclear umbrella" offer of Sep-

[1] TASS in English to Europe, October 28, 1962, 1611 GMT.

194

tember 1962. However the West's negative response to these proposals and Washington's plans for a NATO nuclear force were sharply criticized.[2]

Soviet propaganda increasingly noted that within the U.S. government there were opponents of compromise on the test ban issue. In breaking off the private three-power talks in New York on January 31, 1963, on the grounds that the West was not "showing good will," Moscow, citing Edward Teller and Nelson Rockefeller, emphasized that the U.S. administration was under "strong pressure" not to conclude a test ban agreement.[3] The American test resumption soon thereafter was assailed as an attempt to poison the atmosphere at Geneva, and it was implied that this move was due to pressure from the "right."[4]

While the ground was being prepared for the partial test ban treaty in private talks among the three powers, the Soviet propaganda line on the ENDC was basically antagonistic. The tendency, in the period December 1962 to February 1963, to imply that the Kennedy administration did not have a free hand in negotiating a test ban was subordinated in March and April to attacks on "aggressive" Western moves outside the negotiating forum. The good faith of the Western negotiators in Geneva was questioned in charges of "procrastination." Although Soviet propaganda obliquely indicated that Washington might favor a test ban,[5] Moscow generally stressed the West's refusal to consider "constructive" Soviet proposals at the ENDC. Particular attention was given to the negative Western response to the Soviet proposal

---

[2] Cf. TASS in English to Europe, December 4, 1962, 1748 GMT.

[3] Cf. editorial, "Transferred to Geneva," *New Times*, No. 6 (February 13, 1963).

[4] Editorial, "Nevada and Geneva," *ibid.*, No. 7 (February 20, 1963).

[5] Editorial, "Vicious Circle," *New Times*, No. 15 (April 17, 1963). On this occasion Moscow noted that "influential elements" were exerting pressure on the Kennedy administration not to sign a test ban.

of a nuclear-free zone in the Mediterranean, again with explicit references to Polaris and to possible MLF deployment.

A less hostile approach to the West characterized Soviet propaganda from June to October 1963. After Khrushchev's favorable comments of June 15, 1963 on President Kennedy's American University speech of June 10, and his proposal of a partial test ban at Berlin on July 2, Soviet statements began to play down U.S. "aggressiveness," and indicated instead a recognition that the governments with which they were negotiating were under pressure from "militarist 'ultras' and the big war monopolies" not to enter into agreements or move toward a *détente*.[6] The signing of the hot line agreement was termed a "bright spot" in the work of the ENDC and proof of Moscow's good will in seeking agreements with the West.[7]

With the initialing of the test ban treaty on July 25, 1963 and the subsequent debate on this issue in the United States, Soviet propaganda emphasized two main themes: the agreement furthered a relaxation of tensions and created favorable conditions for the solution of other East-West problems,[8] and it "exposed" the "reactionary" groups in the West that were most opposed to agreements and *détente*. By contrast Soviet media said relatively little about the majority of "sober-moderate" individuals and groups that supported the partial test ban. The treaty was seen as a means of "tying the hands" of those in the West who were most vociferous in their opposition to the "socialist" states,[9] while at the same time the "forces of peace" had been strengthened. In this connection Soviet commentators emphasized that American political

[6] See, for example, "The Test Ban Talks," *New Times*, No. 29 (July 1963).

[7] *Izvestiia*, June 22, 1963.

[8] See, for example, Moscow Domestic Service in Russian, July 26, 1963, 1400 GMT; TASS in Russian to Europe, July 29, 1963, 0310 GMT; TASS in English to Europe, August 3, 1963, 1900 GMT; Moscow Domestic Service in Russian, August 5, 1963, 0600 GMT; and TASS in English to Europe, August 5, 1963, 1619 GMT.

[9] Moscow Domestic Service in Russian, April 18, 1963, 1400 GMT.

leaders were showing an increased understanding of the need for policies of coexistence rather than policies of force. This view complemented the other main Soviet propaganda line to the effect that a start had been made toward a relaxation of tensions and the step-by-step negotiation of other outstanding East-West problems.

Soviet domestic commentary on the test ban made the point that the relaxing effect of the test ban on the international situation inhibited the formation of new multilateral NATO or European nuclear forces.[10] It was also asserted that the Soviet negotiating proposals that accompanied the test ban had provoked "a tense struggle" among the NATO powers.[11] Noting the line-up of the NATO members on the issue of a nonaggression pact, Moscow added that this struggle was "going on not only inside NATO but in every Atlantic country."[12] The Federal Republic of Germany was consistently portrayed as the chief obstruction to further East-West agreement and, on occasion, as "blackmailing" the United States to this end.[13] French opposition to further East-West agreements was also stressed.[14]

Perhaps most interesting, however, was the Soviet propaganda treatment of the resumption of underground testing by the United States almost immediately after the limited test ban was signed. It is understood that Soviet news agencies were directed not to publish a statement by Professor J. D.

[10] Moscow Domestic Service in Russian, August 12, 1963, 1900 GMT; *Krasnaia zvezda,* August 16, 1963.

[11] Moscow Domestic Service in Russian, September 1, 1963, 1400 GMT.

[12] *Ibid.* The division on a nonaggression pact at the NATO Council session in Paris late in August 1963 was reported as follows: the United States, Britain, Belgium, Canada, Luxembourg, Denmark, and Italy for the pact; the Netherlands, Portugal, and Iceland for the pact but with reservations; France, West Germany, Greece, and Turkey opposed to the pact and even to East-West talks about it.

[13] See, for example, Moscow Domestic Service in Russian, September 1, 1963, 1400 GMT.

[14] See, for example, Moscow in English to eastern North America, August 12, 1963, 0030 GMT.

Bernal, president of the World Peace Council, charging that
the U.S. test resumption was "an affront to humanity" and
"a direct blow against the spirit of the agreement." Soviet
media appear to have continued the moratorium on propaganda opposing the U.S. underground tests until October 12,
1963 when, in a broadcast to Italy, the tests were criticized by
Moscow as not being in the spirit of the limited test ban
treaty.[15]

As in the Bernal case, Radio Moscow played down the fact
that the U.S. government did not feel ready to push for a
treaty on banning bombs in orbit, although it would agree to a
U.N. resolution to that effect.[16] Soviet propaganda on the
resolution indicated it had been received with "indignation"
and "disappointment" by Senator Goldwater and "the most
aggressive-minded elements of U.S. military quarters."[17]

On October 21, 1963, as talks on East-West problems
continued between Washington and Moscow, and as Khrushchev continued to seek a conference of the international Communist movement to excommunicate the Chinese, TASS released the first major threat to the West since the test ban was
signed — a warning that the NATO talks begun on October 11 to set up the MLF could obstruct progress toward
further East-West agreements.[18] TASS emphasized that the
Western powers could not verbally oppose the spread of
nuclear weapons while in practice seeking to supply them to
the *Bundeswehr*.

This slight hardening of the line was also reflected in new
activity by the Communist peace fronts, which had been
dormant since the "World Congress of Women" in Moscow
in June 1963. Thus Khrushchev's October 25 warning against

[15] Moscow in Italian to Italy, October 12, 1963, 1900 GMT.
[16] See Moscow Domestic Service in Russian, October 10, 1963,
0600 GMT. TASS in English to Europe, October 17, 1963, 1759
GMT.
[17] TASS in English to Europe, October 19, 1963, 1433 GMT.
[18] TASS in English to Europe, October 21, 1963, 1213 GMT.

allowing the *détente* to lead to the "moral and spiritual de-mobilization of the forces of disarmament"[19] was followed by "Peace Week" (November 17–24) in France and the Warsaw session of the World Peace Council (November 28–December 1). The latter called for renewed mass actions, emphasizing a comprehensive test ban, opposition to nuclear proliferation including the MLF, nuclear-free zones, and the mobilization of "pressure" on the ENDC to progress toward a GCD treaty.[20]

Khrushchev's December 13 announcements of a cut in the Soviet military budget and a possible unilateral force reduction were characterized by Soviet media as tension-reducing moves designed to influence the MLF discussions at the Paris NATO Ministerial Council session of December 16 and 17. Khrushchev by the end of the year was speaking in terms of further agreements by "mutual example."

As the ENDC resumed in January 1964, Moscow proposed a series of partial measures that were advertised as facilitating GCD. By March, as the Soviet Union began again to seek support for a world Communist conference and as the ENDC settled down to unproductive discussion, Mr. Gromyko attacked the West for barring all progress in Geneva while Radio Moscow asserted that the Soviet draft GCD treaty was "the only plan" that could form the basis of negotiation.[21]

On April 20, 1964 the joint declaration of intent to reduce production of fissionable materials was announced by the Soviets as "a major new step toward easing international tension."[22] Further arms controls, formal or informal, were not achieved during the remainder of the period before

[19] Observer, "Moscow Programme," *New Times,* No. 44 (November 4, 1963).

[20] Mikhail Kotov, "The Widening Peace Front," *New Times,* No. 50 (December 18, 1963).

[21] Moscow in German to Germany, March 10, 1964, 1245 GMT.

[22] *Pravda,* April 23, 1964.

Khrushchev was deposed, as Soviet propaganda continued to stress both the dangers inherent in the MLF and Western obstruction in the ENDC.

Thus in its approach to arms control in the period between the Cuban missile venture and Khrushchev's removal two years later, Soviet conduct was marked by significant change within narrow margins. On the one hand, there was a heightened interest in certain forms of agreement, and a more conciliatory posture toward the United States. On the other hand, Soviet conduct was restricted by a host of factors that were not significantly illuminated by either the record of the negotiations or Soviet pronouncements. To determine more precisely the extent of change and continuity in Moscow's policy in this period we turn to the various factors that conditioned the basic Soviet approach to arms control and disarmament.

15

The Implications of Strategic Inferiority

Considerable evidence exists, as noted earlier, that both in terms of the Soviet strategic position at the time and of the prospective ICBM capability, military considerations in 1955 strongly influenced Soviet arms control policy. In the period 1957–1962 the Soviet propensity to negotiate seemed to fluctuate with the confidence that the leaders derived from their strategic power, that is, with high confidence they tended to negotiate more earnestly, with waning confidence their interest in negotiation seemed to fall off, and with the imminence of strategic inferiority they began to take negotiations more seriously again. What then was the relevance of the military-strategic situation to Soviet arms control policy in 1963–1964, once the failure at Cuba had dictated the acceptance of inferiority?

Strategic Forces in Being and in Development

Figure 15.1 shows the approximate gross strategic force levels for the United States and the Soviet Union as of August 17, 1964. As Figures 6.1–6.4 indicated earlier (pp.

201

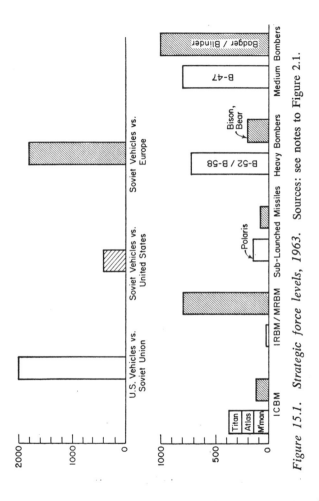

Figure 15.1. Strategic force levels, 1963. Sources: see notes to Figure 2.1.

94–95), the variety and quantity of Soviet strategic delivery vehicles increased substantially over the eight-year period after 1955. Although the diligently fostered notion of the "missile gap" had been exploded by 1961, it was nonetheless true in the post-"gap" period of the early and mid-1960's that the Soviet Union had the unquestioned capacity to deliver nuclear weapons on target in the United States.

By 1963 the Soviet strategic force was built primarily on ballistic missiles (ICBM's, IRBM's, MRBM's), secondarily on missile-carrying submarines,[1] and, to a much smaller degree, on strategic aircraft armed with air-to-surface missiles.[2] The approximate numbers of all these forces in 1963 are displayed in Figure 15.1. As has been indicated,[3] the Soviet MRBM/IRBM force grew only slowly, and a site-hardening program might have been required to make this force into a credible deterrent.

Moscow appeared in the mid-1960's to have a number of options in the further development of offensive weapons systems. These included the following in particular:

Improvement and enlargement of the Soviet ICBM force by deploying a larger number of hardened second-generation ICBM's or by developing an ICBM delivery system for the high-yield warheads under testing since 1961.

Modernization and enlargement of the ballistic missile-firing submarine fleet.

Statements of American officials have shown little concern over a Soviet weapons-in-space program or any significant development and deployment of an ABM system. Consequently, given the slow but steady rise reported in Soviet ICBM and submarine-launched weapons, improvements and

[1] See Table 6.2, p. 94.

[2] Statement of Secretary of Defense Robert S. McNamara before House Armed Services Committee, January 30, 1963. See also Marshal V. D. Sokolovsky, ed., *Soviet Military Strategy* (Englewood Cliffs, N.J.: Prentice-Hall, 1963), p. 309.

[3] See Figures 6.3 and 6.4, p. 95.

numerical increases in the latter systems probably represented the most likely course of action for the Soviet Union in the mid- and perhaps the late 1960's. Although drastic technological innovation in the weapons field seemed unlikely, it was certain that the Soviet Union's strategic deliverable megatonnage, invulnerability, and flexibility would increase throughout the 1960's, particularly if its missile-submarine capability were improved and expanded.

The Search for Political Advantage

Because of its strategic inferiority, Moscow sought to gain maximum political advantage from the military force it had or was likely to have. Soviet political use of military force — the space rockets, the Soviet 61-megaton nuclear blast in October 1961, and Khrushchev's various claims about a "fantastic new weapon," a "global rocket," and a 100-megaton bomb — seems to have been designed in large part to sharpen the concern of American leaders for U.S. vulnerability; this aim emerges rather clearly from Khrushchev's speeches of the period.[4]

After the decisive failure at Cuba and Moscow's at least provisional resignation to military-strategic inferiority,[5] other factors bearing on Soviet security grew in importance. For one thing, there was an intensified interest in averting any continued deterioration of the Soviet strategic position. This concern implied policy moves to inhibit further increases in U.S. nuclear strength, the consolidation of the NATO alliance through the multilateral force (MLF), and the spread of nuclear weapons to West Germany. It also implied steps

[4] See, for example, his speeches of March 16, 1962; December 12, 1962; and January 16, 1963. Moscow Domestic Service in Russian, March 16, 1962, 1500 GMT; Moscow Domestic Service in Russian, December 12, 1962, 1405 GMT; and New Times, No. 4 (January 30, 1963), supplement.

[5] See Thomas W. Wolfe, Soviet Strategy at the Crossroads (Cambridge, Mass.: Harvard University Press, 1964).

to offset Chinese progress toward a strategic capability. Moreover, barring a successful stratagem on the Cuban model or a technological breakthrough, the necessity to live with major U.S. strategic superiority made certain forms of arms control a more palatable policy alternative for Moscow. Thus, in modifying the relationship with the chief adversary by means of both *détente* and limited arms control measures, Moscow could hope to alter a strategic balance that had shifted steadily to its disadvantage.

The Strategic Implications of Soviet Policy

The four limited arms controls into which Moscow entered in 1963–1964 were essentially preventive in nature, and did not disturb the existing military balance[6] or the strategic research and development plans of either side. They represented an increasing strategic rapport between the two chief adversaries, and signified some willingness on both sides to refrain from destabilizing moves.

As to the limited nuclear test ban, Soviet atmospheric testing in 1961 and 1962 apparently yielded significant advances in nuclear warhead design, to the extent that the Soviet government could later assert with some degree of credibility that it possessed "all the necessary requisites for maintaining our defense potential at the proper level that is

[6] It was recently authoritatively reported that in the Cuban missile crisis President Kennedy was more concerned that the presence of Soviet missiles in Cuba would contribute to the "appearance" of a change in the over-all balance of power than to any change "in fact." He later referred to the missiles as threatening the balance of power "materially and politically." The same biographer also reported that Kennedy ruled out inaction because he believed Khrushchev was determined to make the United States appear weak and irresolute, willing to acquiesce in increased "Communist sway" in Latin America, thus clearing the way for a more important challenge against West Berlin or against U.S. bases around the Soviet Union. See Theodore C. Sorensen, *Kennedy* (New York: Harper & Row, 1965), pp. 678 ff.

or may be required by the situation."[7] Although Moscow was willing indirectly to acknowledge that the United States possessed a lead in underground testing,[8] it apparently decided that such tests offered only marginal gains at relatively high cost. As for further atmospheric testing, a key objective would have been to develop ABM systems. Quite apart from the practicality and expense of all-out competition in that realm, Moscow may have believed that as of 1963 it possessed the advantage in high-yield warheads, making it advisable to forestall additional U.S. testing that would lead toward refinements in the penetrability and reliability of U.S. ICBM's.

Aside from foreclosing certain moves in the arms race, the effect of the limited test ban treaty on the Soviet strategic situation seems to have been largely political. The agreement served to lower the perceived military threat from the United States and thus to reduce the effect of the Soviet strategic disadvantage. While it could have little direct military relevance for China, the test ban did raise political obstacles to Peking's nuclear program. Perhaps even more to the point, the agreement served Soviet strategic interests by dividing the United States from France and inhibiting West German development of a nuclear capability either independently or by transfer from the United States. Similarly, by lowering the level of East-West tension the limited test ban could help to undermine Western efforts to create a multilateral nuclear force.

Soviet interest in the hot line would seem to have arisen in part from the realization after Cuba of the need for a rapid and reliable form of communication in crisis management with the United States. Here Moscow seems to have been moved by a desire to stabilize the military environment

[7] Soviet Statement of August 21, 1963 in reply to Chinese Government Statement of August 15, 1963; TASS in English to Europe, August 20, 1963, 2122 GMT.

[8] Moscow in English to Britain, November 14, 1962, 2000 GMT.

by providing a safeguard against the possibility of accidental war, and by strengthening with a formal and less controversial measure the existing tacit understanding on its avoidance.

While the understanding not to orbit nuclear weapons in space did not provide for inspection, and was thus open to evasion, it marked, in common with the test ban, an apparent Soviet interest in closing off possible avenues of weapons development. As in the case of ABM's, the orbiting of nuclear weapons would introduce an element of instability into the military-strategic picture the precise effects of which would be difficult to calculate. Confronted with the uncertaintics and cost of such a program, Moscow may have perceived an interest in not provoking, and in possibly inhibiting, U.S. moves in this direction. Moreover the informal nature of the measure made it possible for Moscow to pursue such objectives without the cost of inspection and with freedom to proceed with an orbiting program if circumstances required.

As to the parallel announcement of intent to reduce fissionable materials production, once again formal restraints were not placed on Moscow. As with the limited test ban, a central Soviet interest in this measure was probably to inhibit the emergence of a race to develop ABM systems, given that the production of high-yield warheads necessary for antimissiles would require substantial supplies of fissionable materials. Unilaterally, Moscow could also hope to exert a restraining influence on American readiness to increase its strategic strength.

Soviet willingness to enter into the test ban, bombs-in-orbit, and nuclear production cutback agreements suggested a judgment that Moscow's military strength was sufficient to back its foreign policies in conditions of *détente,* and also that no breakthrough in the existing technology was imminent for either side.

The modification of the Soviet GCD program, first in

1962 and again in 1963, to allow for retention through the disarmament process of a strictly limited number of nuclear delivery systems by the Soviet Union and United States, was in accord with the immediate Soviet interest in reducing the U.S. strategic advantage and excluding other aspirants from the nuclear club: the one state stronger than Russia would be made weaker, while the Soviet advantage over all others — including China and Germany — would be maintained until disarmament was completed. Thus, in an oblique manner of communication, Moscow appeared to display an interest in the American idea of "stabilized deterrence," so long criticized by Soviet spokesmen. It can also be speculated that the aggravation of the Sino-Soviet relationship in 1962–1963 prompted a greater Soviet interest in the retention of a deterrent force to offset Chinese manpower superiority — an interest also implied by the "nuclear umbrella" proposal. Finally, in the perspective of disarmament, Soviet inability to rely upon Chinese conventional support in a conflict with the West probably increased the incentives to retain a nuclear deterrent.

Although the introduction of the "nuclear umbrella" into the Soviet negotiating stand did not make GCD appear any less remote, and although the various arms control measures arrived at after Cuba seemed very limited in scope, the overall effect of these moves was substantial. They helped to stabilize the Soviet-American confrontation, strengthening barriers to the outbreak of accidental war and the spread of nuclear weapons, and, most important, directing the attention of both sides away from new avenues of development in the arms race. In a manner reminiscent of Moscow's introduction of the ground control proposal into the disarmament dialogue in 1955 to communicate the desire for a joint understanding against surprise attack, the various proposals and agreements of 1963–1964 indicated a strong Soviet interest in moves to stabilize the military environment to utmost advantage.

16

Foreign Policy: Constraints and Opportunities

The failure at Cuba, forcing Moscow as it did to live with an adverse strategic balance, destroyed the basis of a further political-military offensive against the Western alliance. At the same time, the responsiveness of the Kennedy administration to the conciliatory element in the Soviet post-Cuba policy line, combined with the existence of mounting centrifugal forces in NATO, offered Moscow increasingly good reasons to seek a *détente* and even certain agreements with the West. But the Soviet approach to arms controls was also conditioned by an awareness that the balance of forces within NATO and in the NATO capitals made all but the most limited of East-West agreements improbable.[1] These

---

[1] According to Robert F. Kennedy, President Kennedy considered that "the greatest failure during the first two and one-half years of his presidency was the fact that we had reached no concrete agreement with the Soviet Union in the direction of a lessening of international tensions. After the Cuban nuclear confrontation, however, he felt the world had changed and that perhaps there would be less opposition to a renewed effort for agreement. This view was not

constraints and opportunities were matched by influences on Soviet policy arising from the conflict with China. Khrushchev's apparent readiness to rupture relations with the Chinese, rather than make the domestic and foreign policy changes demanded by them, seems to have militated for an accommodation with the West. Yet in seeking to free his hands to deal with the situation to the East, Khrushchev also made himself more vulnerable to criticism from the orthodox throughout the Communist world. The external political situation thus exerted a contradictory effect on Soviet interests in arms control and disarmament.

Perceptions of the United States

The appearance in 1959 of esoteric Lenin documents stressing an instrumental use of the disarmament-peace issue both to split Western elites and to strengthen the less anti-Soviet elements within them, and the amplification of these materials in 1962 and 1964, coincided with Soviet policy statements to the effect that it was "not a matter of indifference" whether Moscow had to deal with aggressive and uncompromising Western leaders or with those who took a more moderate approach to East-West relations.[2]

Soviet statements after the Cuban missile crisis suggested

shared in many quarters of the government, although it was shared by Averell Harriman, among others. Based on this view and on the encouragement he received from Averell Harriman, President Kennedy made the speech at American University [on June 10, 1963]. . . ." See *Toward a Strategy of Peace*, Walter C. Clemens, Jr., ed. (Chicago, Ill.: Rand McNally & Company, 1965), pp. xiii–xiv; see also Sorensen, *op. cit.*, pp. 719–746; Arthur M. Schlesinger, Jr., *A Thousand Days* (Boston: Houghton Mifflin Company, 1965), pp. 889–923; also interview with McGeorge Bundy in *The Christian Science Monitor*, February 28, 1966, p. 1.

[2] In addition to Kuusinen's 1960 Lenin Anniversary Address, (*Pravda*, April 23, 1960), see Khrushchev's speech of January 6, 1961 (*World Marxist Review*, Vol. IV, No. 1, 1961), Ponomarev's speech of April 23, 1963 (in *Pravda* of that date), and N. Inozemtsev, "Nadezhdy i trevogi amerikantsev," *Pravda*, December 25, 1963.

that Moscow perceived a sharp struggle in progress between conflicting leadership groups in the United States. Indeed Khrushchev described the resolution of the Cuban crisis in terms of Soviet manipulation of exploitable differences within the top U.S. leadership:

> Among the ruling circles of the United States there are politicians whom one rightly calls mad. . . . *Is it not clear that if we had adopted an uncompromising position it would only have helped the camp of the rabid ones to utilize the situation* to inflict a blow against Cuba and to unleash a world war? For the sake of justice, it should be observed that among the leading circles of the United States, there are also people who evaluate the situation more soberly. . . .[3]

Khrushchev also chose to emphasize the entirely novel "sobering" effect that this brush with thermonuclear war had had on both the U.S. leadership and the American people generally. Whereas at the Twenty-second Congress in October 1961 he had advanced the line that the U.S. elite was not yet sufficiently "reasonable" in its understanding of the foreign policy consequences of modern weapons developments, after the Cuban crisis he began to advertise that there were those in the U.S. government who now seemed to understand what was at stake.[4]

At the same time Khrushchev made clear his belief that President Kennedy was not entirely a free agent as far as East-West security agreements were concerned, noting that "the Soviet Government takes into account the complexity and many-sidedness of the problems facing various states, displays the necessary restraint, and adheres to constructive

[3] Speech of December 12 to the Supreme Soviet (italics added). Moscow Domestic Service in Russian, December 12, 1962, 1405 GMT. See also Kuusinen's address at the Eighth Hungarian Party Congress on November 21, 1962, Moscow Domestic Service in Russian, November 22, 1962, 0920 GMT.

[4] Compare speech of October 17, 1961 (*Current Digest of the Soviet Press*, Vol. XII, No. 41, 1961) with that of December 12, 1962 (Moscow Domestic Service in Russian, December 12, 1962, 1405 GMT).

views. But we strongly emphasize that there are problems of first priority whose solution brooks no procrastination. . . ."[5] As indicated earlier, this perception of the political situation in Washington intermittently characterized Soviet views on the West in the months prior to the initialing of the limited test ban treaty on July 25, 1963. By that time, however, Khrushchev had gone out of his way to comment favorably on President Kennedy's American University speech of June 10,[6] and *Pravda* had come out with a new and very clear statement of the need to distinguish between various groups in Western capitals:

> In our time, in connection with the possible consequences of thermonuclear war, there has been a marked intensification of the struggle between two tendencies among the bourgeoisie: the aggressive adventuristic tendency and the moderate-sober one. After all, world war has become essentially unthinkable for the imperialist aggressor. . . . *Communists and all the progressive forces are interested in strengthening the moderate-sober tendency in bourgeois policy,* which is dictated by an understanding of the pointlessness of thermonuclear war. . . . The problem is, while not allowing war to be unleashed, at the same time to use the existing situation to the maximum in the interests of the struggle for world socialism.[7]

During the U.S. Senate debate on ratification of the limited test ban, Soviet media provided a good deal of evidence to suggest that Moscow perceived sharp distinctions between the "reasonable" individuals supporting the treaty and the various "madmen" who were said to be at work in the American political system. This distinction was voiced again by Khrushchev in December 1963, soon after the Soviet-American expression of intent not to orbit nuclear weapons

[5] Speech of December 12, 1962, *op. cit.* See also Khrushchev's letter of December 19, 1962 to President Kennedy concerning the test ban (*Pravda,* January 21, 1963).
[6] *Pravda,* June 15, 1963.
[7] F. Burlatskii, "Konkretnyi analyz — vazhneishee trebovanie leninizma," *Pravda,* July 25, 1963 (italics added).

in space, at the moment when he announced a reduction in the Soviet military budget and a possible troop cut:

> I would like to believe that the sensible forces in the United States, those who think realistically and realize the responsibility of their country for the fate of the world, *will show the will and find the means* to rebuff the aggressive militaristic circles, the "madmen," and thereby bar a dangerous development of events which would inevitably involve both the United States and other countries.[8]

As Khrushchev spoke favorably of President Johnson, Secretary Rusk, and Senator Fulbright early in 1964, a new group of Lenin documents was released almost simultaneously with the announcement of the Soviet, U.S., and British intent to reduce the production of fissionable materials.[9] These new materials sanctioned more clearly than ever before Soviet policies designed to enhance the influence of the "sensible forces" in the U.S. leadership.

The preceding evidence clearly associates Khrushchev's differentiated view of the chief adversary with a political use of arms control and disarmament throughout 1962–1964. This gives rise to two questions that go to the basis of the Soviet approach to arms control during the period.

In the first place, to what extent did Khrushchev and his associates in fact perceive the existence of dual tendencies in the U.S. political process? Here it may be suggested that the "conservative" Soviet mentality, as is sometimes the case in the West too, is unlikely to perceive the existence of a significant differentiation within the adversary group. Nor is it likely that even the less "conservative" of Soviet decision makers perceived specific groups in Washington or elsewhere in the United States that consistently represented "sober-

---

[8] Speech to Central Committee plenum, December 13, 1963. Moscow Domestic Service in Russian, December 15, 1963, 0700 GMT (italics added). See also Inozemtsev, "Nadezhdy i trevogi amerikantsev," *op. cit.*

[9] *Pravda* and *Izvestiia,* April 12, 1964; *Pravda,* April 22, 1964.

moderate" or "aggressive" tendencies in the American political system. Presumably Khrushchev had the wit to recognize that on various issues an individual will vary in his willingness to compromise: as one member of the National Security Council observed after the many decisions on the Cuban missile crisis, rather than "hawks" and "doves" there were in the end only " 'dawks' and 'hoves.' " Moreover, the fact that the American "madmen" and "aggressive circles" were often represented in Soviet statements by individuals who were clearly extremists or unsuccessful advocates of a more forward policy against Communism suggested an awareness on Khrushchev's part that his difficulties with the United States arose from a situation far more complex than was explained by the notions of "state-monopoly capitalism" or "aggressive circles of U.S. imperialism."[10]

Khrushchev evidently recognized that certain individuals in Washington represented tendencies that could be influenced. Secretary of State Rusk was presumably seen as a more "sober" and reasonable man than Secretary Dulles; it was doubtless understood that Soviet antagonism toward the West and in the "third world" would tend to revive the influence of those in the United States who thought like Mr. Dulles. And Khrushchev and his associates may have expected that the Soviet *détente* posture would continue to provide President Johnson and his advisers with reason to act with restraint. United States policy in Vietnam was not able completely to cancel out this view during the period, even though it put the *détente* posture under considerable strain in Soviet eyes. We might even conclude that Soviet military and economic interests in arms control in the period were not negligible, nor readily circumvented, and that the

[10] Thus, for example, Mr. Gromyko betrayed a certain realism (or at least lack of ideological distortion) in his remark that some American political leaders pursued an anti-Soviet line because their "political careers" had been built on anti-Communism. Speech of December 13, 1962, to the Supreme Soviet, TASS in English to Europe, December 13, 1962, 1645 GMT.

notion of using formal security agreements in the struggle with an adversary made it appear that a good deal of cooperation could in fact be incorporated into the Communist concept of "struggle."

Germany and NATO

Before the Cuban crisis, Khrushchev doubtless recognized that a political struggle was developing in West Germany as Adenauer's retirement drew nearer. To paraphrase the esoteric Leninist line of this period, it could not have been "a matter of indifference" to him whether he had to deal with Strauss and other German Gaullists, who were rumored to favor independent German possession of strategic nuclear weapons, or with Erhard and Schroeder, who tended to take a somewhat more passive policy line. Khrushchev may have reasoned that under conditions of *détente* and the reduction of the "Soviet threat" the Erhard-Schroeder tendency would become more influential.

In addition to the desirability of a foreign policy posture calculated to influence the political balance of forces within the U.S. and West German leaderships, Moscow was also confronted by mid-1962 with the development of significant differences between the major NATO allies. Divisions of interest between France and the United States had gathered momentum after 1958, and intensified in 1962 as Washington began to press the initial version of its proposal for an MLF. The depth of differences within NATO was revealed to all in the French veto of British participation in the European Economic Community, in January 1963, as well as in the Franco-German treaty of cooperation of the same month.

The extent to which Moscow could attune its policies to openings in the West was, however, significantly influenced by sharpening Chinese resistance to Khrushchev's foreign policy line.

Chinese Restraints on Relations with the West

Following the failure at Cuba, the rising antagonism with China exerted greater influence on Khrushchev to secure his Western flank. As had been the case since 1959, Khrushchev's efforts to lower tensions with the West served further to inflame the Sino-Soviet relationship. Thus while Chinese pressure stimulated Soviet interest in a *détente* with the West, it is not clear what effects the post-Cuba aggravation of the Sino-Soviet rift might have had on the attitude of Soviet leaders toward East-West security agreements. Those of a more "conservative" cast of mind may have considered such agreements inappropriate before a sustained attempt — undoubtedly involving a less conciliatory policy line toward the West — had been made to heal the breach with China. Others, possibly Khrushchev among them, may have viewed arms control agreements as a way of intensifying Chinese alienation and thus of reducing effective Chinese political pressure.

To throw some light on the question of the restraints that China placed on Soviet relations with the West, it is useful to examine in the context of the Sino-Soviet polemic Khrushchev's key proposition that Moscow's foreign relations should be oriented to the promotion of "sober-moderate" thinking in Western capitals.

Following the Twenty-second Party Congress in October 1961 Albania expanded its criticism of Khrushchev's approach to the West, charging that the Soviet premier had "almost completely halted the struggle to unmask American imperialism, hoping, it seems, that in this way the imperialist government of the United States would become peaceful."[11] Similar attacks on Khrushchev's policies continued throughout 1962, with special exception being taken to his August

---

[11] Editorial, "A Year of Historic Proofs," *Zëri i Popullit,* December 6, 1961, in William E. Griffith, *Albania and the Sino-Soviet Rift* (Cambridge, Mass.: The M.I.T. Press, 1963), pp. 273–274.

1962 statement on economic integration, which asserted that the capitalists had in fact taken up the Soviet challenge to compete peacefully.[12] Here again the Albanian Party criticized the alleged belief of the Khrushchev group that an "opportunist" line of conciliation toward the Western governments would make the latter "peaceable" and "sensible," and thus create conditions for a *rapprochement*.[13]

The Soviet response to accusations from the Chinese following the Cuban crisis and the Sino-Indian conflict was to reject the allegation that it had "hopes of persuading imperialism," pointing out that, given changes in the balance of power, "imperialism" had ceased to be the dominant force in determining the course of international events.[14] This seemed a reasonably safe line to take. But, as we have seen, Khrushchev accompanied it in December 1962 and June 1963 with references to responsible political leaders in the West and the desirability of mutual compromises with Western governments. As the test ban agreement drew near, the Soviets began to reply to the various Chinese criticisms more directly.[15] Noting on July 14, 1963 that China had criticized

[12] *Kommunist,* No. 12 (August 1962).

[13] Editorial, "Modern Revisionism to the Aid of the Basic Strategy of American Imperialism," *Zëri i Popullit,* September 19 and 20, 1962, in Griffith, *op. cit.,* pp. 366–369. See also editorial, "Whom do N. Khrushchev's Views and Actions Serve?" *Zëri i Popullit,* March 2, 1962, and "Enver Hoxha's Speech to his constituents," *Zëri i Popullit,* May 31, 1962. Both statements are in Griffith, *op. cit.,* pp. 321–323 and 347–348.

[14] Boris Ponomarev, "The Victorious Banner of World Communists," *Pravda,* November 18, 1962; Moscow Domestic Service in Russian, November 18, 1962, 0600 GMT. Kuusinen, however, emphasized Khrushchev's "force of persuasion" in the settlement of the Cuban missile crisis; Moscow Domestic Service in Russian, November 22, 1962, 0920 GMT. See also Khrushchev's speech of December 12, 1962; Moscow Domestic Service, December 12, 1962, 1405 GMT.

[15] Editorial, "The Differences Between Comrade Togliatti and Us," *Renmin Ribao,* December 31, 1962, in *Peking Review,* No. 1 (January 4, 1963); "More on the Differences Between Comrade Togliatti and Us — Some Important Problems of Leninism in the

Khrushchev's view that President Kennedy "had displayed a certain amount of good sense, a reasonable approach in the course of the Cuban crisis," Moscow now asked, "do they seriously think that all bourgeois governments are completely devoid of reason in all their affairs?"[16]

By April 1964, with the publication of the new Lenin materials on Genoa, Khrushchev seemed to be actually defending President Kennedy against Chinese attack. Asserting that the representatives of the United States had "not been deprived of good sense when it is a question of life or death for their state," he referred to President Kennedy's American University speech and added: "I have been criticized for praising this speech of Kennedy's. But we must not take a primitive approach to events, we must not feel that we are clever and all our opponents are fools."[17] In the same spirit he made favorable comments about President Johnson, Secretary Rusk, and Senator Fulbright.[18]

In the international Communist debate Khrushchev was obviously unable to admit that for various reasons he wanted a *détente* and certain kinds of agreements with the United States, and was prepared to inhibit Communist activities around the world to that end. For Communist-led armed "national liberation" movements in the "third world" — like the pursuit of aggressive "anti-imperialism" by the Communist Parties of Western Europe — would revive a sense of threat in the West; it would help to reconstitute anti-Soviet sentiments within Western states, neutralizing whatever "de-

Contemporary World," *Peking Review,* Nos. 10–11 (March 15, 1963), pp. 8–57; and editorial, "A Comment on the Statement of the Communist Party of the U.S.A.," *Renmin Ribao,* March 8, 1963, in *Peking Review,* Nos. 10–11, pp. 58–62.

[16] *Pravda,* July 14, 1963. To this the Chinese offered the impeccable reply: "There is no reason that can transcend class." "Two Different Lines on the Question of War and Peace — Comment . . . (5)," *Peking Review,* No. 47 (November 22, 1963).

[17] "Rech' tovarishcha N. S. Khrushcheva," *Pravda,* April 7, 1963.

[18] *Ibid.* See also, 'O nekotorykh storonakh partiinoi zhizni v kompartii kitaia," *Pravda,* April 28, 1964.

mobilizing" effect Moscow might have achieved as a result
of its policies of *détente* and negotiation.

Khrushchev was thus obliged to rationalize his conciliatory
foreign policy line with the notion that the use of concessions
to exploit internal divisions within the Western capitals was
a form of "struggle." By attacking the heart of Khrushchev's
rationalization — the assertion that different tendencies could
in fact be distinguished — the Chinese maneuvered Khrushchev into the tactically weak position of appearing to defend
"U.S. imperialism" against doctrinally pure arguments and
of being more interested in collaboration with the adversary
than in the conflict made mandatory by orthodox Marxism-
Leninism.

Implications for Arms Control Policy

From the foregoing it is apparent that the makers of Soviet
decisions on arms control and disarmament found themselves
in a situation of some ambiguity in 1962–1964. In looking
to the West Moscow perceived certain basic interests in
agreement, but presumably recognized that the political situation in the various Western capitals severely restricted the
areas in which the Soviet interest in arms control could be
satisfied. And while ideological pressure from Peking may
have been responsible for some of the restraint in Khrushchev's approach to East-West security agreements, the growth
of an antagonistic China eventually possessing a credible nuclear capability and vying with Moscow for influence in the
"third world" surely strengthened his interest in coming to
terms with the West.

In opting for a rather sobered relationship with the West
after Cuba, Khrushchev found that the need to revise Soviet
positions so as to expand the areas of possible agreement
heightened his vulnerability to attacks from defenders of
Communist orthodoxy. This was particularly so when Moscow sought support for a world Communist conference with

the apparent purpose of ostracizing Peking — a factor that may have contributed to the slight hardening of the Soviet line toward the West in October 1963 and more emphatically in March 1964. But, in the large sense, the arms controls of 1963–1964 with their highly political overtones represented a means of creating an international climate in which the Chinese foreign policy line would appear increasingly inappropriate.

Given these external pressures narrowing the scope of possible agreement, Khrushchev sought to turn to Soviet advantage the opportunities available in the West. In adopting an increasingly conciliatory stance toward Washington after Cuba, he endeavored to diminish the Western sense of a Soviet threat and to neutralize U.S. leadership opinion that favored a continued line of antagonism to Moscow. The Kremlin's interest in influencing the American decision-making process by means of arms control policy was strikingly demonstrated, for example, by Soviet propaganda restraint, which we have noted, first on U.S. underground testing after the limited ban was signed, and subsequently on the manner in which both sides dealt with the measure not to orbit nuclear weapons in space.

A TASS broadcast of August 30, 1963 reported a commentary in *Krasnaia zvezda* to the effect that the Pentagon "curiously" was presenting the new program of underground testing as "an attempt to strengthen the positions of the supporters of the test ban treaty," since the test resumption was aimed "to meet the demands of certain Senators for guaranteeing the security of the United States when the treaty becomes operational."[19] Several days later *Pravda* made a similar observation.[20] This Soviet action and, more positively, the cancellation of the Bernal condemnation (referred to earlier), which would have injected a note of an-

[19] TASS in English to Europe, August 30, 1963, 0618 GMT.
[20] *Pravda* dispatch from Washington as reported by TASS in English to Europe, September 3, 1963, 1624 GMT.

tagonism into the international climate, indicated Moscow's wish not to complicate the President's effort to deal with internal difficulties.

Similarly, Soviet willingness to accept without public comment an "expression of intent" not to orbit nuclear weapons in space when an "agreement in principle" had presumably already been achieved also suggests a strong interest in cultivating a moderate attitude within the U.S. government. The political aim of the measures achieved was to deepen the sense of East-West relaxation desired by Khrushchev in dealing with the Western alliance as a whole. In particular, the reduction of the apparent Soviet threat could have been expected to further the disarray within NATO, especially in the deterioration of relations between the United States and France, which seemed to have a momentum of its own. In addition to creating a climate of opinion inimical to the establishment of the MLF, a *détente* might complicate France's efforts to develop its *force de frappe,* and would amplify sentiment in Britain favoring abandonment of the independent British deterrent.

In the light of these comments on the nature of the Soviet approach to arms control and disarmament in the period, we can proceed to consider Moscow's political interest in comprehensive and partial measures — including those on which agreement was not reached.

Comprehensive Disarmament

It seems reasonable to suggest — and one Soviet writer has all but done so[21] — that the Soviet propaganda campaign on GCD, which continued intermittently throughout the 1962–1964 period, was closely related to the Soviet interest

[21] V. A. Zorin, "Problemy razoruzheniia i manevry Pekina," *Izvestiia,* June 30, 1964; and V. A. Zorin, "Marksizm-Leninizm i problema razoruzheniia," *Mirovaia ekonomika i mezhdunarodnye otnosheniia,* No. 9 (1963).

in cultivating Western leadership groups. Soviet commitment to the "struggle" for GCD via the Communist front organizations, and indeed the generally rather recriminatory Soviet propaganda line on the Geneva negotiations, served as a shield, albeit an imperfect one, against orthodox Communist criticism of Moscow's moves for a *détente* and limited agreements with the West. Certainly without its advocacy of GCD the Kremlin would have been harder put to defend its moves on partial measures during the 1962–1964 period.

In addition, Moscow had an interest in GCD as a useful political backdrop for Soviet negotiating moves on less far-reaching measures that were of more immediate significance to both the United States and the Soviet Union, and the discussions of GCD also offered the Kremlin a means of probing for more immediate mutual interests in the dialogue with the United States. The nuclear umbrella was a case in point. Thus, while GCD did not hold ready appeal for influential opinion in the West, it could provide Moscow with a direct means of influencing the atmosphere in which the implications of limited arms control agreements were discussed.

On a more routine level, Soviet sponsorship of GCD served the various Moscow-oriented peace movements as a tool to mobilize support for Soviet policies in the West. It was also emphasized by Soviet propagandists to promote the image of a progressive and peace-loving Soviet Union to the populations of the developed and underdeveloped countries alike. To the latter, Moscow sought to gain influence by championing the cause of increased economic assistance flowing from disarmament.

Partial Measures

The political as well as the military objectives behind the limited agreements of 1963–1964 have already been discussed. There is reason to think Moscow also had strong political reasons to advocate, if not sign, other measures that it proposed in this period. Negotiation of a nonaggression pact would promote Soviet interests in the light of differences among the NATO allies on this point; agreement on it would lower the perceived threat and deepen the relaxation of tensions for disruptive — or arms control — purposes.

Similarly, stabilizing moves in Central Europe such as measures to prevent surprise attack, the gradual removal of foreign troops from both Germanies, and the exchange of troop representatives among foreign forces stationed in both Germanies, would help to solidify the *status quo* in this region while avoiding the greater risks of the Rapacki Plan, especially for the Ulbricht regime. In achieving these limited but relaxing measures, Moscow would satisfy its interest in obstructing West German acquisition of nuclear weapons.

Other Soviet proposals of partial measures in this period seemed to be primarily of agitational interest to Moscow. The call for the prohibition of nuclear delivery vehicles or servicing facilities on foreign territories was clearly aimed at raising popular opposition in Western Europe and the Mediterranean to the deployment of U.S. Polaris submarines. Similarly, the traditional demand for the abandonment of foreign bases was aimed at destabilizing American missile and bomber facilities abroad. Given its appeal to the "third world," agitation of this proposal also served to counter Chinese attacks on Khrushchev's coexistence line in the various Communist front organizations.

(It might be added that the Soviet government in July 1964 proposed that an international peacekeeping force be established under the U.N. Security Council from contingents provided by neutralist, Western, and Communist powers — excluding the five permanent members of the Council.[22] While this move was part of the attempt to shore up the Soviet position in the United Nations' financial crisis, and to cast doubt on a peacekeeping conference then being organized by Canada, it may also have indicated a nascent interest

[22] *The New York Times,* July 5, 1964.

in limiting violence in the "third world" through cooperation with the United States in the Security Council.)

Thus, while there seemed to be substantial political interests moving Moscow toward an accommodation with the West, Soviet conduct did not eschew the political uses of arms control and disarmament that serve as a means of struggle against the adversary. The complex of constraints and opportunities that both East and West posed for Moscow, while sustaining the duality of Soviet political tactics on arms control, was also responsible for the more basic ambivalence that we have discussed in Soviet intentions toward the United States. Some further light may, however, be cast on the blend of conflict and collaboration in Soviet policy by examining the impact of economic and domestic political affairs on the Soviet posture.

17

Economic Factors in Soviet Policy

Defense Expenditures

After 1956 estimated military expenditures started to increase rapidly: by 1962 defense outlays were about 40 per cent higher than in 1957 (see Figure 3.1, p. 52). In 1960 and 1961 an attempt may have been made to stabilize defense outlays, but it was abandoned, perhaps in response to the first Kennedy budget. The principal cause of this observed increase in spending was undoubtedly the accelerated effort in the development of rocket technology; ICBM's received great and increasing emphasis, while IRBM's and tactical missiles probably retained an important place in the Soviet advanced-weapons program.

Antimissile technology may also have played an increasing role in escalating the costs. The development of advanced aircraft, while de-emphasized in Soviet military doctrine, in all likelihood continued to play a role throughout the current period although one of decreasing importance. The proportion of total defense outlays devoted to the procurement of conventional equipment for the ground forces was certainly much lower in the period 1958–1963 than in earlier years, although the Soviet Union continued to devote some attention to the improvement of its conventional armaments. In the period 1962–1963 the commanding objectives of the Soviet defense effort were probably (a) to develop and place in serial production a second-generation ICBM system, an effort begun before first-generation systems became fully available; and (b) to advance the development of a missile-submarine capability.

Very little can be said about trends in total defense outlays in 1963 and 1964 on the basis of data yet available. The published outlay for defense in 1963 was 13.9 billion rubles, that is, 10 per cent more than in 1962.[1] In December 1963, however, Khrushchev announced a reduction of the defense budget to 13.3 billion rubles, a reduction of about 5 per cent.[2] At the same time the Soviet Premier stated that his government was considering the "possibility" of a troop cut as well.[3]

Despite the dramatic increase in the Soviet defense effort during the Khrushchev decade, the weight of defense expenditure as a share of GNP was probably lower in 1962 than in 1955. A 10–12 per cent range appears reasonable for 1962 when hidden spending above the published budgetary level is taken into account.

Apart from its relation to GNP, however, the "burden of defense" should be evaluated by its effect on the rate of economic growth generally and in terms of real resources denied to other sectors of the economy. In 1961–1963 a broad deceleration from the rapid growth rates of the mid-1950's was apparent in most sectors. In industry — the priority

---

[1] *Narodnoe khoziastvo SSSR v 1962 godu: statisticheskii ezhegodnik* (Moscow: Gosstatizdat TsSU SSSR, 1963).

[2] *Pravda*, December 16, 1963. In 1965 the official Soviet military budget declined to 12.8 billion rubles. It was to be raised 5 per cent to 13.4 billion rubles in 1966 as part of a general increase in the Soviet budget (*The New York Times*, December 8, 1965, p. 1).

[3] *Izvestiia*, December 15, 1963.

sector for the Soviet economy — the slowdown was marked.[4] In agriculture, after the bumper harvest of 1958 a series of mediocre years followed and finally the catastrophe of 1963. It appears to have been increasingly recognized, especially in 1963, that better and stable harvests were dependent upon irrigation and the expansion of the chemical industry and thus required the allocation of additional investment resources. In regard to consumption the regime's policy was to allow moderate improvement to follow the growth rate of the economy as a whole. With the general economic slowdown, growth of consumption appeared almost to have ceased, consumer-goods output rising only 5 per cent in 1963.

The broad slowdown in the Soviet economy may have been in part a product of trends unrelated to defense production. Nevertheless, since growth has been one of the most urgent priorities of the Soviet regime, we believe that the diversion of valuable resources to armaments became increasingly burdensome — even though the percentage of GNP devoted to defense may have declined. It is likely that the need to allocate increasing resources to arms has been at least partially responsible for the stagnation of other sectors of the economy. Clearly the channeling of engineering and other trained personnel to the arms effort has tended to restrain civilian technological progress and inhibit the main-

---

[4] See TASS report in *The New York Times,* October 21, 1964. The Greenslade-Wallace index shows an annual average growth rate of aggregate civilian industrial output of 10.7 per cent for the years 1954–1957 but only 6.7 per cent for 1959–1962. The official Soviet index, which includes military output and is inconsistent in other ways with most Western indexes, shows an annual rate of industrial growth of 11 per cent for the years 1955–1957 and only 9.5 per cent for 1960–1962. Soviet figures on plan fulfillment in 1963 claim a growth rate for that year of 8.5 per cent. See Rush V. Greenslade and Phyllis Wallace, "Industrial Production in the USSR," in U.S. Congress, Joint Economic Committee, *Dimensions of Soviet Economic Power* (Washington: 1962), p. 120; and *Narodnoe khoziastvo SSSR 1962,* p. 119.

tenance of existing plants. Military production has also cut into civilian machinery production; this in turn has hampered investment, which is increasingly dependent upon the supply of new machinery. In 1963 the machinery supply component of Soviet investment plans was not mentioned in plan-fulfillment data, suggesting a large margin of underfulfillment. Similarly it is likely that expansion of the chemical industry, a priority since 1958, was restrained by the Soviet arms effort.

Further evidence that the arms burden was felt to be placing pressure on the Soviet economy was suggested by the appearance in March 1962 of statements in the Soviet media implying that President Kennedy had intensified the U.S. commitment to the arms race. Such statements were apparently made to justify diverting "considerable funds" from Soviet economic development to arms.[5]

By April 1964 Khrushchev, for political reasons that will be considered later, pointed explicitly to an inhibiting effect of military expenditures on Soviet agriculture and consumer goods production:

> Doesn't the need to support the defense might of the USSR at the present-day level hinder raising the well-being of the people? With all straightforwardness I reply: Yes, it hinders it. Rockets and cannons — these are not meat, not milk, not butter, not bread, and not *kasha*. If it were not necessary constantly to strengthen the might of the Soviet armed forces, we could sharply raise the living standard of our people, make it in the very near future the highest of the world.[6]

More precise relations between armaments and the overall deceleration of the Soviet growth rate are not easily determined. It is probably accurate to suggest, however, that the burden of military expenditures on the economy has in

[5] Moscow Domestic Service in Russian, March 11, 1962, 1400 GMT; and election speech of A. Kosygin on March 14, Moscow Domestic Service in Russian, March 14, 1962.

[6] N. S. Khrushchev, "O mire i mirnom sosushchestvovanii," *Kommunist,* No. 7 (May 1964).

general increased in recent years and has consequently impinged increasingly on other goals of the Soviet leadership. In short, there can be little doubt (*a*) that the Soviet arms effort since the late 1950's has inhibited the capacity of the regime to counteract trends causing deceleration of the economic growth rate, and (*b*) that reduction or at least stabilization of arms expenditures would have some favorable effects on growth.

Implications of a Declining Growth Rate

There is evidence to suggest that the reduction in the Soviet growth rate and conflicting demands on scarce resources generated internal conflicts on foreign policy. It is useful to consider the possible relations between Khrushchev's efforts to deal with domestic economic problems and the foreign policies of *détente* and limited arms control that he pursued in the period under consideration.

By 1962 Khrushchev's attitude on resource allocation was to some extent consumer oriented.[7] In this respect he differed from "some comrades" who had "an appetite for metals that could only unbalance the economy."[8] Given the very low probability that the adverse strategic balance could be easily reversed, and given his propensity to resist major increases in resource allocation to armaments, it was not surprising that Khrushchev in March and April 1962 proposed an intensified Soviet commitment to policies seeking to exploit differences within Western elites. By June–July 1962, following the major food-price riots near Rostov on June 1 and the decision, apparently made in the summer of 1962, to place Soviet missiles in Cuba, Khrushchev with seeming reluctance affirmed that Soviet arms expenditures would have to be con-

[7] See Carl Linden, "Khrushchev and the Party Battle," *Problems of Communism*, Vol. XII, No. 5 (May 1963).

[8] Speech of January 6, 1961 (*Pravda*, January 21, 1961).

tinued at the expense of investment in animal husbandry and consumer goods.[9] Subsequently the thaw in the Soviet policy line immediately after Cuba, with its emphasis on concessions and *rapprochement* with Washington, was definitely associated with renewed but apparently unsuccessful moves on Khrushchev's part to stress the domestic consumer economy.[10] For the moment, however, he succeeded in a major reorganization of the party and in making further gestures toward a test ban agreement.

Rather than accelerate a very costly arms race in which the lead of the opponent was considerable, Khrushchev apparently chose in the immediate post-Cuban relaxation with the West to moderate the arms race, to stabilize — if not to reduce — Soviet arms expenditures, and to promote the growth of the consumer economy. This last objective was reflected in a renewed emphasis on the theme that the economic achievements of the Soviet Union represented its greatest contribution to the "world revolutionary process."

In the following months Khrushchev was evidently forced to retreat on his line of limited *rapprochement* with the United States and on his domestic economic program. As we noted earlier, following the Soviet test ban concessions of December 1962 Moscow canceled the three-power test ban talks at the end of January 1963. In his election speech of February 27, 1963 Khrushchev pleaded with his electors to "give us time" in providing consumer goods and openly stated that the "spending of enormous funds" required for the Soviet military program "reduces and cannot help but reduce the

[9] Speech to Cuban students in Russia, June 3, 1962 (*Pravda,* June 4), and speech at Grivita Rosie Plant in Romania, June 19, 1962 (*Pravda,* June 20), both cited in *Problems of Communism,* Vol. XII, No. 6 (June 1963), and *Pravda,* July 6, 1962 (speech to military academy graduates).

[10] Although Khrushchev affirmed the primacy of heavy industry at the November 1962 plenum, it was not without complaints about those who cried "steel, steel!" Linden, *op. cit.*

people's possibilities of obtaining direct benefits."[11] The trend of events against Khrushchev seemed to be strengthened in March 1963, when the Supreme Council of the National Economy of the USSR (VSNKh) was established. The creation of this organization recentralized planning and evidently neutralized some of the advantages Khrushchev gained through the November 1962 Party reform.[12] The Chairman of the Supreme Council, Dimitri Ustinov, for some two decades previously had been directing Soviet armament industries.

As the East-West *détente* deepened following the signing of the limited test ban treaty and the understanding not to orbit nuclear weapons, Khrushchev sought a return to the defense of his domestic economic line. At the December 1963 plenum heavy emphasis was placed on an ambitious program for the development of the chemical industry, and a cut in the Soviet military budget was announced. And at the open plenum of February 1964 Khrushchev attempted to argue the point that growth in the chemical industry and agriculture would strengthen Soviet defense capability.[13]

Toward the end of April 1964, as has been indicated, Khrushchev came more directly to the point in opposing the maintenance of high levels of Soviet military spending. Having asserted that "certain ruling parties and leaders of

[11] *Pravda*, February 28, 1963. See *Pravda*, January 7, 1963, editorial comment on the defense burden: "Bearing such a burden is no easy matter; the Soviet people are quite often obliged to deny themselves necessities."

[12] Leon Smolenski and Peter Wiles, "The Soviet Planning Pendulum," *Problems of Communism*, Vol. XII, No. 6 (1963).

[13] Speech of February 14, 1964 to Central Committee plenum, *Pravda*, February 15, 1964. Khrushchev used an elliptical technique in making his point by referring to Western views that "the Soviet Union has been forced to reduce its arms and armed forces because of difficulties in economic development. Attempts are also being made to propound the theory that the Soviet Union is incapable of simultaneously developing its economy and strengthening its defenses. . . ."

the biggest capitalist states "were coming to recognize that force could not be used to settle international disputes, Khrushchev made it clear that the Soviet defense budget stood in the way of his plans for the development of agriculture and light industry.[14] This statement appeared in the Party's theoretical journal shortly after the publication of new esoteric documents advocating a foreign policy of compromise, and the joint announcement of intent to reduce the production of fissionable materials.

In the following months, as the East-West *détente* continued its uncertain course, Khrushchev gave increasing emphasis to consumer goods. Shortly before he was removed he called upon Soviet economic planners to place "the satisfaction of the growing material and spiritual requirements of men at the forefront in working out the long-term plan for developing our economy."[15] This may well have been interpreted by the heavy-industry and military interests as an open bid for popular support for a Malenkovite "new course" in economic policy.

It seems reasonable to conclude that during the period under review, the pressure of the arms burden on the Soviet economy was a contributing factor in Khrushchev's pursuit of both *détente* and perhaps even a long-term attenuation of the conflict with the United States. In seeking a *détente* Khrushchev evidently sought to reduce the military threat to the Soviet Union from the West; in reducing the military threat he must have hoped to be in a stronger position to press for, among other things, a reduction of the Soviet military budget and thus eventually a more rapid expansion of the civilian economy.

In addition to such budgetary relief as might follow from a *détente* with the West, Khrushchev's apparent desire to avoid increasing the burden of Soviet military spending seems

[14] Khrushchev, "O mire i mirnom sosushchestvovanii," *op. cit.*

[15] Moscow Domestic Service in Russian, October 2, 1964, 0600 GMT.

to have been directly related to three of the four arms controls achieved in 1963–1964. The limited test ban, the statement of intent not to orbit nuclear weapons in space, and the joint announcement of readiness to reduce fissionable materials production probably reflected, in part, an interest in foreclosing new and costly developments in the arms race. Insofar as these measures succeeded in closing off the remaining major avenues of weapons development for East and West, their effect over time may give some satisfaction to the Soviet desire for relief from the economic burden of defense.

18

Internal Political Pressures

Our cautions regarding the obscurity of the Soviet political system are particularly applicable here, where the perspective of events is so short. But some tentative judgments are possible.

While many Western observers had regarded Khrushchev's position as unassailable, his abrupt removal suggested that significant independent political power resided in the institutions that he formally controlled. One can speculate on the possible parallel between the internal political struggle of 1954 and 1955, which led to Malenkov's downfall, and the circumstances under which Khrushchev operated in 1962–1964. As we have seen, both men were committed to unsuccessful domestic policies tending to stress light industry and some increase in consumer investment. But where Malenkov failed to secure the kind of *détente* that in his view the "new course" and Moscow's foreign political situation required, Khrushchev made some progress in the form of arms control agreements. Without stretching the point, the parallel might be relevant in looking for the sources of internal oppo-

sition to Khrushchev's foreign policy line and in attempting
to calculate their effect on his ability to enter into agreements.

Sources of Opposition

Khrushchev throughout this period seems to have been engaged in a running battle with the so-called "metal eaters" —
the proponents of continued emphasis on investment in heavy
industry — plus the representatives of the armaments industry and possibly some of the military establishments as
well. These groups were essentially technocratic, associated
with the state as opposed to the party machinery and, in the
opinion of some, sufficiently powerful to dominate the economy — with the exception of agriculture.[1]

It may be significant that the fall of Khrushchev was
presaged by the publication in *Pravda* of a letter indicating
that the Ministry of Finance had refused to comply with the
decentralized planning decisions and the introduction of
profit-based accounting.[2] Moreover, shortly before the appearance of Khrushchev's "new course" statement on October 2, 1964, the Soviet military press apparently expressed
an opposing view.[3] Accordingly, part of the military establishment, if the events of 1954 and 1955 are any indication of
the characteristic opposition to a "new course" for the Soviet
economy, may previously have combined with the technocrats
in some manner to resist Khrushchev's attempted modifications in domestic and foreign policy.

In opposing Khrushchev's economic moves, the "statist"
opposition as a whole may have sought to inhibit or restrain
his accompanying efforts to establish a *modus vivendi* with
the United States. In this some presumably reasoned that the

[1] L. Smolenski and P. Wiles, "The Soviet Planning Pendulum,"
Problems of Communism, Vol. XII, No. 6 (November-December
1963).
[2] *The Christian Science Monitor,* October 16, 1964.
[3] *Ibid.;* also Chapter 17, footnote 15.

greater the apparent reduction of the external "threat," the more easily the internal economic changes desired by Khrushchev could be effected. It may also reasonably be assumed that some of Khrushchev's opponents believed significant shifts in Soviet resource allocation would institute the moral and physical disarmament of the Soviet Union in the face of what they perceived to be an essentially unchanged and aggressive United States.

It was thus not wholly surprising that the Soviet Defense Minister, Marshal Malinovsky, implicitly attacked the Khrushchevian theme that "sober-moderate" groups were emerging in the U.S. leadership, and condemned proponents of "pacifism" and the "abstract negation of war" within the Soviet Union.[4] These remarks were made at difficult moments for Khrushchev (February 1963 and 1964), when he was under strong pressure to desist in his moves to reduce allocations to defense.

In February 1963 Khrushchev seems also to have been engaged in a struggle with the late Frol Kozlov, a powerful figure then in the party Presidium and Secretariat, who apparently tended to favor sustained investment in heavy industry.[5] Kozlov's disappearance from the political scene in April 1963 due to a stroke may have assisted Khrushchev in moving for a test ban agreement.[6] In February 1964 Khrush-

[4] Speeches of February 22, 1963 (*Pravda,* February 23, 1963) and February 7, 1964 (*Krasnaia zvezda,* February 9, 1964). On the former occasion, Malinovsky emphasized that "time has taught the imperialists nothing," and warned: "It must not be naïvely supposed that the imperialists have laid down their arms. The events we are witnessing today show that not everyone has yet learned to assess soberly the balance of forces that has taken shape on the international scene. . . ."

[5] C. Linden, "Khrushchev and the Party Battle," *Problems of Communism,* Vol. XII, No. 5 (September-October 1963).

[6] Testimony of Marshall D. Shulman, *Hearings before the Committee on Foreign Relations, United States Senate on Executive M, 88th Congress, 1st Session* (Washington: U.S. Government Printing Office, 1963), p. 795.

chev clearly acknowledged that he differed with members of the party on matters of foreign policy:

> We must not deny the paramount importance of economic construction in the socialist countries and oppose it to the class struggle against imperialism. To do this is to confuse different concepts.[7]

The implication seemed to be that certain party members regarded the foreign affairs corollaries of Khrushchev's economic program as contrary to correct foreign policies oriented to the struggle against "imperialism."

Since it was reportedly Suslov who delivered the main attack on Khrushchev in October 1964, he may have been one of those who tended to oppose Khrushchev's line of conciliation and limited agreements with the United States. Quite apart from concern for the practical problems of Sino-Soviet and international Communist relations that continued to rise throughout the 1962-1964 period, Suslov was no doubt voicing a more widespread sentiment in the CPSU that Khrushchev's *détente* policies were unpalatable. The proclivity in the international Communist movement to view coexistence in a tactical and instrumental light[8] underscores the likelihood that opposition within the Soviet Communist Party may have been substantial where permament arms control agreements with the United States were concerned.

In addition, resistance may also have been focused on Khrushchev's efforts to restrain the "anti-imperialist" propaganda and to play down "wars of national liberation." The fact that the Bernal condemnation of U.S. underground testing after the partial test ban was transmitted and then re-

[7] Speech of February 14, 1964; *Pravda*, February 15, 1964. The context here is one of domestic policy.

[8] See, for example, Ezio Santarelli, in "The Debate in the Central Committee and the Central Control Commission of the PCI on the XXII CPSU Congress," *L'Unità*, November 12, 1961. Document given in Alexander Dallin *et al.*, eds., *Diversity in International Communism: A Documentary Record, 1961–1963* (New York: Columbia University Press, 1963), p. 422.

scinded by Moscow may also have indicated the existence of differences of opinion. Similarly the tendency — perhaps most clearly associated with Mikoyan[9] — to emphasize Soviet arms shipments to new states and to assert that Soviet general disarmament proposals would not disarm the new states suggests that continuing concern existed within the Soviet leadership over the issue of national-liberation wars (although Mikoyan could have been equally or even more concerned to cover the left flank against Chinese criticism). The very active but indirect Soviet arms aid to Congolese rebels after Khrushchev's removal also strongly implied the existence of internal opposition to his relative restraint on the national-liberation issue.

Above all, opposition to Khrushchev's approach to East-West relations must be interpreted in terms both of relations with China and of the erosion of Soviet control in Eastern Europe and in the nonruling parties. It was crystal clear that energetic pursuit of the Khrushchev line on coexistence and arms agreements served to sustain Sino-Soviet antagonisms, to create conditions favoring the further disintegration of Soviet influence in the bloc, and to aggravate the divisions within the international movement. Given Khrushchev's apparent inability to cope with these problems in 1963–1964, it would hardly have been surprising for some Soviet state and party officials to have altered their preferences from a *détente* that was at best left unconsolidated toward definite resistance to arms control agreements.

The Effects of Internal Dissension

Given these potential forms of opposition to Khrushchev, the continued publication in 1962–1964 of archival materials on the 1922 Soviet disarmament and peace proposals at

[9] See, for example, speeches of March 14, 1962, and July 2, 1964: TASS in English to Europe, March 14, 1962, 1957 GMT; and *Pravda*, July 3, 1964.

Genoa must have reflected an effort on Khrushchev's part to legitimize and broaden support for his innovations in relations with the West. In March and April 1962 those who were less well informed about the nature of the Genoa documents were asked to accept them as evidence of literal commitment on Lenin's part to the pursuit of disarmament agreements and the kind of coexistence being sought by Khrushchev. This was at a time when Khrushchev seemed to be attacking Kozlov's base in Leningrad by associating himself personally with an effort to unseat Spiridonov (one of Kozlov's associates) from the Secretariat of the Central Committee.[10] The success of this move in April, accompanied by the return of Kirilenko to the Presidium, may have eventually given Khrushchev sufficient influence to take steps on the test ban and reportedly on the spread of nuclear weapons in August and September 1962, while at the same time preparing the Cuban missile venture. The November reform of the party also seemed to mark a further advance for Khrushchev.

However, this progress was apparently not made without loss of political bargaining power. Although Khrushchev retained some latitude in foreign policy, criticisms of anti-Stalinism appeared late in 1962 when the November plenum emphasized the priority of heavy industry, and Khrushchev himself led a new assault on freedom in literature and the arts. By March 1963 Khrushchev had announced that advances in consumer goods production were to be postponed in favor of defense and heavy industry, the establishment of the VSNKh had neutralized some of the organizational advances of the November 1962 party reform, and the internal climate seemed generally less favorable for East-West arms control agreements. Nonetheless private talks on a test ban continued in 1963; an agreement on satellite cooperation was signed with the United States on March 20; and on April 5 the proposal for a direct communication link with Washington was accepted in principle.

[10] Linden, *op. cit.*

In April 1963 the internal political picture apparently improved for Khrushchev and with it the prospects for arms control agreement. On April 8 *Pravda* in a routine advance printing of the May Day slogans failed to note that Yugoslavia was "building socialism." Shortly afterwards Kozlov disappeared from public view, and on April 11 *Pravda* set the May Day slogans right. The implied reassertion of the moderate line in foreign affairs was soon followed by Khrushchev's criticism of what had in effect been Kozlov's demand for increased investment in heavy machine-building equipment.

Additional light on Khrushchev's internal posture was shed during a seven-hour interview he granted Norman Cousins on April 12, 1963 at the Black Sea retreat of Gagra, sixty miles from Sochi. Cousins had been asked by President Kennedy to clarify the Soviet misunderstanding on the U.S. position on a test ban. Khrushchev contended there was no possibility of a "misunderstanding" and that the United States had simply raised its demands as soon as he had agreed to three on-site inspections — even though none were scientifically required in the Soviet view. Khrushchev declared:

> We wanted a treaty and the U.S. said we couldn't get one without inspections. So we agreed, only to have you change your position.

The Premier went on to say that following the Cuban crisis he had gone to the Council of Ministers and argued:

> We can have an agreement with the United States to stop nuclear tests if we agree to three inspections. I know that three inspections are not necessary, and that the policing can be done adequately from outside our borders. But the American Congress has convinced itself that on-site inspection is necessary and that the President cannot get a treaty through the Senate without it. Very well, then, let us accommodate the President.
>
> The Council asked me if I was certain that we could have a treaty if we agreed to three inspections and I told them yes. Finally, I persuaded them. . . .
>
> People in the United States seem to think I am a dictator

who can put into practice any policy I wish. . . . Not so. I've got to persuade before I can govern. Anyway the Council of Ministers agreed to my urgent recommendation. Then I notified the United States I would accept three inspections. Back came the American rejection. They now wanted — not three inspections or even six. They wanted eight. And so once again I was made to look foolish. But I can tell you this; it won't happen again. . . .

We cannot make another offer. I cannot go back to the Council. It is now up to the United States. Frankly, we feel we were misled. If we change our position at all, it will not be in the direction of making it more generous. It will be less generous. When I go up to Moscow next week I expect to serve notice that we will not consider ourselves bound by three inspections. If you can go from three to eight, we can go from three to zero.

Khrushchev also threatened that he would accede to the demands of his atomic scientists to resume nuclear testing, but he finally told Cousins that if the United States agreed to a comprehensive test ban treaty Moscow would concur and permit some on-site inspections. He reiterated, however, his refusal to ask the Council of Ministers to permit more than three inspections annually.[11]

Later, on the Lenin Anniversary in April 1963, Ponomorev, normally associated with a conservative line on foreign affairs owing to his primary concern for international communism, called for "sensible agreements" with the moderate Westerners.[12] In May a further agreement was signed with the United States (on cooperation in the peaceful uses of atomic energy), and in June a further strengthening of

[11] Norman Cousins, "Notes on a 1963 Visit with Khrushchev," *Saturday Review*, November 7, 1964, pp. 16–21, 58–60, at pp. 20, 21, 58. It is not excluded that Khrushchev exaggerated some aspects of his position and that the relevant policy body was the CPSU Presidium rather than the Council of Ministers, but the story probably gives the basic thrust of Khrushchev's thinking at the time.

[12] *Pravda*, April 23, 1963. The *World Marxist Review* also returned to this line for the first time since the Khrushchev statement of August 1962 on economic integration. Santiago Carillo, "Some International Problems of the Day," *World Marxist Review*, No. 5 (April 1963).

Khrushchev's position was reflected in the appointment of Brezhnev and Podgorny to the Secretariat of the Central Committee. Khrushchev seemed to have sufficient leverage to rebuff the Chinese and to enter into the test ban agreement with the United States. It is to be noted, however, that he still avoided concessions on inspection.

With the signing of the test ban, Khrushchev proposed several partial measures that he considered susceptible to East-West agreement.[13] From the internal standpoint he probably stood to gain from any one of them, since all were essentially political undertakings without direct impact on Soviet force levels. Most attractive would have been a non-aggression pact or a military budget freeze. The latter would presumably have given him some support in the internal political struggle, and the former, by strengthening the *détente,* might have had a favorable effect on his domestic economic policies. As it was, however, Khrushchev emerged with an understanding not to orbit nuclear weapons in space, which could have helped in restraining those who favored offensive military use of space.

In the meanwhile Sino-Soviet relations had continued to deteriorate, and the Soviet grain harvest had proven catastrophic. Thus, as Khrushchev began to move in October 1963 for a conference of the Communist parties, the balance of internal political forces may have begun once again to swing against him. Although the effort to convene a conference soon ended in failure, Khrushchev's line on the chemical industry and agriculture was emphasized in December when he announced a cut in the military budget and a possible Soviet force reduction.

By 1964 Khrushchev was speaking of East-West arms con-

---

[13] As indicated, these included a nonaggression pact; a freeze on military budgets; measures to prevent surprise attack; a cut in foreign troops stationed in both Germanies; and an exchange of troop representatives among the foreign forces in both Germanies. It is noteworthy that at the ENDC in August the Soviet negotiator tied the control post proposal to progress on other measures.

trol agreements in terms of "the policy of mutual example." This approach may have been in deference to what he considered to be President Johnson's political position, but it also suggested certain restraints on Khrushchev's ability to enter into formal agreements. No doubt those responsible for the Soviet armaments industry, some of the military, and the advocates of the primacy of heavy industry had to some degree been alienated by the budgetary cut and by Khrushchev's accompanying demand for substantially increased investment in chemicals.[14] The party conservatives may have become concerned by Peking's aggravation of the Sino-Soviet differences to the point of instigating border disturbances and by Khrushchev's failure to cope successfully with the situation. Those responsible for agriculture were doubtless perturbed by the showing of 1963. Thus, by the time of the February 1964 plenum and the renewed commitment of the CPSU to an international Communist conference of excommunication, Khrushchev was again pleading for resources for light industry and agriculture and for a foreign policy line of conciliation toward the West.

We can only speculate on the future course of Soviet policy had Khrushchev remained in power beyond October 1964. Kuusinen's death in May deprived him of needed support in both the Presidium and the Secretariat. Mounting economic problems and Russia's waning position in international communism would have strengthened internal opponents of Khrushchev, but it is impossible to know whether the contradictory forces within the Soviet power structure would have pointed toward a retrenchment in U.S.-Soviet relations or toward greater accommodation to relieve certain pressures. In any event, the rising tensions in Southeast Asia would surely have presented a Khrushchev still in power with the same kinds of inhibitions that have troubled his successors in their dealings with the West.

[14] See Thomas W. Wolfe, *Soviet Strategy at the Crossroads* (Cambridge, Mass.: Harvard University Press, 1964), pp. 149–152.

19

The Soviet Interest in Détente *and Agreements*

The Soviet approach to arms control and disarmament after the Cuban missile adventure was shaped by a contradictory process in which the pursuit of policies of conciliation and limited arms controls with the United States was countered by, and indeed sometimes stimulated, resistance to policy change. The evidence suggests (1) that Khrushchev and some of his associates were interested in a prolonged attenuation of the conflict with the United States; and (2) that such interest was only partially sufficient to overcome the many inhibitions to formal agreements. In the summary that follows, we first examine the nature of Soviet interests in a *détente,* then consider restraints on the Soviet ability to enter into formal agreements, and finally seek to place the conflict of interests on *détente* and arms control into the over-all framework that combined both conciliation and antagonism in the Soviet approach to the West during the period.

244

The Factors at Work

By mid-1962 the Soviet leaders were confronted with the prospect of strategic inferiority for the foreseeable future, plus a faltering Soviet growth rate that seemed to require some form of reallocation of resource priorities to the detriment of heavy industry and defense. These posed two problems of long-term significance that Soviet investment and output could not solve simultaneously. Accompanying them were strong political pressure from the Chinese, the advent of an American administration that seemed more interested than its predecessors in exploring stable relations with Moscow, and a growing disunity among the NATO powers.

Moscow seemed aware that the arms race had reached the point where the enormous investments involved were returning increasingly marginal gains in security. A drastic rise in ICBM production or a wholesale commitment to the development and deployment of antiballistic missiles, civil defense, or weapons in space may have struck Khrushchev as an increasingly questionable proposition. And of course to some extent, the arms race was creating a pause of its own, so to speak, given the enormous striking power that had been accumulated on both sides, and given also the absence for the moment of any radically new weapons systems promising a ready and economically acceptable improvement in strategic power.

Of the several factors at work, apart from the fluctuation of internal differences on foreign policy, the Soviet perception of the adverse military balance — and what to do about it — seems to have been the most important element influencing Soviet leadership in 1962–1964. When it came time to translate the implications of the strategic balance into foreign policy, however, the military factor could not be divorced from economic determinants and the limitations that they imposed on Soviet choices. Thus, while considering the strategic balance to be of fundamental importance in determining Soviet conduct on the arms control and disarmament issue, it was in this sense little less significant than the pressure of economic considerations. And certainly of key importance were both the political opportunities and constraints that the West placed before Moscow and the political and potentially military pressures that China mobilized against Khrushchev.

During Khrushchev's last two years in the Kremlin, Soviet policy toward arms control thus appears to have been based more firmly on enduring national interests than were the previous, possibly "tactical," Soviet attempts to achieve a *détente* in 1955 and in 1959–1960. But the precise extent to which it was based on long-lived conditioning factors was a function of the distribution of power within the Soviet leadership, which in turn was influenced by the other conditioning factors we have mentioned. For instance, Khrushchev presumably found it more difficult to deal with internal resistance to his domestic economic policies and to his interest in further limited arms control agreements after the partial test ban treaty, when the failure of the Soviet harvest in 1963 was forcing him simultaneously to negotiate an enormous purchase of wheat from the chief adversary.

Alternatives for Soviet Policy

Despite new dimensions in virtually all the determining factors, the fundamental alternatives facing Soviet policy during the period were in many ways comparable to those of the past. Moscow could seek to rectify the military balance by entering into a costly arms race with a wealthier opponent, thus requiring that economic growth be given second place and a more antagonistic posture be adopted toward the West. Alternatively, Moscow could seek to alter the political character of the strategic confrontation, through *détente* and possible limited agreements, to offset the growing Western strategic advantage. The latter course would probably strengthen the resolve of the Kennedy administration to reciprocate in seeking new East-West relations; it would, however, involve a repudiation of the Soviet association with the Chinese Communists, and thus a repudiation of "conservative" communism in Soviet domestic and foreign policy generally.

But one variation of these alternatives took the form of a seeming short cut, through which Moscow could seek to circumvent the problem of Soviet strategic and economic deficiencies by attempting to gain an immediate increment in Soviet strategic power through the redeployment of existing forces. If successful, the internal pressure for sustained levels of Soviet military expenditures would presumably slacken, thereby allowing some redirection of resources to lagging sectors of the Soviet economy, particularly agriculture.

In Cuba the Soviet leaders sought the third alternative. With the test ban and the other limited agreements, Khrushchev pursued the second alternative. And after Khrushchev's removal it was not clear which direction was to be favored.

The failure in Cuba underscored the improbability of either offsetting U.S. strategic superiority or gaining political advantage of that sort from Soviet military strength. Cuba may thus have legitimized some of the pressure Khrushchev exerted for reallocation of Soviet resources away from defense. At the same time, the rise in U.S. missile strength in 1961 and 1962 and the advertisement of the military balance by the Kennedy administration served to emphasize the depressing effects of Soviet military and economic weakness on a continued foreign policy offensive. The psychological aftermath of the Cuban confrontation favored a positive American response to Soviet expressions of interest in stabilizing East-West relations. Similarly the growth of centrifugal tendencies within NATO, in part the result of Khrushchev's efforts over the years to reduce the appearance of a blatant Soviet "threat" to the West, probably gained importance in the Soviet perspective after Cuba.

From Khrushchev's point of view, relief from both strategic adversity and economic scarcity may have lain in a relatively enduring *détente,* for only over time could a relaxation of East-West tensions blunt the threatening edge of Western strategic superiority. Only over time could mutual reduction of military budgets be promoted in the hope of gradually achieving a measure of reallocation of Soviet resources to the chemical and light industries. The partial test ban agreement was intended to place obstacles in the way of increases in the strategic capability of West Germany and China. Together with the other Soviet-American agreements it implied a reciprocated interest in cutting off expensive developments in the arms race, both defensively in the case of the antimissile missile and offensively in prohibiting the emplacement of nuclear weapons in space. The agreements presumably reflected a Soviet interest both in a gradual reduction of military budgets and in maintaining an international political environment suitable to this end.

By the end of the year the need to obtain wheat from the United States had compounded Khrushchev's problems: in February 1964 he seemed to be under severe pressure not to cut the Soviet military budget as he had begun to do in December 1963, and therefore not to proceed with investment in the chemical industry and agriculture as he clearly desired. Nonetheless Khrushchev evidently preserved sufficient strength to enter into the reciprocal cutback in fissionable materials production, this being his last major move in the arms control field before October 1964.

Collaboration Over Conflict

It has been observed that the conciliatory Soviet moves of 1963–1964 arose in part from a desire to aid the fragmentation of the Atlantic Alliance. While Soviet conduct in 1963–1964 gave priority to dealing with the United States on the German problem, Moscow throughout the period retained the option of negotiating directly with West Germany and France in an effort to reduce American influence on European affairs. In the longer term, depending on how their differences were managed by the Western powers, Moscow might have expected to find itself in a position to make renewed demands on the German question with greater chances of success. In any event, the achievement and continuation of an East-West *détente* could in the Soviet view be expected to stimulate a *détente* within the various West European countries, allowing greater local Communist success by broad-front tactics.

In principle, the Soviet leadership also remained free throughout the period to support armed "national liberation" struggles in the new states, even to support them somewhat more energetically by drawing carefully on the new stability in Soviet-American relations to take greater risks in the "third world." More practically, perhaps, Moscow stood to gain from the fact that American military intervention into the "third world" would be made with greater difficulty under conditions of *détente,* and that in this event it would be easier to mobilize diplomatic and popular opinion against the United States. While Khrushchev's policy in the short term was basically one of limited verbal commitment to wars of "national liberation" and restraint in practice, Moscow could in the longer view calculate that a *détente*-oriented international environment would be conducive to advantageous political and social change in the "third world."

Furthermore, the options did remain of developing anti-ballistic missiles or attempting clandestinely to orbit nuclear weapons in space. Should a military-strategic breakthrough be possible, however expensive or technically unlikely, a political offensive could be resumed at a time when NATO had fallen into desuetude, and the level of Western political and military mobilization to withstand Soviet threats had declined. Although Soviet conduct in 1963–1964 seemed to reflect a desire to check the arms race, these possibilities could not be ruled out. Nor, of course, was it entirely a matter of Soviet volition, since Moscow's activity in the military-strategic sphere, and in foreign relations generally, was contingent also on Western behavior. Clearly, then, it would be illusory to imagine that the limited arms controls and various manifestations of restraint in Soviet foreign and military policy in 1962–1964 had brought into sight the end of Soviet hard-line policies.

We are led in the end to the conclusion that, in the mixture of antagonism and collaboration in the Soviet approach to arms control in 1963–1964, Moscow's interest in collaboration to satisfy persistent and relatively long-lasting national needs may have in fact begun to outweigh the outlook that saw accommodation with the adversary as always tactical. Although a return to policies of "struggle" against the West remained a distinct possibility, the accommodations of 1963–1964 evidently offered some satisfaction to persistent Soviet needs. And where needs are satisfied, the policy changes that assure them often come to have a rationale of their own.

PART IV

THE KHRUSHCHEV DECADE IN RETROSPECT: THE DRIVING FORCES

The ten years ending with the limited arms controls of 1963–1964 and Khrushchev's removal soon thereafter, constitute a distinctive chapter in the evolution of both Soviet foreign policy and Soviet interest in arms control and disarmament. The rise of Khrushchev by 1955 coincided with a number of epochal developments affecting the basic outlook of Soviet foreign policy: the end of the West's nuclear monopoly and the imminence of both the missile and space ages; accumulated Stalin-fatigue in the Soviet Union; a U.S. President devoted to creating a new "spirit" in East-West relations; new vacuums in the "third world"; and the beginnings of the Sino-Soviet rift. The composition of the United Nations was about to be irrevocably altered; and under the monolithic façade of international communism there were surging eddies of polycentrism that would swell into a current of rebellion against Soviet hegemony. But of all the forces creating an environment for wholesale change in Soviet policy, the most significant was the growing conviction on both sides that general thermonuclear war was not to be permitted.

These opportunities and problems in the international field registered a sharp impact upon Soviet foreign relations and on arms control policy in particular. By 1955 and for several years thereafter the Soviet mood was one of rising expectations and of optimism. The expectations derived primarily from the calculation that something like atomic parity with the West had been achieved, that with an all-out research and production effort on ICBM's the military balance would soon shift further to the Soviet advantage, and that it could pursue a political and economic offensive aimed at expanding the "zone of peace" and contracting the capitalist camp while avoiding general war. In the realm of arms control and disarmament Soviet policy began to shift in 1954–1956 concurrently with the new look in foreign policy. Heavy-handed "exposure" tactics of the Stalin era were modified, but not replaced, by greater emphasis on a "reasonable" and conciliatory appearance in the style and substance of Soviet disarmament proposals and propaganda; toward accommodation with Western positions and the adoption of partial-measures approaches instead of the "ban the bomb" slogans of the late Stalin period.

At a minimum it appeared that the shift in arms control policy was aimed at undermining the West's will and ability to maintain its defenses. But the increased feasibility and realism in Soviet proposals suggested there might also be a qualified but growing Soviet interest in enacting certain measures that might reduce the danger of surprise attack, impede German rearmament, and freeze research and development of nuclear weapons at a moment favorable to the Soviet Union. From 1957 to 1960, even after the world began to talk of a "missile gap" in Moscow's favor, manifest Soviet interest in various partial measures, particularly a cessation or ban on nuclear testing, continued.

1955 was a time when multiple opportunities seemed to be opening up to influence events in conformity with the revised desires and expectations of the Soviet leaders. But even by

*1956 the limits to their prospects were beginning to appear.
By 1959 a sense of reality was returning and, as the 1960's
began, a protracted morning-after set in. 1955 may have
marked a sharp decline in the paranoia so long characteristic
of the Soviet outlook; but it left a dualism in that outlook that
bordered on the schizoid.*

*The reasons were several. One was that by the very nature
of the situation the desires and expectations of the Soviet
leaders were essentially contradictory, and each had the effect
of setting in action a countervailing force. Even in inner
Soviet reasoning one senses internal tensions. For every
reasonable measure of agreement with the adversary to warm
up the atmosphere, save money, or ward off the threat of later
annihilation, there was always a new argument against appearing weak, a danger on a new flank, a new difficulty raised
by the enemy, or a new temptation to exploit.*

*From 1954 to 1961 the Soviet Union thus endeavored to
relax tensions with the West even while seeking to bury it by
economic and political competition. It tried to keep China
within the fold even while refusing it nuclear weapons and
attempting to restrain Peking's military and foreign policy. It
endeavored to avoid a showdown with either Washington or
Peking, while maintaining and increasing Soviet influence to
the east and to the west, and to the south as well. Détente
with the West was the logical policy expression of the renewed
"peaceful coexistence" doctrine, implying "struggle" short of
major war while the zone of Communist influence expanded.
But détente contributed to erosion of the leading strings from
Moscow to the satellite capitals both in the east and west.
Agreements that controlled China's force levels or inhibited
its capacity to test nuclear weapons were desirable from the
standpoint of Russian national security; but disarmament
propaganda had the effect of further alienating an increasingly
militant Peking.*

*If in 1955 détente was paramount, the opening opportunity
to leapfrog the northern tier of U.S. treaty states in the Middle*

East and penetrate into the African vacuum at the same point in time was close to being paramount. If in 1959 and 1960 the spirit of Camp David and the GCD line were highly functional to Soviet strategy, the chance to consolidate a new client state ninety miles off the coast of Florida was too good to miss. If in 1961 Moscow's touted missile lead proved by and large to be nonexistent, nevertheless the exigencies of keeping East Germany in camp required the most serious risks to be run in Berlin that year.

Arms control policy had a greater or lesser role to play in all these operations, either in neutralizing forces inimical to Moscow or in cultivating sentiment favorable to the Soviet government. Indeed, disarmament in some form may have been the logical policy expression of the new appreciation of the nonutility of general nuclear war. But it ran afoul of accumulated suspicion of the West, the tempting political uses of the threat of force, the powerful military factions in the Soviet Union, and the extraordinary functional difficulty in arriving at formulas that satisfied both the Western need for reassurance and the Soviet wish for secrecy. If in 1962 the more sophisticated Soviet leaders had marked, absorbed, and digested the contemporary American school of strategy featuring minimum deterrence and the arms control doctrine, the chance drastically to revise the strategic equation with an end run via Cuba proved too tempting.

But the narrowing of alternatives open to the Soviets was not just a product of their own schizoid view of things. From 1956 to 1961 the bases of Soviet optimism were undermined one after another by events not of their own immediate making. First, the Polish uprisings and then the Hungarian revolution of 1956 shook the foundations both of the empire gathered by Stalin and of Moscow's leadership in international communism. Following these shocks came a more profound threat — ideological, political, and even military — from Peking, creating for Moscow even as early as 1957 the classic spectre of a two-front struggle. The Western front was proving unyielding in the face of Soviet pressure on Berlin, and the military and economic power of the West during the rest of the 1950's grew stronger and more integrated despite the autonomous course steered by Paris after 1958.

Undoubtedly Moscow marked well the new and potentially disastrous political fissures opening in NATO as the 1960's began. But the overriding reality was that by 1960 Washington was about to reverse whatever missile gap there may have been, and this at a time when a downturn in the Soviet economy made the relative weight of military expenditures more onerous. Finally, the attempted leap into the "third world" had reaped little fruit: the emerging nations appeared as little susceptible to Soviet as to Western influence. As for arms control and disarmament, failure of the 1955 approach, Western disinterest in disengagement, and the start of the ICBM and space races all reinforced the growing sense of the unreality of the debate, culminating in Khrushchev's 1959–1960 initiative in proposing sweeping general disarmament.

By 1961 and 1962 the Soviet government thus seemed to be faced with some new choices to make. Given its narrowing alternatives, what policy course could it pursue realistically? Could it seek accommodation with both Peking and the West? Should it concentrate on internal or external development? And what arms control measures, if any, remained relevant to its still-changing strategic and political circumstances? The 1961 joint-principles statement represented surprising consensus. But other pressures within the Kremlin seemed to militate for short cuts to redressing the strategic balance vis-à-vis the West, first by the testing of some very high-yield bombs in 1961 and then by the Cuban missile gamble in 1962. It must have seemed that only from a position of power would the problems on both eastern and western fronts prove more amenable to solution on Soviet terms. While Soviet diplomacy stalled for time, Moscow's apparent interest in partial disarmament measures seemed to decline as the Kremlin in-

creasingly returned to the propaganda of general and complete disarmament.

The failure of the 1962 Cuban venture to yield an improved bargaining position for the Soviets again narrowed the alternatives but this time seemed to indicate with new clarity the desirability of at least a temporary accommodation with the West. This option was made the more feasible by Washington's apparent willingness to forgo a more aggressive strategy designed to exploit the Soviet retreat; by the deterioration of Sino-Soviet relations; and by the economic difficulties that pressed hard on Russia in 1963.

In 1963 many of the essential conditions for serious Soviet interest in arms control agreements in fact came together. Moscow possessed a minimum deterrent braced with some multimegaton bombs, but had no prospect of attaining superiority over the United States. Washington indicated its willingness to collaborate with Moscow to keep the peace and control the arms race. No rapprochement *seemed possible with China. A success for "peaceful coexistence" could help Khrushchev internally. Economic incentives were strong to lower defense spending by such moves as a ban on nuclear testing, keeping the arms race from outer space, and slowing the production of fissionable materials.*

The Khrushchev decade had begun with Moscow confident that it was riding a tide of history and would soon vanquish capitalism in political and economic competition. It ended with Moscow apparently pleased just to stabilize the military-political situation with the West and to cut the losses within the international Communist movement, accepting, at least up to Khrushchev's removal, the consequences of the defection of China.

20

The Decisive Factors in Arms Control Policy

To draw specific conclusions regarding Soviet interests in arms control during the Khrushchev decade, it is necessary to return to the assumptions with which this analysis began. With these as a starting point, a close look has been taken at several forces that underlay Soviet interests in arms control, namely the changes over time in the strategic-military situation, in the external political outlook, and in the economic and the internal leadership situations. Our conclusions center on the nature of these factors and their interaction, as they influence the formation of Soviet interest — or disinterest — in arms control in the decade under study.

A few explanatory words should be said about these factors and the relationship between them. Although they are treated in similar fashion, and have even been rank-ordered in accordance with their apparent relative saliency as determinants, they are not in fact completely comparable. The first three factors — military, external political, and economic — represent both objective situations with which Soviet leaders must deal and policy goals for which arms controls might be functional. This pertains particularly clearly to the first and second factors.

To illustrate: the desire for military security represents a constant and fixed goal of the Soviet Union; Soviet policy must adapt to and try to influence the military-strategic balance that prevails at any given time. It seems apparent that arms control and disarmament take their primary meaning from the ways in which they serve the security goal by altering the military situation. However, it is perhaps less readily apparent that they may alter the military situation in two different but closely interrelated ways: (1) imposing formal and tacit measures of control on the international military environment; and (2) influencing the will of the opponent to make use of military force, by the use of concessions and agreements against a backdrop of military threats. Apart from their value in serving the various ends of Soviet political strategy, the "manifest" changes in Soviet arms control policies in 1954–1956 appeared to constitute the beginnings of a trend toward greater feasibility and realism and, more basically, the beginnings of an awareness that adversaries could share a common interest in confining their military competition and containing possible military confrontations. Thus, of the several determinants, the military-strategic factor stands out as the primary force accounting for continuity and change in Soviet arms control interests during the Khrushchev decade.

The second factor likewise represents a fundamental objective of Soviet policy: the manipulation of the external political environment to serve the twin ends of Soviet security and political strategy. Arms control policy in the period was a reasonably flexible instrument for the pursuit of security objectives, whether through propaganda that would psychologically disarm others or through measures to improve Soviet security by actually affecting the military dispositions of others. Arms control and disarmament policy was in the period a potent support for the strategy of *détente* vis-à-vis the West; there disarmament was presented as a way of ensuring peace and prosperity. To the Communist world it was justified in these terms and also as the best means of advancing the cause of revolution — but by peaceful means. Soviet arms control and disarmament policies were thus aimed at inhibiting the arms race, influencing the level of international tension, impeding Western unity, dealing with the mounting challenge from China, and winning support for Soviet policy in Eastern Europe and in the underdeveloped countries.

The economic factor enjoys a more distant but still functional relationship with arms control policy. Significant arms reductions can obviously have a direct feedback effect upon the domestic economy. But for the period in question we would rate as considerably lower in importance than the other factors any incentive for serious arms controls that may have been supplied by the slowly mounting drag of military expenditures upon the Soviet economy. The economic situation probably constituted an increasingly distinct incentive to *détente* and arms control after 1961. But the point cannot be made too often that the tempting Western assessment of Soviet defense costs as "burdensome" always requires correction to account for the totalitarian ability to mobilize, force sacrifices, and suppress demand.

The fourth factor — political differences within the Soviet leadership — is of a different order. One might have treated the three factors discussed above as though they represented an objective reality somehow independent of the perceptions of the Soviet leaders. But this is a valid approach only if one can assume that the leaders all perceived reality in the same way. Since the Soviet elite has in the past decade demonstrably not been monolithic in its view of things, the policy significance of the other factors must be qualified by a specific examination of the internal controversies within the Soviet Union. The internal power struggle has therefore to be considered as a separate influence on arms control policies, even though from a purely logical standpoint it is not parallel to the other factors considered. There is persuasive evidence that the manner in which the contending Soviet elites perceived the domestic and world situations and attempted to act upon them exerted on occasion a strong influence upon the specific arms control policies followed.

One more thing must be said about the four factors and the way in which they are treated here. For the period under review, 1954–1964, these four make sense as determinants of Soviet interest in arms control and disarmament measures. It might even be inferred that one could predict the *future* course of Soviet arms control policy by analyzing the particular configuration of determinants in 1954–1964, under the assumption that a similar constellation of factors at a future time might produce comparable results in terms of Soviet interest in certain types of arms control or disarmament. That may be true. But the warning is self-evident: the way these particular factors interacted and were perceived by Moscow at any given moment in this period will not necessarily recur.

The Military-Strategic Factor

Of the four main factors we have studied, the military-strategic factor best accounts for both the stability and the fluctuations in Soviet policy toward arms control. Moscow's deep concern to avoid general war and its acquisition of a credible minimum deterrent account in large part for the fixed elements among Soviet interests and policies on arms control, while the changing balance between Soviet and U.S. strategic forces appears to have been the key factor in inducing the shifts in Soviet arms control policies throughout the decade.

Two notions, of the class the Soviets like to call "permanently operating," shaped Moscow's evaluation of the changing military balance: the recognition of the potential destruction nuclear war could inflict; and Soviet acquisition of an effective minimum deterrent to create a functioning balance of terror — mutual deterrence. Neither of these strategic constants operated in Stalin's time. Both were characteristic of a new realism in Soviet strategic thinking — a coming to grips with the restraints as well as the opportunities of the atomic age. This realism spilled over into Soviet arms control thinking as well, most significantly in the realization that in certain circumstances security might be served by limited agreements with the adversary over and above propaganda alone.

The first of these two notions to become constants in Soviet military thought was the belated recognition in 1954–1956 of the decisive role that surprise nuclear attack could play in modern war. Despite occasional bravura assertions that only capitalism would perish in a nuclear exchange, Soviet political thinking also acknowledged an awareness that general war under modern conditions would destroy Communist as well as capitalist society. Since a nuclear first strike could be decisive to the whole course of the war and not just to a single operation, it behooved Kremlin policy to make greater efforts to control the military-political environment so that the West would not attack the Soviet Union on grounds either that it was weak or that it was soon to overtake and bury the capitalist system. It therefore served Soviet interests to pursue a political-military line that both lowered manifest danger to the West and raised the threat of crushing retribution. The first aim could be partially effected by a somewhat more reasonable posture in arms control negotiations, while the second led Moscow to maintain an impressive military machine, which the Kremlin warned could pre-empt Western plans for aggression.

As for limited war, the Soviet government appeared genuinely concerned that such a war might escalate or that another power such as Germany or China might by catalytic action involve the great powers in a direct confrontation. It

thus may not have wished to give carte blanche in the For-
mosa Strait, and declared Soviet neutrality in the Sino-Indian
border clashes in 1959. Such concerns seem in part to have
underlain a whole series of Soviet arms control proposals,
from ground control posts to symbolic acts such as a nonaggression pact or a ban on the use of nuclear weapons. In
part, but not entirely for propaganda purposes, Soviet theory
also belittled the chances of containing a war fought with
"tactical" nuclear weapons.

Throughout the decade Soviet policy makers generally
sought to avoid or at least to keep under control conflicts that
could lead to war. Soviet interests were to be promoted
primarily by political and economic competition, thereby
making a virtue of the necessity of avoiding war. While Moscow occasionally brandished a big stick, it tended to speak
softly. At times the Kremlin dealt out threats and ultimatums,
but only in Berlin and Cuba, in 1961 and 1962, did Moscow
approach the brink — and then only when desperate to redress its diminishing bargaining power, and in the process
evidently making a serious miscalculation of the probable
U.S. response under President Kennedy. In order to avoid
great power confrontations, Moscow tended to limit its actual
support to national liberation movements well below the level
suggested by its propaganda. The objective of controlling
East-West tensions to avoid war was served generally by the
very existence of arms control negotiations. More specifically,
it was served by cultivating personal contacts with Western
leaders, reiterated expressions of concern for the consequences of thermonuclear war, the growing East-West experience in crisis management, and — eventually — by a direct
communications link with Washington.

A second strategic notion that seemed to be "permanently
operating" in Moscow's outlook was the confidence that the
Soviet state, for the first time since 1917, possessed the means
decisively to deter attack upon it. The potential destruction
that could be wrought by surprise nuclear attack had changed

the "laws of war." But the equally striking fact was that in 1953–1955 the Soviet Union developed hydrogen as well as nuclear bombs, plus the means to deliver them to Europe, to SAC bases around Russia and — at least on one-way missions — to the United States itself. Throughout the decade, the actual number of U.S. bombers and missiles capable of striking the Soviet Union far outnumbered the Russian strategic delivery vehicles that could reach the United States. But, the Soviet government possessed a credible minimum deterrent from about 1954, the magnitude of which was vastly exaggerated in the Western and the Soviet press at least until 1961. Further, a very large number of Soviet medium-range bombers and, later, missiles held Western Europe hostage. Not by accident is the concept "deterrence" rendered in Russian as "terrorization." Soviet confidence that the West did not plan or want war was also reinforced by personal contacts with Western leaders and visits to Western countries.

Feeling relatively secure against calculated attack by a nuclear power, and perhaps even believing some of its own propaganda about the "bomber gap" and the "missile gap," the Soviet government shed much of the paranoia of Stalinist times. But while Moscow's new deterrent may have allayed long-standing fears arising from Russian vulnerability, the over-all effect was to raise Moscow's political strategy to a new level of importance because there was now a diminished belief that the West would respond to Moscow's political-economic offensive by military intervention — at least not by attack upon Soviet territory.

Depending on how "minimum" the Soviet deterrent appeared to the West, the Kremlin could also press for political concessions. Furthermore, in disarmament negotiations the Soviet Union could consider dispensing with arms — present or potential — not considered essential to preserve the Soviet minimum deterrent, provided of course that the West reciprocated or had already eliminated such equipment. Moscow could now approach the negotiations with a *quid pro quo* to match Western concessions, in contrast to the wholly negative Soviet stance when confronted with the Baruch Plan in 1946. Finally, Moscow's realization that both sides acknowledged an effective balance of terror helped Khrushchev to revise Lenin's 1916 dictum that disarmament was neither possible nor desirable so long as capitalism endured; peaceful co-existence was now dictated by "life itself."

The Strategic Balance

Interacting with the Kremlin's acknowledgment of mutual deterrence in East-West relations, the changing nature of the military balance precipitated certain specific Soviet interests in achieving some concrete forms of arms control. We judge that the Kremlin's interest in achieving such measures was relatively high from 1955 to 1960, low from 1960 to 1962, and highest between 1962 and 1964. In the first period the seemingly high Soviet interest in arms control appears to have been based upon an expectation of significant improved relative strength and the bargaining power this would carry with it vis-à-vis the West. The low point occurred when Moscow's military and political advantages were being rapidly undermined and the Kremlin leadership sought by desperate measures to regain them. But when after the Cuban debacle Moscow had resigned itself for the time being to reliance on a minimum deterrent considerably smaller than U.S. strategic might, the Soviet interest in arms control measures reached a high point for the decade.

Closer analysis of this pattern reveals more concretely the strategic rationale behind Soviet interests at different times. From 1954 to 1960 Soviet strategic expectations were high, even though the United States far outnumbered the Soviet Union in strategic delivery vehicles — mainly bombers. It appears that for a time in late 1959 and early 1960 Moscow may have had a slight lead in the number of ICBM's on launchers. In any event the Soviet Union was far ahead of the

United States from 1957 through 1964 in the development of powerful boosters capable of shooting large payloads into space. The Kremlin obviously intended to exploit this situation in political bargaining; but Soviet interest was also evidenced in the advocacy of the kinds of arms controls championed in Soviet diplomacy from 1955 to 1960, that is, reductions of conventional forces and a nuclear test ban. Given secondary attention but nonetheless reflective of strategic interests were measures regarding bases and calls for disengagement in Central Europe.

The first step in implementing that strategic interest was the reduction in conventional forces. A large infantry was no longer necessary to hold Europe hostage, and Soviet armed forces were unilaterally cut from over 5 million to just over 3 million men from 1955 to 1961. The Soviet bases in Austria, Porkkala-Udd, and Port Arthur were eliminated in 1955. By 1960 Khrushchev went further: he talked of the obsolescence of surface naval vessels and bombers as well as of large ground forces, and pointed to the economies their reduction would allow while at the same time Soviet firepower actually increased due to nuclear technology. Soviet official statements in 1956 and 1960 also noted the economy's need for the manpower resources resulting from demobilization. In 1960 a fifth branch of the armed forces was formed — the Strategic Rocket Forces. Khrushchev's "atomic fetishism," as the Chinese called it, was only partially checked by the influence of more conservative marshals who insisted that "balanced" forces be maintained, armed of course with the latest weapons.

From 1955 to 1960 Moscow often called on the West to reciprocate in the reduction of armed forces (and the elimination of foreign bases), and Soviet disarmament proposals emphasized such measures. The point most stressed by Soviet propaganda about the May 10, 1955 proposal was its endorsement of Western-proposed force levels of 1–1.5 million men for the United States, the Soviet Union, and China. Such a measure would have forced greater reductions upon Moscow than upon Washington, but it would also have effectively forced U.S. troops to withdraw to a "Fortress America" by the end of 1957. (Complete nuclear disarmament was to begin in mid-1957 and be completed at the end of the year.)

In the same vein, perhaps because of Moscow's imminent space triumphs, the Soviet proposals of March 27, 1956 dealt exclusively with conventional force reductions, plus the banning of hydrogen bomb tests (just before London planned its first tests) and the prohibition of nuclear weapons in Central Europe. Beginning at the 1955 Summit Conference, Moscow also espoused a ceiling of 200,000 men for states other than the big five — a move clearly aimed at thwarting plans for a German *Bundeswehr* of 500,000 men.

The second principal arms control measure flowing directly from Soviet strategic interests was to halt nuclear testing and thus to inhibit both the refinement and spread of nuclear weapons. By the time Moscow completed its March 1958 test series, the Kremlin seems to have concluded that a moratorium on further testing would help to keep what it considered to be its lead in strategic rocketry and prevent the refinement of U.S. tactical nuclear weapons. Since the Soviet Union could shoot larger payloads into space, Moscow was concerned to prevent warhead miniaturization by the United States. A test cessation would also slow the development of small, "clean," mobile bombs for use in limited war. So long as this strategic situation prevailed it was in Moscow's interest to accept a test ban that had these desired effects provided excessive international inspection on Soviet territory were not required.

As to the third set of measures reflecting strategic interests, Moscow endeavored also to keep U.S. weapons from being stationed in other countries and to prevent nuclear spread, especially to Germany and China. In 1955 and 1956, while SAC bases were still a vivid threat to Soviet security, Moscow advocated control posts in air fields and other designated locations, but — in this pre-Sputnik period — said nothing about missile launchers. And the Soviet concern to reduce the general danger of war, economize on conventional forces, drive the United States out of Europe, prevent German re-armament, and capitalize on Soviet medium-range and long-range rockets was reflected by Moscow's almost constant advocacy of disengagement and the denuclearization of Central Europe together with inspection and ground control posts.

The threat posed by China to Soviet strategic interests seems to have been of special concern to Moscow. In the short run China might involve Russia in a war with the West or, at the least, undermine Soviet efforts for *détente*, as in 1958–1959. In the long run there was the possibility of territorial disputes and, more important, the prospect of great conventional and nuclear Chinese military power. Moscow tried to keep Peking militarily dependent upon a nuclear shield based in the Soviet Union, and from 1957 to 1959 placated Chinese nuclear aspirations by some kinds of long-term aid in developing a new defense technology.

In June 1959, according to Chinese sources, Moscow flatly refused to provide a sample atomic bomb or the technical data required to produce one. Soviet proposals for a nuclear-free zone in the Far East and Moscow's espousal of peaceful coexistence as the highest form of international class struggle were both aimed in part, although with little prospect of success, at inhibiting China's military pretensions. There seems however to be little evidence for the idea advanced in Peking and elsewhere that Khrushchev sought in 1962 or 1963 to impose with the West a nonproliferation agreement upon China. France's acquisition of a nuclear capability seemed less threatening and more inevitable, but Moscow did what it could to promote nuclear-free zones where France planned to test.

By 1961 most of the optimistic calculations that accompanied the shift in Soviet arms control policy in 1955 had been undermined or had proved illusory. The salient strategic fact was that while Moscow still possessed a credible minimum deterrent, its political bargaining position was seriously eroded by a sharp and mounting U.S. lead in the production of ICBM's, a lead that was publicized as establishing a real missile gap but this time in Russia's disfavor. The Soviet response could have been to negotiate more earnestly on arms control in order to check the U.S. lead. But Moscow opted instead to kill the test ban talks by trying to link them with GCD, and to resume nuclear testing in the atmosphere. If the Soviet Union could not produce more missiles than the United States, it chose to test larger warheads than Washington considered a sound military investment. Regardless of military utility, the up-to-61-megaton tests were fully exploited by Moscow to terrorize public opinion and thus to add to the power base on which Soviet diplomacy rested.

After Moscow's tests had been completed, a year of drift and ambivalence in Soviet foreign policy ensued, a year in which the Kremlin appeared unsure whether to strive again for a bold move to enhance its power position, or for some accommodation with the West that included agreements on arms control. Apparently content with the results of its own nuclear tests, the Kremlin moved in November 1961 and again in September 1962 to ban all nuclear tests, with at least a moratorium on underground testing. But Moscow was willing to pay little for such a ban, and rejected the principle of even limited on-site inspection until the winter of 1962. The lack of commitment to immediately feasible partial measures was manifested by Moscow's emphasis on GCD in the Eighteen Nation talks in 1962. The Soviet GCD program, however, was in turn made increasingly reasonable by a number of modifications, notably Gromyko's endorsement in September 1962 of the principle of retaining nuclear weapons in the disarming process.

But while Moscow stalled for time on the disarmament issue, the strategic imbalance tilted still more to Russia's disfavor, and the Kremlin decided on another bold move to improve its psychological and strategic position against the West: the emplacement of missiles in Cuba, which ended in humiliating retreat.

The point of maximum arms control activity came after Cuba. The limited arms control agreements of 1963–1964 — the hot line, the partial test ban, the ban on bombs in orbit, the pledge to slow fissionable material production — followed the Soviet failure dramatically to modify the strategic equation via the Caribbean, and all reflected a desire to freeze or at least slow down a race in armaments in which the West was rapidly outpacing the Soviet Union. The hot line may in part have reflected Moscow's desire, based on its traumatic experience in Cuba, to reduce the danger of war by miscalculation or inadvertence.

Soviet leaders declared that if either side were to benefit from the test ban it would be the Soviet Union, since it held the lead in testing huge warheads. Although the Soviet Union could not presently hope to match the United States in ICBM's, to freeze the number of strategic delivery vehicles on each side, as Washington proposed early in 1964, would rule out all prospect of parity. What the Soviet Union could accept would be a reduction of forces on both sides toward a common level — the idea of a nuclear umbrella, which Moscow agreed in September 1963 should be maintained until the very end of the process of general and complete disarmament. The idea of relying upon a minimum deterrent of the same size as Washington's had become increasingly attractive for Moscow in a world where the United States outproduced the Soviet Union and where Peking and the NATO allies threatened to obtain nuclear forces of their own. However, the interests of both sides would probably require that a minimum nuclear deterrent possessed by Moscow and Washington be accompanied by a nonproliferation agreement accepted by or imposed on the rest of the world.

Because of Moscow's interest in avoiding war, and its

confidence — at least in 1955–1959 — in a "peaceful victory for communism," there may have been more than propaganda in its espousal of general and complete disarmament. In theory disarmament was an appropriate adjunct to the pursuit of the "peaceful offensive" under the changed "objective conditions." However, if implemented it would have deprived the Soviet Union of the extraordinary bargaining power obtained from the political uses of nuclear weapons through threats, deterrence, and implied actions. Moreover, serious disarmament might have had the effect of vitiating Communist *élan* in many countries.

In any case, there is little evidence that Moscow regarded GCD as a feasible program actually to carry out in the foreseeable future. All that can be said about it is that, with a nuclear umbrella sustained throughout the process, some version of GCD, no matter how utopian it seems today, is no longer unthinkable in terms of Soviet security interests.

The major limitations to Soviet interest in arms control were, like the inducements, also military in nature. As long as Moscow enjoyed a lead in the research and development of rockets, the Soviet Union wanted to keep both its strengths and weaknesses veiled by military secrecy. Therefore it rejected aerial inspection except with heavy qualifications, and turned down any other form of "inspection over armaments." Further, Soviet production of fissionable materials was behind that of the United States, and Moscow refused to tie a test ban to a nuclear production cutoff; only by 1964 was it ready to announce a slowdown in the production of fissionable materials.

21

External Political Perspectives

The opportunities and constraints that the Soviet leaders perceived as they looked to the east, to the west, and to the south exerted a powerful influence on their evaluation of both the military and the political uses of the disarmament issue. The Kremlin's perception of the political environment provided above all the basic sense of the possible and the desirable that gave direct guidance to Soviet arms control policy.

The roles that policy toward Western, Communist, and nonaligned states played in the shaping of Soviet arms control interests cannot be directly compared since the arms control problem arose primarily in relations with the West. However, because the Soviet Union was engaged in a two-front campaign and was facing substantial political and even military challenges from Peking, an opportunity or difficulty on the Western front became doubly significant. The role of the southern front — the "third world" — was marginal but cannot be ignored.

Toward the West

A profound change took place in the Kremlin's political perspective in 1954–1956 that conditioned Soviet interests in arms control throughout the remainder of the Khrushchev decade. Soviet policy toward the West from 1954 to 1964 endeavored to avoid the mistakes of Stalin's antagonistic line and to capitalize on the opportunities it had previously underrated. Since the West's political and military unity (including German participation in NATO and the Western European Union) had been spurred by a sense of threat, the Kremlin now sought generally to reverse this trend by lowering the threat and stressing the advantages of accommodation with the new Soviet line. Whereas Stalin's policies often tended to treat the Western elites as a homogeneous antagonist, the Khrushchev regime recognized diversity within and between the NATO governments, and sought to cultivate and exploit these differences, using as a key instrument a more reasonable stance on arms control and disarmament.

A central Soviet objective in arms control policy was to strengthen moderate, "sober" forces in the West who could move their governments away from an arms build-up and a forward strategy toward accommodation with the Soviet Union. Disarmament propaganda, concessions, and eventually agreements were used instrumentally to isolate the "hards" and strengthen the "softs" in the West, particularly in the United States. Such measures were also used to create propaganda that would put pressure on U.S. overseas base policy, U.S. reliance on nuclear weapons, German rearmament, and other aspects of Western military planning. Proposals for disengagement helped to foster anti-German sentiment in Britain and France. Advocacy of a nuclear test ban helped to stir differences between Washington and London on the one hand and Paris on the other because of the latter's lag in nuclear testing. Working in the opposite direction, Moscow's proposal in June 1960 to abolish all nuclear delivery systems in the first stage of GCD was evidently calculated to be welcome in Paris but not in London or Washington, thereby increasing friction among them.

Khrushchev staked much of his foreign policy upon the calculation that "moderates" existed in the West and that their hand could be strengthened; this premise had to be defended against critics in Moscow as well as in Peking. Khrushchev may have been chastened several times in the decade by the apparent stiffening of Western policy (as in late 1955, mid-1960, and 1961), but he seemed to assume that a more moderate orientation would eventually prevail.

The "permanently operating factor" in Moscow's view of the external political situation since 1955 has, on the evidence, been the premise that some kind of accommodation with moderate forces in the West is both desirable and possible. From 1955 to about 1960 this orientation was qualified by the Kremlin's belief that the influence of international communism, guided by the socialist fatherland, would gradually expand while the sphere of capitalism contracted. As Peking posed a more intense threat from 1959 to 1962, and as the "third world" showed by 1961 its resistance to Soviet penetration, the narrowing of alternatives and the impact of reality were intensified for Soviet decision makers. First in theory, after 1959, and then also in practice, after the abortive "quick fix" attempt in Cuba, Moscow's interest in stimulating Western and particularly American tendencies to moderate the East-West conflict took on increasingly an aspect of collaboration as well as "struggle," intensifying the Soviet political interest in partial measures of arms control and tacit arrangements to preserve peace and slacken the arms race.

Toward the East

Whereas there was diversity in the West that offered a possibility of manipulation to Soviet advantage, Peking presented a more monolithic front that opposed Khrushchev's efforts toward peaceful coexistence and arms control agreements with the West. That opposition ran squarely athwart Moscow's potent interest in maximizing its position of leadership in the international Communist movement, initially by keeping China within the Soviet camp, and, as this failed, in keeping ahead of Peking both in the international Communist movement and in influencing the "gray zones." A third set of Soviet interests derived from the military desideratum of preventing Chinese moves that could involve Russia in a major war, which in turn involved inhibiting China from acquiring nuclear weapons. Clearly, depending on the priority accorded to one or another of these basic interests, the effect of China could be either to restrain or accelerate Moscow's posture of accommodation with the West.

Moscow at first, from 1956 to 1959, endeavored to mollify Peking's political and military aspirations by adding tough phrases to Communist pronouncements on East-West relations and by offering some assistance in developing a nuclear program. No doubt many Soviet party and military officials found their own reasons to oppose *détente* and arms control reinforced by the realization that such an orientation was alienating Peking. Even after 1959, a faint hope of *rapprochement* with the world's most populous nation may have exerted some drag on Soviet policy, if only because it added to other conservative pressures that opposed moving toward a more conciliatory coexistence.

The net result of China's military and political threat was, however, to push Moscow steadily westward, to increase its interest in arriving at a test ban and other agreements to impede proliferation and further developments of the arms race. By mid-1959 the die was cast as Moscow declined to spread nuclear weapons to China and sought to rebut forcefully the latter's ideological critique. Even after the U-2 incident and the Paris Summit debacle in 1960 Moscow gave no quarter to Chinese orthodoxy. At Bucharest in June and in Moscow later on in the year Khrushchev assailed dogmatic insistence that imperialism remained unchanged. The deterioration of Sino-Soviet relations in late 1962 and the evident abandonment of Soviet hopes of mending the breach probably helped remove the last inhibitions in Moscow against moves toward *détente* and arms control with the West. The 1963 "Treaty of Moscow" was then used against Peking — even in propaganda to the "third world" — likening the Chinese opponents of the test ban to "madmen" in the West such as Goldwater and Adenauer.

Just as Moscow seemed willing to sacrifice political interests in relations with China in order to pursue *détente* — and appropriate arms control agreements — with the West, so the Kremlin may even have been willing to risk the probable loss of considerable political control in Eastern Europe in exchange for the high-priority strategic desideratum of neutralizing Germany. But even here there were potential political payoffs. A clear benefit of favoring German neutralization was its popularity in Eastern Europe. Rapacki's (later Gomulka's) proposals, for example, gave a semblance of autonomy to Polish foreign policy, and their rejection by the West deepened Eastern Europe's sense of dependence upon the Soviet Union. Even more important, the Soviet campaign for disarmament probably won some favor for Moscow among the war-weary peoples of Eastern Europe.

Toward the South

The influence of the "third world" upon Soviet arms control policies was also quite marginal and indirect during the decade. Virtually no Soviet security interests have been at stake in these areas, except perhaps that of complicating the maintenance of Western bases or the carrying out of French nuclear testing. The major relationship of this zone to Soviet arms control interest emerged in 1954–1955 when Moscow decided that opportunities for penetration in Africa and Asia could fruitfully be exploited to accelerate the departure of

Western colonialism and to win a foothold for communism. The Soviet decision to move into this "gray zone," partly by arms shipments but mainly by political and economic means, increased the importance of desensitizing the West by a conciliatory disarmament posture. The object of winning favor for Soviet policy added to Moscow's reasons for posing as the champion of a test ban, a nuclear-free Africa, and the liquidation of Western bases, and as the supporter of national independence (although in 1961 the Soviet government ignored the sentiments of the nonaligned nations meeting at Belgrade and the U.N. resolution appealing to Moscow not to test its giant warheads).

After 1961 the task of Soviet propaganda was to persuade the nonaligned nations that the Soviet policy of peaceful coexistence was more in their interest than either the bellicose ways favored by Peking, or Western "neo-colonialism." To strengthen its revolutionary image the Soviet Union continued to qualify its support for a warless world and the renunciation of force by insisting on the unavoidability and justness of wars of national liberation. In practice, however, Moscow sought to impose a broad-front policy on the Communist parties in the "third world," and has shown some restraint even in exploiting unstable situations in the new states, as in the Congo in 1960–1961, Laos in 1961–1962, and Vietnam as of mid-1965. All of this has contributed to the image Moscow wishes to convey to the West, and specifically to the possibility of continued arms control agreements.

22

Internal Influences on Policy

The Economic Factor

Analysis of the Khrushchev decade corroborates the supposition that a powerful centralized government would probably never allow internal economic pressures to dissuade it from policies considered essential to state security. The historic interaction of economic incentives for reduction in defense expenditures and Soviet policies on arms control demonstrates that such incentives could have an impact on Moscow's negotiating posture only at a time when the Kremlin felt secure from imminent external attack or when it had no prospect of a significant strategic gain from greater investments in defense.

The "economic burden of defense" does not appear in 1954–1956 to have been a strong force motivating the Kremlin to seek a reduction of defense expenditures. Moscow's general sense that it could triumph in economic competition with the West was, however, an important premise of the softer turn in Soviet foreign policy generally, one which tended to persist even after the optimistic expectations underlying it had cause to falter.

Some economic incentives to reduce military spending existed even in 1955–1958, when Soviet economic growth was continuing at a high rate. Moscow was confronted with a number of scarcities in agriculture, housing, light industry, and in manpower, which could be alleviated by the transfer of human and material resources from defense. These economic factors helped to reinforce Moscow's military interests in the reduction of conventional ground forces and the limitation of nuclear testing. More important, an atmosphere of East-West *détente* was absolutely essential if the Soviet military posture was to rely upon a minimum deterrent of prototype bombers and first-generation missiles instead of striving immediately to mass produce these weapons.

From 1958 to 1961 the economic incentives to cut defense spending increased as the Soviet economy's over-all growth rate slowed, at a time when the investment required for military and space technological development was soaring. The pronouncements in 1959 that Soviet production would soon surpass that of the United States in many areas added to the pressures to keep economic growth at a high rate. By 1961, however, it appeared that Russia's efforts to overtake the United States militarily as well as economically had landed the Soviet Union on a treadmill; the chances for keeping up with, much less surpassing, the West seemed dim indeed. The United States was producing large numbers of ICBM's and other advanced equipment, and the European economies showed strong prospects of integration and dynamic growth that contrasted sharply with the situation in the Comecon countries.

By 1961, therefore, Moscow had even stronger economic as well as military reasons to seek a stabilization of the arms race. But it was precisely in 1961 and 1962 that the Soviet government increased its military spending, raised food prices, and took a more intransigent stand on arms control negotiations. This seems powerful evidence that economic incentives by themselves could not be decisive in shaping Soviet foreign and arms control policy.

On the other hand, in 1963, when the strategic situation seemed neither so threatening nor so promising as before Cuba, the same economic reasons to reduce or stabilize defense spending could reinforce the weight of the military and political factors in favor of limited arms control agreements with the West. An end to nuclear testing, a promise to keep bombs out of orbit, and a slowdown of fissionable material production could all ease the drag that defense — along with other economic problems — exerted upon Soviet growth. Two additional political and economic goals could also be served by the limited agreements of 1963–1964. First, if a lengthy *détente* made it possible gradually to lower the Soviet military budget, Moscow might be able to accelerate its economic growth, strengthen its claim to be a model of scientific socialism, and enhance its ability to influence the developing nations. An upturn in Soviet growth would also mean a stronger capacity for an intensified defense effort after the breathing space was over. Second, the goal of greater growth and prosperity could also be served by the long-term trade credits from the West that Moscow might hope to obtain in the improved political climate following the arms controls of 1963–1964.

Whether the Soviet economy would soon become stronger and, if so, whether this strength would again be intensively applied to surpassing the West militarily would of course depend upon many variables, including the manner in which a new generation of Soviet leaders assessed their problems to both east and west. But other measures of arms control might be influenced by the economic factor. Moscow has indicated an interest in some formal undertaking to reduce military budgets. And the time may have been developing for some more explicit understanding between Moscow and Washington not to intensify the arms race by efforts to build antimissile defense systems.

Political Factors

Our knowledge about the internal workings of Soviet policy is limited like that of the shadow watcher in Plato's cave. But the available evidence suggests that domestic political factors have been an important conditioner of Soviet interests and policies in arms control. The way in which the men in the Kremlin perceive arms controls is of course the primary determinant of policy that may be adopted, and if the leadership is divided in its assessment, or under conflicting demands from the pressure of other goals, powerful limitations will be set up. Furthermore the peace and disarmament issues become entangled on occasion in the political in-fighting within the Kremlin itself, serving as weapons in the internal power struggle.

For Khrushchev to hold office and, a fortiori, for his preferred policies to be implemented, his own perception of the world had to be shared by many of his colleagues, since his power was by no means so unlimited as Stalin's. The main opposition to a policy favoring *détente* and arms control probably came from certain military and party leaders and possibly managers in defense production and heavy industry. Khrushchev's critics saw in his policies threats to various of their interests. In any event they used as a basis of their criticisms the alleged or threatened inroads in defense spending, the preservation of military and economic secrecy, defense against foreign intrusion, or the avoidance of debilitating effects of prolonged *détente* on the international movement. The loosening of Soviet influence upon China and Eastern Europe as a result of *détente* with the West would also concern these groups.

There were some countervailing internal forces, but they were less coherent. Certain pressures arose out of Soviet society for a relaxation of international and internal tensions and for peace and prosperity, desires that gained momentum with de-Stalinization, and were articulated increasingly by Soviet writers and some scientists.

There is evidence that the peace and disarmament issue was used most clearly in power struggles within the Kremlin in 1955, in 1957, and perhaps in 1962–1964. Thus Khrushchev gained power in 1954 by accusing Malenkov of shortcutting defense requirements, but then used the issue of *détente* to isolate Molotov after Malenkov was removed. This power play coincided with a hard Soviet line on disarmament from September 1954 to February 1955 while Malenkov's star was falling and Molotov's rising, and with renewed concessions in the negotiations from March to May 1955 as Khrushchev edged out his second rival. Again in 1957 Khrushchev accused his heterogeneous opposition in the "antiparty group" of opposing "peaceful coexistence."

It is likely that internal power struggles induced some of the sharp zigs and zags in Soviet arms control policy in 1960–1962 and may well have stimulated the desperate measures Soviet foreign policy took to redress its waning power. We do not yet have enough information about this period, however, to establish a clear relationship between these moves and the rise and fall of particular forces in the Kremlin. Following the Cuban fiasco and the Party reorganization of November 1962, internal opposition to Khrushchev's policies seemed once more pronounced. Kozlov in particular seemed to be opposed to a policy of conciliating the West and diverting resources from heavy industry. Kozlov's eventually fatal illness in April 1963 coincided with a softer line signaled by a change in the May Day slogans. The removal of this critic may have been a key factor that allowed Khrushchev to agree to the hot line and the nuclear test ban and to break off negotiations with the Chinese.

By early 1964, however, Khrushchev seemed again to be under pressure from the defense and heavy industries and from the marshals not to make reductions in the defense budget or in the number of military personnel (and, we may speculate, to pursue the development of an antimissile defense). By this time Khrushchev was also publicly indicating differences of opinion among Party members over foreign policy. Nonetheless he apparently preserved sufficient freedom of action to enter into a commitment to cut back the production of fissionable materials.

On balance, it appears that Khrushchev generally enjoyed sufficient power to carry out far-reaching innovations in foreign and military affairs and in arms control policy, overriding whatever internal opposition may have existed. Thus he engineered concessions to Austria, Finland, and Yugoslavia prior to the 1955 Summit Conference; he himself announced in June 1957 that Moscow would accept limited on-site inspection over a test ban; his power determined Soviet entry into a moratorium on nuclear testing from 1958 to 1961. It was Khrushchev who pushed through the reduction of conventional forces in 1955, 1956, and 1960 and the establishment of the Strategic Rocket Forces; upon his initiative the Soviet military budget was allegedly reduced in December 1963 and the Soviet government stated in April 1964 its intention to slow production of fissionable materials.

Most important perhaps, Khrushchev's peaceful coexistence line, which had represented a central problem exacerbating Sino-Soviet relations from 1956 to 1964, continued to prevail. In each case Khrushchev had to overcome some domestic opposition and persuade the members of the elite close to the seat of power to go along with his policies. Although the evidence indicates that he often succeeded, there may well have been occasions when domestic opposition forced Khrushchev to take a harder stand than he otherwise would have preferred — for instance, the refusal in 1961 to stand by the principle of limited on-site inspection and the later insistence that there be no more than three such inspections. At other times internal opposition may simply have prevented a concession the First Secretary wanted in order to spur the arms control negotiations. Such suggestions of "things that never happened" obviously cannot be documented, but they seem inherently possible. In general the domestic political situation seems to have served as a key factor that could either open or close the door to some policy alternative suggested by external considerations. Usually the door seems to have been open to the policies favored by Khrushchev, but perhaps not always as far as he may have liked. Occasionally he himself was probably forced to slam it shut in the face of internal dissension. And in Cuba he certainly proved to be as hair-raising a gambler himself as any leader of modern times.

The forces and problems confronting the Kremlin after Stalin's death were in a sense larger than the individuals who succeeded him to power. Certainly the high optimism and ebullient style of Soviet foreign policy throughout most of the decade bore the personal stamp of Khrushchev. That there was broad support for his policies was due in large part to the necessity of coming to grips with the hard realities of the nuclear age, economic scarcity, and the existence of enormous problems on the eastern and western fronts. The management of power in the Kremlin will always, until constitutionalism comes, involve an inextricable combination of high policy and base impulses and tactics of personal ambition and power seeking. We can guess that the primary reasons for Khrushchev's eventual removal in 1964 had more to do with his personal style and his domestic policy — plus his inability to cope with the problem created for the international Communist movement by the Chinese — than with the orientation of his policy toward the West. But the squalid and Byzantine style of succession in the Kremlin must leave as "not proven" any attempts to correlate the internal power struggle with rational policy choices.

23

The Thrust of Events

The impression is strong that in the period under review the Kremlin's interests called for at least some tangible measures of arms control to be achieved. The first reason lay in the degree to which the Kremlin's proposals were probably consistent with Soviet strategic theory, military posture, and strategic expectations, particularly in that they would have preserved Soviet strengths while limiting those of the West. Second, the conflicts of political and military interests between Moscow and Peking gave the Soviet leadership good cause to stabilize relations with the West and to endeavor to prevent nuclear spread. Third, the mounting cost of defense reinforced the external military and political reasons to seek arms controls, *détente,* and East-West trade. Fourth, the leadership appeared to believe, at least tentatively, that the Soviet economic system could compete better in a disarming than in an arming world. None of these four inducements to arms control could be fully gratified by a mere relaxation of East-West tensions. Only specific arms control agreements could secure the strategic, political, or economic desiderata arising from these diverse factors.

Moscow continued to have strong inducements to move

toward the West. The latter could not be readily defeated; an ally against China might be needed; there were increasingly shared interests; and it was not clear that either side was going to win the game involving the developing nations. On balance, emphasis on collaboration rather than struggle might prove to be the more useful approach in Moscow's relations with the West.

Only the unfolding of history will tell whether or not Soviet policy during the Khrushchev decade acquired a genuinely new orientation that might bring it permanently into a less hostile general relationship with the West. The world of Khrushchev's successors still bore family resemblances to that of the past; the visage of peaceful coexistence could still from time to time be dominated by the familiar earmarks of the older, harsher outlook. The de-Stalinization process could still turn out, as could the Sino-Soviet schism, to be reversible in terms of some things that count for the West. Soviet moves toward accommodation with the West could still be interpreted as temporary steps backward to prepare for a subsequent offensive. And comprehensive disarmament — even if qualified by provision for a U.S. and Soviet minimum deterrent — still seemed remote.

Yet other forces continued to work for sobriety regarding the arms race. The implicit threat in the very existence of nuclear arsenals remained. The potential dangers for Soviet policy in the expansion of the nuclear club continued to threaten. The traditional elements of friction in Sino-Russian relations remained implicit in state relations vis-à-vis China, fortified by the differential in their respective stages of development as exemplars of "scientific socialism." And the growth of expectations and habits of modernity on the part of both people and leaders in the Soviet Union could be expected to have at least some effect on policy. In short, many of the same forces that militated for limited arms controls in 1963 would continue to weigh upon Soviet decision makers.

Soviet leaders in the decade after Khrushchev live, as he did, within two general representations of reality. They have to mediate between these two sets of pressures as part of the process of retaining power — which makes internal conditions so potent a factor. As the Tsars did, they once again have to calculate their futures, if only in contingency planning, in terms of the two-front nightmare. The prospects for arms control and disarmament remain a secondary, derivative feature of these sets of interactions as they change and mature over time. That in 1963–1964 several modest agreements could be reached with the West — the hot line, the limited test ban, the undertaking not to orbit nuclear weapons, and the subsequently announced mutual cutbacks in production of fissionable material for military purposes — described the limits of the possible, if not the desirable, in Moscow's military-political outlook toward the West.

To go beyond these statements to the realm of specific prediction is hazardous. There is no general rule of thumb one can apply to historical prediction and, a fortiori, to prediction of the behavior of Soviet Communist leaders. One must look at each event that arises in its full historic context to read sense and meaning into it. Above all, one cannot help being sobered by the highly ambiguous nature of the relationship between the Soviet drive for some kind of *détente* on the one hand, and concrete measures to moderate the arms race on the other. One plausible way to view the two is as points on a continuum that runs from relaxation of tensions to arms control and perhaps disarmament. The crucial question remains how far the Soviet leadership is prepared to go from the atmospherics of *détente* to concrete arms control measures; Westerners are notably ill equipped to measure the probabilities with any predictive exactitude.

At the same time, the crucial factors explored here will undoubtedly continue to operate. Their relative saliency to Soviet arms control policy may supply useful systematic guides to behavior. It seems not unreasonable to proceed in the post-Khrushchev era with the assumption that the achievement of significant arms control will depend on the optimum configuration of the four factors studied here. This would mean, for example, a high degree of saliency for a particular arms control measure to Soviet military-strategic imperatives; a high degree of responsiveness on the part of the West; a submissive Peking, or conversely a Peking sufficiently hostile to force Moscow into a serious entente with the United States; a significant degree of economic pressure; and collective backing in the Kremlin for such a policy.

Of course, nothing could be more dangerous than the blind assumption that such an arrangement of factors will in fact produce the anticipated results. An already present element may subsequently acquire a new dimension of importance. An example of this is the escalation of the Vietnamese conflict, leading Moscow at times to put its revolutionary image over the goal of *détente* with the West. One cannot foretell the manner in which Soviet planners will react to new variables, such as China's growing nuclear capacity or the possibility of nuclear sharing in the West. Finally, unpredictable changes in the Soviet power structure and unforeseen technological innovations will add further uncertainties to our already cloudy vision. If history repeats itself, it is usually in a way one could not have foretold. The only genuine intellectual sin would be to abandon the search for systematic understanding.

SOURCES FOR THE STUDY OF
SOVIET DISARMAMENT POLICY

On Analyzing Soviet Disarmament Policy

What follows is a discussion of the major materials used in the present work. It may also serve as a guide to further study of Soviet disarmament policy, whether for the period studied here or for subsequent periods. It is therefore structured to parallel the kinds of problems studied in each part of the book, beginning with declaratory policy and propaganda, followed by the underlying determinants of Soviet policy, and ending with analyses that endeavor to interpret and integrate these two sets of information. Full references to particular authors or works mentioned in the essay may generally be found in the bibliography that follows. Where additional references are suggested, the reader will be referred to the more comprehensive listing in *Soviet Disarmament Policy, 1917–1963: An Annotated Bibliography of Soviet and Western Sources.*[1]

In order to come to grips with the issues of arms control

---

[1] Compiled with an introduction by Walter C. Clemens, Jr. (Stanford, Calif.: The Hoover Institution, 1965).

292   SOURCES FOR STUDY OF SOVIET POLICY

and disarmament, scholars must be prepared to tackle a wide assortment of diverse social and scientific data. For those would penetrate the particular enigmas of Soviet disarmament policy the obstacles are still more numerous and diverse in character. Not only must researchers deal with economic and military questions, but they must enter in the ways of Byzantine power struggles and intra-Communist polemics, esoteric and otherwise.

Sooner or later, however, students of Soviet arms control affairs must examine what we have called "manifest" or declaratory policy. Both secondary and primary sources must be consulted. Bechhoefer's long narrative *Postwar Negotiations for Arms Control* tells the story objectively for the period 1945–1960, but gives no special emphasis to the Soviet position or, more important, to the factors that conditioned it.[2] The most solid account of Moscow's negotiating record in a brief span is *The Soviet Union and Disarmament* by Dallin and others, the outgrowth of a conference organized by Columbia University and sponsored by the U.S. Arms Control and Disarmament Agency in 1963. Two divergent approaches are exemplified by the work of Jensen, on the one hand, and Spanier and Nogee, on the other. Jensen provides a stimulating essay charting the "concessions" and "retractions" in the U.S. and Soviet negotiating positions. Much of the thrust of his conclusions is borne out by the present analysis, but the scope of his effort has precluded sufficient attention to some of the moves being plotted, thus resulting in some distortion of certain problems and periods. Spanier and Nogee by contrast argue a priori that the ne-

[2] An equally objective but briefer narrative that takes the story through 1961 is available in German, with a companion volume of documents in both German and English. See Hermann Volle and Claus-Jürgen Duisberg, *Probleme der internationalen Abrüstung: die Bemühungen der Vereinten Nationen, 1945–1961*, introduction by Ulrich Scheuner (2 vols.; Berlin: Alfred Metzner Verlag, 1964). These two volumes are the first in a series on Arms Limitation and Security produced by the Deutsche Gesellschaft für Auswärtige Politik in Bonn.

gotiating positions of each side are constructed for tactical propaganda gain only, a view that may not have been entirely adequate to explain the events of 1963–1964. A no less suspicious and pessimistic view of arms control developments is laid out in two chapters by James E. Dougherty in *Détente*, edited by Dulles and Crane, providing perhaps the most up-to-date critique of more optimistic views.

On the particular issue of the nuclear test ban negotiations, Zoppo, Mark, Jacobson, and Stein offer specialized and useful accounts showing the complex interaction between technical and political factors. On the special questions of disengagement in Europe and nuclear-free zones in Asia, the analyses of Hinterhoff and Hsieh remain outstanding.

Soviet histories of disarmament have improved in quality and increased in number, at least from 1959 to 1963, but are still too one-sided and riddled with omissions to serve as a reliable research tool.[3] Their main value lies first in making the best possible case for Moscow's stand, and second in providing occasional insights into the Kremlin's disarmament gamesmanship (some of them thus serving to confirm part of the Spanier-Nogee analysis). Third, however, they also reveal something of the cynical manner in which Moscow has perceived the zigs and zags in Western policy. The collection of essays edited by V. Zorin serves as a kind of Soviet counterpart to Bechhoefer's history.

After studying the outlines of Soviet negotiating history in Soviet and Western secondary works, the student of Soviet arms control policy must turn to the verbatim records and conference documents of U.N. and other negotiating forums. At a minimum it is necessary to examine and compare the resolutions introduced by Moscow and the other major powers. But to appreciate the drift of the argument (and, quite frequently, the semantic problems involved) the verbatim records themselves must be read with care. The present study has utilized particularly the verbatim records of the

[3] *Ibid.*, pp. 51 ff.

U.N. Disarmament Subcommittee for 1955–1957 and the records of the Eighteen Nation Disarmament Committee for 1962–1964.[4] Amplification of the Soviet position may often be found in Soviet periodicals, particularly in *International Affairs* and *New Times*.

As one departs from the negotiating arena to the domain of mass media, one crosses a somewhat artificial line distinguishing "declaratory" policy from what this study has termed the "propaganda and ideology" of disarmament. A diplomat may of course propagandize. But mass media may also transmit official declaratory policy, albeit in more popular fashion. Soviet journals published in English give easy access to the Kremlin's propaganda position on current disarmament problems. The *World Marxist Review* (published in Prague in many languages, generally under the title "Problems of Peace and Socialism") gives a more revolutionary interpretation than the Moscow-based *International Affairs* and *New Times*. Several journals available only in Russian, such as *Mirovaia ekonomika i mezhdunarodnye otnosheniia*,[5] may be slightly more reflective of Kremlin views because of their more restricted readership. Monitored radio broadcasts translated into English from the Russian domestic as well as overseas service go far toward providing a running account of the current Soviet line.

Other major sources for the study of Soviet propaganda and ideology concerning disarmament are the resolutions and records of party congresses; the speeches of Soviet leaders (often more loquacious abroad than at home); and — a source to be considered in greater detail below — the polemics within the Communist world on matters of war and peace.

In addition to the surface manifestations of Soviet policy, it is necessary to look at the conditioning factors that repre-

[4] For fuller discussion and citation see *ibid.*, pp. x–xii, 39–50, esp. 41–42.
[5] *World Economics and International Relations*.

sent the bulk of the iceberg beneath Soviet diplomacy and propaganda.

For a full picture of the strategic-military factor, one must consult a wide variety of Soviet and Western materials. Many of these are noted in excellent bibliographies published by the U.S. government and in Western works on Soviet military doctrine such as those by Garthoff, Dinerstein, Wolfe, and others. It is important to read not only the current Soviet press such as *Krasnaia zvezda* but to analyze authoritative works such as *Military Doctrine* edited by Marshal Sokolovsky, and to compare one edition with another. A positive sign, the interfaces between strategy and arms control are discussed with increasing frequency by Soviet military as well as political commentators in *International Affairs*. For yearly reports on the military balance the publications of the Institute for Strategic Studies are invaluable. The ISS analysis of the impact upon European security of enactment of the first stage of the Soviet and U.S. GCD plans is uniquely illuminating. Additional information on the East-West balance and the strategies of both sides is increasingly found in testimony to U.S. Congressional committees, especially the House and Senate Subcommittees on Military Appropriations.

A second major determinant of Soviet arms control policy is the nature of Moscow's external relations with the Western and Communist worlds. A primary source for the 1954–1964 period is provided by the many statements of Khrushchev having to do with both disarmament and world politics and published on virtually an annual basis from 1957 to 1963.[6]

The Cousins interview with Khrushchev in early 1963 (published after the latter's fall) reveals something of the man beneath the mask. The memoirs of Western leaders, such as Eden and Eisenhower, plus the insightful histories of the Kennedy era by Schlesinger and Sorensen, go far toward

[6] See Clemens, *Soviet Disarmament Policy, 1917–1963*, pp. 27–31.

illuminating the manner in which Western leaders perceived Khrushchev's foreign policy.

Perhaps the greatest windfall for students of Communist affairs generally, including researchers on arms control matters, has been the Sino-Soviet polemics. In the materials released by Peking and Moscow since the signing of the limited test ban treaty in 1963, one finds invaluable data for a reconstruction of Sino-Soviet relations since 1955, as well as a far better appreciation of the role played by nuclear issues in the deterioration of the alliance. Many of these documents have been included in the useful collections assembled by Griffith, Dallin, and others. In many cases, however, the student of arms control will wish to be certain that he has available the entire text of a document and not just excerpts. The *Peking Review* published in China, the *Current Digest of the Soviet Press* published in New York, the Chinese press surveys assembled in Hong Kong, and monitored radio broadcasts provide convenient primary sources in English translation. The growing library of such materials in the files of the International Communism Project at M.I.T.'s Center for International Studies is uniquely useful. One of the first serious efforts to take stock of Sino-Soviet relations and arms control occurred in the summer of 1965 at a conference sponsored by the U.S. Arms Control and Disarmament Agency. A number of the papers, edited by Morton H. Halperin, including one by Oran Young on Soviet and Chinese views regarding nuclear proliferation and one by Clemens on the test ban in Sino-Soviet relations, are to be published by the M.I.T. Press.[7]

Third, we have considered the economic determinants of Soviet policy. The raw material for such analysis is provided by the Soviet press, party decrees, policy speeches by Kremlin leaders (and sometimes by spokesmen for industrial,

[7] The studies by Halperin and Perkins cited in the bibliography represent a great leap forward in the analysis of the problems of China and arms control.

military, and scientific interest groups), and by Soviet statistical yearbooks. The interpretations of the RAND Corporation, the Institute for Defense Analyses, and Western university economists have been extremely useful. In the final analysis, however, Soviet statistics remain a questionable index for measurement, especially where they concern defense expenditures, some of which remain hidden in the official budget. Attempts to plot "real" defense expenditures may of course be too high or too low. But the most basic reason for diffidence about estimates of the "economic burden of defense" is the difficulty in knowing how Soviet leaders rank economic as against other priorities at a given time. The approach suggested in this study is to compare, at different time periods, the state of the Soviet economy generally, the relative weight of estimated defense expenditures, and the extent of apparent Soviet efforts to curtail these expenditures by unilateral or joint arms control measures.

The fourth conditioning factor is domestic politics: who is in power, the stability of the regime, and the pressures for change. In retrospect it seems painfully clear that our knowledge and even the commonly accepted model of the Soviet political scene during the Khrushchev decade have been woefully inadequate. Some developments have been followed from afar with surprising accuracy, particularly the succession crises from 1953 through 1957, but the extent of Khrushchev's power was probably rather widely overestimated after that time. While the definitive history of the Khrushchev era has yet to be written, it may be suggested that an attempt to follow in detail a specific policy problem that has wide ramifications, such as arms control, should be of importance in developing a sounder picture of Kremlin politics generally in the decade since Stalin.

The basic sources for observing domestic Soviet politics have been the daily papers such as *Pravda* and *Izvestiia* (sometimes revealing a conflict between "party" and "government" factions), and journals such as *Kommunist,* all of which are translated to some extent in *Current Digest of the Soviet Press*. *Problems of Communism, Survey,* and other Western periodicals reflect the assessment of foreign soviet-ologists of the struggle for power within the Kremlin. And it has been increasingly the case that revelations in Communist circles outside Russia (and especially in Italy, Yugoslavia, and China) provide us with a "window to the East."

The kinds of cross pressures that arise from Soviet society itself constitute an area between the economic and domestic political factors we have studied. Some discussion of the impact of these pressures upon arms control policy may be found in the works by Dallin, Wiesner, and others. But such study must remain rather impressionistic until more systematic social science research is possible in Soviet society. Since Khrushchev's removal there have been encouraging signs of movement toward a less politicized social science in the Soviet Union, but there is as yet little ground for believing that it is likely to go beyond studies designed to enhance labor productivity.

The study by Brzezinski and Huntington, *Political Power USA/USSR,* constitutes a landmark in the analysis of social change and the prospects of future political development in the Soviet Union. It also contains useful comparisons of foreign-policy decision making in Moscow and Washington during the Khrushchev era. One may object that the authors assign too great a weight to history and hence overlook the possibilities for change implicit in their own findings about Soviet society. But any scholar concerned with the relation between future societal change and arms control must take this book as a point of departure.

In seeking to make a judgment as to the "real" nature of Soviet attitudes and intentions in the field of arms control we have analyzed factors ranging from Moscow's declaratory disarmament diplomacy to pressures for change within Soviet society. For anyone making such an analysis, it is clear that his over-all assessment of Soviet aims is likely to be skewed accordingly if one or another factor is weighted too highly or ignored. Thus, Jensen's emphasis on Moscow's proclivity toward concessions and Spanier-Nogee's concentration on the Kremlin's loaded deck make too much of the negotiating record without consideration of the hidden part of the iceberg. Dougherty's emphasis on ideological conflict between East and West may lead him to underestimate the pressures upon the Kremlin to deal realistically with the Chinese threat and the economic pressures of competing in an arms race with the United States. Similarly, the Brzezinski-Huntington book may rule out too summarily a greater degree of convergence and collaboration between Moscow and the West. In another vein, the analysis by Walter Hahn of historical trends toward secrecy in Russian society may also place excessive emphasis on the past, thus minimizing the role of current strategic considerations, and of pressures from the "military-industrial" complex. It is encouraging perhaps (and has nothing to do with the sponsorship and little to do with partially overlapping personnel) that the two most extensive and expensive studies of Soviet arms control policy to date, those by Columbia University and by M.I.T., come out at about the same point of qualified optimism in appraising the nature of Soviet policy under Khrushchev and by implication, *mutatis mutandis*, under his followers.

It should be added that second-hand knowledge of Soviet policy may often be supplemented to great advantage by direct contact with the negotiations or negotiators. The present study has benefited from conversations with several Western, Soviet, and East European diplomats and governmental advisors. The Westerners concurred broadly with the main theses of the paper. The major specific criticism offered by one Communist official was that our approach has been too rationalistic, looking for complicated explanations where a more elementary one would have sufficed, and seeking to associate top leaders' motives with proposals prepared perfunctorily by foreign office staff. However no Soviet or East European officials or scholars availed themselves of the opportunity offered to criticize the manuscript in detail or in its general approach and conclusions.

Two of the authors of this work contributed to the recommendations of the U.S. committee headed by Dr. Jerome B. Wiesner for the International Cooperation Year in 1965. Many of that Committee's key recommendations rested in part on an assessment of recent and expected technological developments, for example, in antiballistic missile defenses and underground nuclear test identification. To keep abreast of such developments is difficult, but a careful reading of journals such as the *Bulletin of the Atomic Scientists, Missiles and Rockets,* and *Science* provides at least a foundation.

Finally, the student in search of new perspectives on Russian disarmament policy might wish to move in two rather different directions: toward the earlier periods of Soviet and even Tsarist history, on the one hand, and toward the insights of modern behavioral science on the other. The longer one's acquaintance with Russian affairs, the more one may be impressed by the extent of continuity as opposed to change. Some indication of the continuity in Tsarist and Soviet disarmament diplomacy was sketched at the very beginning of this book, and in recent years the Soviet leaders have opened the Lenin archives to defend their case against the Chinese. The volume edited by Lederer entitled *Russian Foreign Policy: Essays in Historical Perspective* demonstrates many of the surprisingly consistent trends in propaganda across the years, the use of international movements, techniques of negotiation, and other areas of tactics and strategy. Deeper study of history, however, will be well complemented if associated with the imaginative work appearing in the *Journal of Conflict Resolution* and other publications drawing on the interdisciplinary insights of operations research, game theory, political socialization, and political behavior.[8] Thus, for example, on-going research by Richard A. Brody and John Vesecky of Stanford University is testing the applicability of the Richardson differential equations[9] to the U.S.-Soviet arms competition in the period covered by the present study. And Gaylor Bonham at M.I.T. is simulating in political exercises the negotiating behavior of U.S. and Soviet disarmament delegations in the mid-1950's. Merely to mention such dimensions of the problem is to acknowledge that this volume and others like it represent but a beginning on the road toward historical understanding, political wisdom, and psychological insight.

[8] See, for example, Roger Fisher, ed., *International Conflict and Behavioral Science* (New York: Basic Books, Inc., 1964); J. David Singer, ed., *Human Behavior and International Politics* (Chicago: Rand McNally & Company, 1965).

[9] L. F. Richardson, *Arms and Insecurity* (Pittsburgh, Pa.: Boxwood Press, 1960).

Bibliography[1]

A. Books and Documents

ABEL, ELIE. *The Missile Crisis.* Philadelphia, Pa.: J. B. Lippincott Co., 1966.

BARRACLOUGH, GEOFFREY, and RACHEL F. WALL. *Survey of International Affairs, 1955–1956.* London: Oxford University Press, 1960.

BECHHOEFER, BERNHARD G. *Postwar Negotiations for Arms Control.* Washington: The Brookings Institution, 1961.

BLOOMFIELD, LINCOLN P. *International Military Forces: The Question of Peacekeeping in an Armed and Disarming World.* Boston: Little, Brown and Company, 1964.

BRZEZINSKI, ZBIGNIEW, and SAMUEL P. HUNTINGTON. *Political Power: USA/USSR.* New York: The Viking Press, 1964.

CLEMENS, WALTER C., JR. *Automated Inspection of Underground Nuclear Testing.* Santa Barbara, Calif.: General Electric Defense Programs Operation, 1962.

———. "Moscow and Arms Control: Evidence from the Sino-Soviet Dispute." Cambridge, Mass.: M.I.T., Center for International Studies, mimeo., 1965.

---

[1] The transliteration from Russian into English accords generally with the Library of Congress system. Exceptions are where names are transliterated differently in Soviet English-language journals, and also where names such as Sokolovsky and Talensky are frequently so used in the American press.

————. *Origins of the Soviet Campaign for Disarmament: The Soviet Position on Peace, Security and Revolution at the Genoa, Moscow and Lausanne Conferences, 1922–1923.* Unpublished Ph.D. thesis, Columbia University, 1961.

————. "The Test Ban in Sino-Soviet Relations." Cambridge, Mass.: Harvard University, Center for International Affairs, mimeo., 1965.

————, ed. *Toward a Strategy of Peace.* Chicago, Ill.: Rand McNally & Co., 1965.

CONQUEST, ROBERT. *Power and Policy in the U.S.S.R.* New York: St. Martin's Press, 1961.

Current Soviet Policies. Vols. I–II, New York: Frederick A. Praeger, Inc., 1953 and 1957; Vols. III-IV, New York: Columbia University Press, 1960 and 1962.

DALLIN, ALEXANDER. *The Soviet Union at the United Nations.* New York: Frederick A. Praeger, Inc., 1962.

————, et al. *Diversity in International Communism: A Documentary Record, 1961–1963.* New York: Columbia University Press, 1963.

————, et al. *The Soviet Union and Disarmament: An Appraisal of Soviet Attitudes and Intentions.* New York: Frederick A. Praeger, Inc., 1965.

DALLIN, DAVID J. *Soviet Foreign Policy after Stalin.* Philadelphia: J. B. Lippincott Co., 1961.

DINERSTEIN, HERBERT S. *The Soviet Military Posture as a Reflection of Soviet Strategy.* Santa Monica, Calif.: RAND Research Memorandum RM-2102, 1958.

————. *War and the Soviet Union.* Rev. ed. New York: Frederick A. Praeger, Inc., 1962.

————, LEON GOURÉ, and THOMAS WOLFE. Introduction to V. D. Sokolovsky, ed., *Soviet Military Strategy [Voennaia Strategiia].* Englewood Cliffs, N.J.: Prentice-Hall, Inc., 1963.

Diplomaticheskii slovar'. 2 vols. Moscow: Gospolitizdat, 1961.

DONOVAN, ROBERT J. *Eisenhower: The Inside Story.* New York: Harper & Row, 1956.

DULLES, ELEANOR L., and ROBERT D. CRANE, eds. *Détente.* New York: Frederick A. Praeger, Inc., 1965.

EDEN, ANTHONY. *Full Circle.* Boston: Houghton Mifflin Company, 1960.

Eighteen Nation Committee on Disarmament. First Interim Progress Report of the Conference of the Eighteen Nation Committee on Disarmament. Covers period March 14 to June 1, 1962. ENDC/42, May 31, 1962. (Also circulated as Document DC/203, June 5, 1962.)

————. General Series. ENDC/1, March 14, 1962 to ENDC/ 126, February 13, 1964.

————. Report of the Conference of the Eighteen Nation Committee on Disarmament. Covers period November 26, 1962 to April 10, 1963, DC/207, April 12, 1963. (Also circulated as Document A/5408.)

————. Report of the Conference of the Eighteen Nation Committee on Disarmament. Covers period April 17 to September 1, 1963, DC/208, September 5, 1963. (Also circulated as Document A/5488.)

————. Second Interim Progress Report of the Conference of the Eighteen Nation Committee on Disarmament. Covers period June 1 to September 8, 1962, ENDC/62, September 7, 1962. (Also circulated as Document DC/205, September 18, 1962.)

————. Verbatim Records. Committee of the Whole. ENDC/ C.1/PV.1, March 28, 1962 to ENDC/C.1/PV.9, July 19, 1962.

————. Verbatim Records. ENDC/PV.1, March 14, 1962 to ENDC/PV.170, February 27, 1964.

————. Verbatim Records. ENDC/SC.1/PV.1, March 21, 1962 to ENDC/SC.1/PV.50, December 18, 1962.

EISENHOWER, DWIGHT D. *Mandate for Change, 1953–1956.* Garden City, N.Y.: Doubleday and Company, Inc., 1963.

————. *Waging Peace, 1956–1961.* Garden City, N.Y.: Doubleday and Company, Inc., 1965.

FAINSOD, MERLE. *How Russia Is Ruled.* Rev. ed. Cambridge, Mass.: Harvard University Press, 1963.

France. *La Conférence d'Experts pour Etudier les Mesures Eventuelles qui Pourraient Contribuer à la Prévention d'une Attaque par Surprise et pour Préparer un Rapport aux Gouvernements sur ce Problème, Genève, 10 novembre–18 décembre 1958.* Paris: La Documentation Française, 1959.

GARTHOFF, RAYMOND L. Introduction to V. D. Sokolovsky, ed. *Military Strategy [Voennaia Strategiia].* New York: Frederick A. Praeger, Inc., 1963.

————. *Soviet Military History.* New York: Frederick A. Praeger, Inc., 1966.

————. *Soviet Strategy in the Nuclear Age.* Rev. ed. New York: Frederick A. Praeger, Inc., 1962.

GILPIN, ROBERT. *American Scientists and Nuclear Weapons Policy.* Princeton, N. J.: Princeton University Press, 1962.

GLAGOLEV, I., ed. *Ekonomicheskie problemy razoruzheniia.* Moscow: Akademiia Nauk SSSR, 1961.

Great Britain. *Conference of the Ten Nation Committee on Disarmament.* Geneva, 1960. Verbatim records of the meetings of the Conference of the Ten Nation Committee on Disarmament held at the Palais des Nations, Geneva, March 15–April 29, 1960 and June 7–June 27, 1960 (1st–48th meetings). London: Her Majesty's Stationery Office, 1960. (Foreign Office, Miscellaneous, 1960, No. 10. Cmd. 1152.)

————. *Further Documents Relating to the Conference of the Eighteen Nation Committee on Disarmament.* London: Her Majesty's Stationery Office, 1963. (Cmd. 2184.)

GRIFFITH, WILLIAM E. *Albania and the Sino-Soviet Rift.* Cambridge, Mass.: The M.I.T. Press, 1963.

————. *Sino-Soviet Relations, 1964–1965.* Cambridge, Mass.: The M.I.T. Press, 1966.

————. *The Sino-Soviet Rift.* Cambridge, Mass.: The M.I.T. Press, 1964.

GRIFFITHS, FRANKLYN. "Proposals of Total Disarmament in Soviet Foreign Policy, 1927–1932 and 1959–1960." Certificate essay, Russian Institute, Columbia University, 1962.

GRULIOW, LEO, ed. *Current Soviet Policies II: A Documentary Record of the 20th Communist Party Congress and Its Aftermath.* New York: Frederick A. Praeger, Inc., 1957.

HALPERIN, MORTON H. *China and the Bomb.* New York: Frederick A. Praeger, Inc., 1965.

————, and DWIGHT H. PERKINS. *Communist China and Arms Control.* New York: Frederick A. Praeger, Inc., 1965.

HART, B. H. LIDDELL. *The Red Army.* New York: Harcourt Brace, 1956.

HILSMAN, ROGER, and ROBERT C. GOOD. *Foreign Policy in the Sixties.* Baltimore, Md.: The Johns Hopkins Press, 1965.

HINTERHOFF, EUGENE. *Disengagement.* London: Stevens and Sons, Ltd., 1959.

HSIEH, ALICE L. *The Chinese Genie: Peking's Role in the Nuclear Test Ban Negotiations.* Santa Monica, Calif.: RAND Corporation P-2022, 1960.

————. *Communist China's Strategy in the Nuclear Age.* Englewood Cliffs, N. J.: Prentice-Hall, Inc., 1962.

HUDSON, G. F., RICHARD LOWENTHAL, and RODERICK MACFARQUHAR. *The Sino-Soviet Dispute.* New York: Frederick A. Praeger, Inc., 1961.

Institute for Strategic Studies. *Disarmament and European Security: The Effect of Implementing the First Stage of the Soviet Draft Treaty and the United States Proposals on General and Complete Disarmament.* 2 vols. London, 1963.

————. *The Military Balance* (1959—— [title varies]).

IVASHIN, I. F. *Bor'ba Sovetskogo Soiuza za vseobshchee i polnoe razoruzhenie.* Moscow: VPSh pri TSK KPSS, 1960.

JACOBSEN, HANS-ADOLF, UWE NERLICH, and HERMANN VOLLE, eds. *Strategie und Abrüstungspolitik der Sowetunion: Ausgewälte sowetische Studien und Reden.* Introduction by Curt Gasteyger. Frankfurt and Berlin: M. Alfred Metzner Verlag, 1964.

JACOBSON, HAROLD KARAN, and ERIC STEIN. *Diplomats, Scientists, and Politicians: The United States and the Nuclear Test Ban Negotiations.* (To be published in 1966.)

Jane's All the World's Aircraft, 1963–1964. New York: McGraw-Hill Book Company, 1963.

JENSEN, LLOYD. *The Postwar Disarmament Negotiations: A Study in American-Soviet Bargaining Behavior.* University of Michigan, Center for Research on Conflict Resolution, preprint, 1962.

JONAS, ANNE M. *The Soviet Union and the Atom: Peaceful Sharing, 1954–1958.* Santa Monica, Calif.: RAND Corporation RM-2290, 1958.

KAUFMANN, WILLIAM W. *The McNamara Strategy.* New York: Harper & Row, 1964.

KHRUSHCHEV, N. S. *Conquest Without War.* Comp. and ed., N. H. Mayer and Jacques Katel. New York: Simon and Schuster, Inc., 1961.

————. *Disarmament and Colonial Freedom.* Speeches and interviews at the United Nations General Assembly, September–October, 1960. London: Lawrence and Wishart, 1961.

————. *K pobede v mirnom sorevnovanii s kapitalizmon.* Moscow: Gospolitizdat, 1959.

————. *Mir bez oruzhiia-mir bez voin.* Moscow: Gospolitizdat, 1960. Vol. I (January–July, 1959); Vol. II (August–December, 1959).

————. *O vneshnei politike Sovetskogo Soiuza, 1960 g.* 2 vols. Moscow: Gospolitizdat, 1961.

————. *Vseobshchee i polnoe razoruzhenie — garantiia mira i bezopasnosti vsekh narodov.* Moscow: Gospolitizdat, 1962.

————. *Za mir, za razoruzhenie, za svobodu narodov!* Moscow: Gospolitizdat, 1960.

————. *Za prochnyi mir i mirnoe sosushchestvovanie.* Moscow: Gospolitizdat, 1958.

KOROL, ALEXANDER G. *Soviet Research and Development: Its Organization, Personnel, and Funds.* Cambridge, Mass.: The M.I.T. Press, 1965.

KOROVIN, E. A., and V. V. EGOR'EV. *Razoruzhenie.* Moscow: Gosizdat, 1930.

KRAMISH, ARNOLD. *The Chinese People's Republic and the Bomb.* Santa Monica, Calif.: RAND Corporation P-1950, 1960.

KRASIN, YU. *Mirnoe sosushchestvovanie — forma klassovoi bor'by.* Moscow: Gospolitizdat, 1961.

LEDERER, IVO J., ed. *Russian Foreign Policy: Essays in Historical Perspective.* New Haven, Conn.: Yale University Press, 1962.

LEITES, NATHAN. *Styles in Negotiation: East and West on Arms Control, 1958–1961.* Santa Monica, Calif.: RAND Corporation RM-2838-ARPA, 1961.

LENIN, V. I. *Leninskii sbornik.* Vol. XXXVI. Moscow: Gospolitizdat, 1959.

————. *Sochineniia.* 2nd ed. 30 vols. Moscow: Gospolitizdat, 1926–1932; 4th ed. 38 vols. Moscow: Gospolitizdat, 1941–1958; 5th ed. Moscow: Gospolitizdat, 1958 ————.

LEONHARD, WOLFGANG. *The Kremlin Since Stalin.* Rev. ed. New York: Frederick A. Praeger, Inc., 1962.

MARX, DAVID E. *Die Einstellung der Kernwaffenversuche: Probleme und Ergebnisse der bisherigen Verhandlungen.* Frankfurt: M. A. Metzner, 1965.

Narodnoe khoziastvo SSSR v 1962 godu: statisticheskii ezhegodnik. Moscow: Gosstatizdat TsSU SSSR, 1963.

NOEL-BAKER, PHILIP. *The Arms Race.* London: Stevens and Sons, Ltd., 1958.

PATCHER, HENRY M. *Collision Course: The Cuban Missile Crisis and Coexistence.* New York: Frederick A. Praeger, Inc., 1963.

PENKOVSKIY, OLEG. *The Penkovskiy Papers.* Garden City, N. Y.: Doubleday & Company, Inc., 1965.

RICHARDSON, L. F. *Arms and Insecurity.* Pittsburgh, Pa.: Boxwood Press, 1960.

SCHLESINGER, ARTHUR M., JR. *A Thousand Days.* Boston: Houghton Mifflin Company, 1965.

SHAPIRO, LEONARD, ed. *Soviet Treaty Series.* Washington: The Georgetown University Press, 1950.

SHULMAN, MARSHALL D. *Beyond the Cold War*. New Haven, Conn.: Yale University Press, 1966.

————. *Stalin's Foreign Policy Reappraised*. Cambridge, Mass.: Harvard University Press, 1963.

SORENSEN, THEODORE C. *Kennedy*. New York: Harper & Row, 1965.

STEBBINS, RICHARD P. *The United States in World Affairs: 1963*. New York: Harper & Row, for Council on Foreign Relations, 1964.

TRISKA, JAN F., ed. *Soviet Communism: Programs and Rules*. San Francisco, Calif.: Chandler, 1962.

TUCKER, ROBERT C. *The Soviet Political Mind*. New York: Frederick A. Praeger, Inc., 1963.

U.S. Congress: House. Statement of Secretary of Defense Robert S. McNamara before House Armed Services Committee, January 30, 1963. Washington: U.S. Government Printing Office, 1963.

————. *United States Defense Policies in 1957* (Document 436, 1958); *ibid.* 1958 (Document 227, 1959); *ibid.* 1959 (Document 432, 1960); *ibid.* 1960 (Document 207, 1961); *ibid.* 1961 (Document 502, 1962); *ibid.* 1962 (Document 155, 1963). Washington: U.S. Government Printing Office, 1958–1963.

U.S. Congress: Senate. *Nuclear Test Ban Treaty . . . 1963*. Hearings before the Committee on Foreign Relations, 88th Congress, 1st session, on Executive M. Washington: U.S. Government Printing Office, 1963.

————. Testimony of Seweryn Bialer to Senate Internal Security Subcommittee, Release of July 11, 1957. Washington: U.S. Government Printing Office, 1957.

————. Testimony of Paul H. Nitze before the Preparedness Investigating Subcommittee of the Committee on Armed Forces, U.S. Senate, January 24–30, 1963. Washington: U.S. Government Printing Office, 1963.

————. Testimony of Marshall D. Shulman at Hearings before the Committee on Foreign Relations, U.S. Senate. Washington: U.S. Government Printing Office, 1963.

U.S. Department of State. *Disarmament at a Glance*. Washington, n.d.

————. *Disarmament: The Intensified Effort, 1955–1958*. Washington, 1960.

————. *Documents on Disarmament, 1945–1959*. Historical Office, Bureau of Public Affairs, 2 vols. Washington: U.S. Government Printing Office, 1960. (Publication 7008.)

————. *Geneva Conference on the Discontinuance of Nuclear Weapons Tests: History and Analysis of Negotiations.* Washington: U.S. Disarmament Administration, October 1961. (Department of State Publication 7258, Disarmament Series 4.)

————. *Official Report of the United States Delegation to the Conference of the Ten Nation Committee on Disarmament.* Washington: Department of State Press Release, August 5, 1960.

————. Arms Control and Disarmament Agency. *Documents on Disarmament, 1961,* Publication 5 (1962); *ibid., 1962,* Publication 19 (1963); *ibid., 1963,* Publication 24 (1964); *ibid.,* 1964, Publication 27 (1965). Washington: U.S. Government Printing Office, 1962–1965.

————. Arms Control and Disarmament Agency. *International Negotiations on Ending Nuclear Weapon Tests, September 1961–September 1962.* Publication 9. Washington: U.S. Government Printing Office, October 1962.

————. Arms Control and Disarmament Agency. *Second Annual Report to Congress, January 1, 1962–December 31, 1962.* Washington: U.S. Government Printing Office, 1963.

VOLLE, HERMANN and CLAUS-JÜRGEN DUISBERG. *Probleme der internationalen Abrüstung: die Bemühungen der Vereinten Nationen, 1945–1961,* introduction by Ulrich Scheuner. 2 vols. Berlin: Alfred Metzner Verlag, 1964.

WIESNER, JEROME B. *Where Science and Politics Meet.* New York: McGraw-Hill Book Company, 1965.

WOLFE, THOMAS W. *Soviet Strategy at the Crossroads.* Cambridge, Mass.: Harvard University Press, 1964.

ZINNER, PAUL E., ed. *National Communism and Popular Revolt in Eastern Europe.* New York: Columbia University Press, 1956.

ZOPPO, CIRO ELLIOT. *The Test Ban: A Study in Arms Control Negotiation.* Unpublished Ph.D. dissertation, Columbia University, 1963.

ZORIN, V., ed. *Bor'ba Sovetskogo Soiuza za razoruzhenie, 1946–1960.* Moscow: Izdatel'stvo instituta mezhdunarodnykh otnoshenii, 1961.

B. *List of Periodicals*

Air & Cosmos. Paris. Weekly.

Australian Outlook. Melbourne: Australian Institute of International Affairs. Three times yearly.

Aviation Week and Space Technology. New York. Weekly.
Bulletin of the Atomic Scientists. Chicago, Ill.: Educational Foundation for Nuclear Science, Inc. Monthly.
China Quarterly. London: Congress for Cultural Freedom. Quarterly.
The Christian Science Monitor. Boston, Mass. Daily.
Current Digest of the Soviet Press. Ann Arbor, Mich.: Joint Committee on Slavic Studies. Weekly.
Disarmament and Arms Control: An International Quarterly Journal. London: Pergamon Press, Ltd. Quarterly.
Department of State Bulletin. Washington: U.S. Department of State. Weekly.
The Economist. London. Weekly.
For a Lasting Peace, for a People's Democracy. Bucharest: Organ of the Information Bureau of the Communist and Workers' Parties. Published only from 1948 to 1956.
Foreign Affairs. New York: Council on Foreign Relations, Inc. Quarterly.
Flying Review International. London. Monthly.
Institute for the Study of the USSR Bulletin. Munich. Monthly.
Interavia. Geneva, Switzerland. Monthly in English, French, German, and Spanish.
International Affairs. London: Royal Institute of International Affairs. Quarterly.
International Affairs. Moscow: Soviet Society for the Popularization of Political and Scientific Knowledge. Monthly in English, French, and Russian.
International Conciliation. New York: Carnegie Endowment for International Peace. Five times yearly.
Izvestiia. Moscow. Daily.
Journal of Conflict Resolution. Ann Arbor, Mich.: University of Michigan, Center for Research on Conflict Resolution. Quarterly.
Kommunist. Moscow: Kommunisticheskaia Partiia Sovetskogo Soiuza. Tsentral'nyi Komitet. Eighteen times yearly.
Mirovaia ekonomika i mezhdunarodnie otnosheniia. Moscow: Akademiia Nauk SSSR. Institut mirovoi ekonomiki i mezhdunarodnykh otnoshenii. Monthly.
The New Leader. New York: American Labor Conference on International Affairs, Inc. Biweekly.
New Times. Moscow: Trud. Weekly in Russian, English, French, German, Spanish, Polish, and Czech. Russian edition: *Novoe vremia.*

The New York Herald Tribune. New York. Daily.
The New York Times. New York. Daily.
Orbis. Philadelphia, Penn.: University of Pennsylvania, Foreign Policy Research Institute. Quarterly.
Peking Review. Peking. Weekly.
Pravda. Moscow. Daily.
Problems of Communism. Washington: U.S. Information Agency. Bimonthly.
Review of International Affairs. Belgrade: The Federation of Yugoslav Journalists. Twice monthly.
Sane World. New York: National Committee for a Sane Nuclear Policy. Twice monthly.
Slavic Review. Seattle, Wash.: University of Washington, American Association for the Advancement of Slavic Studies. Quarterly.
Survey: A Journal of Soviet and East European Studies. London. Monthly.
Survival. London: Institute for Strategic Studies. Bimonthly.
L'Unità. Rome: Organ of the Italian Communist Party.
U.S. News and World Report. Washington. Weekly.
Voprosy ekonomiki. Moscow: Akademiia Nauk SSSR. Monthly.
War/Peace Report. New York. Monthly.
World Marxist Review [title varies]. Toronto, London, Prague. English language edition of monthly journal *Problems of Peace and Socialism,* published in Prague in many languages.
World Politics. Princeton, N. J.: Princeton University, Center of International Studies. Quarterly.
Za rubezhom. Moscow. Weekly.
Zëri i Popullit. Tirana, Albania: Organ of the Albanian Party of Labor. Daily.

C. Articles

"A Comment on the Statement of the Communist Party of the U.S.A.," editorial, *Peking Review,* Nos. 10–11, March 15, 1963.
"After the Elections, the Selection," Commentator, *Pravda,* November 10, 1960.
"A Genuine Peace Programme," editorial, *International Affairs,* No. 2, February 1958.
ALEXANDROV, V. "An Urgent Task," *International Affairs,* No. 6, June 1960.
———. "Some Current International Problems," *International Affairs,* No. 7, July 1958.

312   SOURCES FOR STUDY OF SOVIET POLICY

———. "Western Zigzags on Disarmament," *International Affairs*, No. 8, August 1960.

ALEXAYEV, A. "The U.S.S.R. Disarmament Proposals — A Major Contribution to Peace," *International Affairs*, No. 7, July 1955.

"Amerikanskii senator o soveshchanii," *Pravda*, June 18, 1955.

ANDREYEV, G. "Disarmament and the Inspirers of the Cold War," *International Affairs*, No. 6, June 1958.

———. "Disarmament Talks: Truth and Fiction," *International Affairs*, No. 6, June 1961.

———. "Who Is Stalling on Disarmament," *International Affairs*, No. 10, October 1956.

ANDREYEV, O., and L. LVOV. "The Arms Drive Strategy Cannot Win," *International Affairs*, No. 11, November 1960.

"An Historic Act," editorial, *International Affairs*, No. 5, May 1958.

"A Policy of Perfidy," editorial, *International Affairs*, No. 6, June 1960.

"A Proposal Concerning the General Line of the International Communist Movement — The Letter of the Central Committee of the Communist Party of China in Reply to the Letter of the Central Committee of the Communist Party of the Soviet Union of March 30, 1963 (June 14, 1963)," *Peking Review*, No. 25, June 21, 1963.

ARBATOV, IU. "Imperialisticheskaia propaganda SShA — ugroza miru narodov," *Kommunist*, No. 7, 1955.

ARKADYEV, N. "An Artificial Deadlock," *International Affairs*, No. 8, August 1960.

———. "New Words, Old Tune," *International Affairs*, No. 8, August 1962.

———. and I. MATVEYEV. "Disarmament — Problem No. 1," *New Times*, No. 5, 1957.

ARZUMANYAN, A. "Vernyi put' obespecheniia prochnogo mira mezhdu narodami," *Kommunist*, No. 4, April 1962.

"Atomic War Must be Prevented," *New Times*, No. 19, 1957.

"Atomic Weapons Must be Destroyed," editorial, *International Affairs*, March 1955.

"A Year of Historic Proofs," editorial, *Zëri i Popullit*, December 6, 1961.

"Ban Nuclear Weapons Tests," *New Times*, No. 22, 1957.

BATURIN, M. "Peace and the Status Quo," *International Affairs*, No. 1, January 1958.

BEZYMENSKY, L., and N. MTKOVSKY. "The Peaceful Coexistence Policy — Early Beginnings," *New Times*, No. 11, 1962.

BOLTIN, MAJOR GENERAL E. "Progress Towards Disarmament —
Or Still Bigger Armaments," *New Times*, No. 24, 1957.

BORILA, P. "Peace is our Policy," *World Marxist Review*, Vol. II,
No. 6, June 1959.

BURLATSKII, F. "Konkretnyi analiz — vazhneishee trebovanie
leninizma," *Pravda*, July 25, 1963.

CHARLES, D. A. "The Dismissal of Marshal P'eng Teh-huai,"
China Quarterly, No. 8, October–December 1961.

CLEMENS, WALTER C., JR. "Lenin on Disarmament," *Slavic Review*, Vol. XXIII, No. 3, September 1964.

————. Soviet Disarmament Proposals and the Cadre-Territorial
Army," *Orbis*, Vol. VII, No. 4, Winter 1964.

————. "Ideology in Soviet Disarmament Policy," *Journal of
Conflict Resolution*, Vol. VIII, No. 1 (March 1964), pp.
7–22.

————. "The Sino-Soviet Dispute: Dogma and Dialectics on
Disarmament," *International Affairs* (London), Vol. XLI,
No. 2 (April 1965), pp. 204–222.

————. "The Soviet Militia in the Missile Age," *Orbis*, Vol.
VIII, No. 1, Spring 1964.

"Common Aim," editorial, *New Times*, No. 22, 1957.

CONQUEST, R. "The Struggle Goes On," *Problems of Communism*, Vol. IX, No. 4, July-August 1960.

"Constructive Contribution to Disarmament," Commentator,
International Affairs, No. 7, July 1960.

COUSINS, NORMAN. "Notes on a 1963 Visit with Khrushchev,"
Saturday Review, November 7, 1964.

DALLIN, ALEXANDER. "The Legend of the Chained Nikita," *The
New Leader*, June 1960.

"Department of Defense Statement on U.S. Military Strength,"
April 14, 1964, Release 308-64, *The New York Times*,
April 16, 1964.

"Disarmament Is Not a Utopia," editorial, *World Marxist Review*, Vol. II, No. 11, November 1959.

"Disarmament — Vital Problem of our Time," Symposium, *International Affairs*, No. 11, November 1960.

"End the 'Cold War'!" editorial, *International Affairs*, No. 6,
June 1955.

ENTOV, R. "Military Spending and Monopoly Profits," *International Affairs*, No. 2, February 1961.

"Enver Hoxha's Speech to his Constituents," editorial, *Zëri i
Popullit*, May 31, 1962.

"For a Leninist Peace Policy," editorial, *International Affairs*,
No. 7, July 1957.

FOSTER, W. Z. "Usilenie fashistskikh techenii v SShA," *Kommunist*, No. 1, 1955.

GALAY, N. "The New Reduction in Soviet Armed Forces," *Bulletin*, Institute for Study of the USSR, July 1956.

GALLAGHER, M. P. "Military Manpower: A Case Study," *Problems of Communism*, Vol. XIII, No. 3, May-June 1964.

"Gates Sees U.S. Safe," *The Christian Science Monitor*, January 19, 1960.

"Geneva: Hopes and Prospects," editorial, *International Affairs*, No. 5, May 1962.

GREENSLADE, R. V., and P. WALLACE. "Industrial Production in the USSR," *Dimensions of Soviet Economic Power*. Washington: U.S. Congress Joint Economic Committee, 1962.

GRIFFITHS, FRANKLYN. "Origins of Peaceful Coexistence: A Historical Note," *Survey*, No. 50, January 1964.

GRIGORYEV, I. "An Epoch-Making Programme," *International Affairs*, No. 10, October 1959.

GRIGORYEV, Y. "Bonn and the Treaty," *New Times*, No. 36, 1963.

GROMOV, L. "Our Idea of a World Without Arms," *International Affairs*, No. 7, July 1962.

GROMOV, L., and V. STRIGACHEV. "Invalid Economic 'Arguments' about Disarmament," *International Affairs*, No. 9, September 1962.

———. "Some Economic Aspects of Disarmament," *International Affairs*, No. 3, March 1960.

———. "The Arms Race: Dangers and Consequences," *International Affairs*, No. 12, December 1960.

HAHN, WALTER. "The Mainsprings of Soviet Secrecy," *Orbis*, Vol. VII, No. 4 (Winter 1964), pp. 719–747.

HAVLICEK, F., and L. GRUPPI. "The Growing International Significance of Communist Construction," *World Marxist Review*, Vol. II, No. 3, March 1959.

HOTZ, R. "Air Force Takes Key Role in U.S. Policy," *Aviation Week*, Vol. LX, No. 11, March 15, 1954.

INOZEMTSEV, N. "Amerikanskaia politika s pozitsii sily i Zapadnaia Evropa," *Kommunist*, No. 9, 1955.

———. "Mirnoe sosushchestvovanie — vazhneishii vopros sovremennosti," *Pravda*, January 11, 1962.

———. "Nadezhdy i trevogi amerikantsev," *Pravda*, December 25, 1963.

———. "International Notes," *New Times*, No. 12, 1957.

———. "Iskliuchit' mirovuiu voinu iz zhizni obshchestva," editorial, *Kommunist*, No. 9, 1959.

IVANOV, K., M. KALUGIN, and B. BATSANOV. "Economic Programme for Disarmament," *International Affairs*, No. 12, December 1962.

KAIGL, V. "The Economic Possibility of Disarmament," *World Marxist Review*, Vol. III, No. 11, November 1960.

"Khrushchev Bares Troop Data," *The New York Times*, January 25, 1960.

KHRUSHCHEV, N. S. Concluding Remarks of, to the Twenty-Second Party Congress, October 27, 1961, *Current Digest of the Soviet Press*, No. 40, 1961.

————. "Nasushchnye voprosy razvitiia mirovoi sotsialisticheskoi sistemy," *Kommunist*, No. 12, 1962.

————. "O mire i mirnom sosuschestvovanii," *Kommunist*, No. 7, 1964.

————. "On the Control Figures for Development of the U.S.S.R. National Economy in 1959–1965," *Current Digest of the Soviet Press*, No. 4, 1959.

————. "On the International Situation and the Foreign Policy of the Soviet Union," *Current Digest of the Soviet Press*, No. 44, 1959.

————. "Rech' toverishcha N. S. Khrushcheva," *Pravda*, April 7, 1963.

————. Report by, on October 17, 1961, *Current Digest of the Soviet Press*, No. 41, 1961.

————. Report of the Central Committee of the CPSU to the Twentieth Party Congress, *Current Digest of the Soviet Press*, No. 4, 1956.

————. Report of the Central Committee, CPSU, *Pravda*, October 18, 1961.

————. Speech at Grivita Rosie Plant in Romania, June 19, 1962, *Pravda*, June 20, 1962.

————. Speech of January 6, 1961, *Pravda*, January 21, 1961.

————. Speech of January 6, 1961, *World Marxist Review*, January 1961.

————. Speech of February 14, 1964 to Central Committee Plenum, *Pravda*, February 15, 1964.

————. Speech to Cuban students in Russia, June 3, 1962, *Pravda*, June 4, 1962.

————. Speech to military academy graduates, *Pravda*, July 6, 1963.

————. Speech to the Supreme Soviet, *Current Digest of the Soviet Press*, No. 2, 1960.

————. "Za novye pobedy mirovogo kommunisticheskogo dvizheniia," *Kommunist*, No. 1, 1961.

KHVOSTOV, V. "Disarmament Negotiations: History of the Problem," *International Affairs,* No. 2, February 1961.

————. "The Prospects of Disarmament," *International Affairs,* No. 11, November 1962.

KIRILLOV, V. "The Peoples Want an End to Nuclear Tests," *International Affairs,* No. 12, December 1959.

————. "The Post War Disarmament Problem," *International Affairs,* No. 10, September 1959.

————. "The Western Powers Oppose Discontinuation of Nuclear Tests," *International Affairs,* No. 3, March 1959.

KONSTANTINOV, F., and KH. MOMDZHYAN. "Dialektika i sovremennost'," *Kommunist,* No. 10, 1960.

KOROVIN, E. "The A-Weapons vs. International Law," *International Affairs,* No. 5, May 1955.

KOTOV, M. "The Widening Peace Front," *New Times,* No. 50, 1963.

KRAMINOV, D. "New Tactics, Old Policy," *Za rubezhom,* February 25, 1961.

KREMENTSOV, M., and G. STARKO. "Military Bases in Foreign Territories," *New Times,* No. 21, 1955.

KUUSINEN, O. V. "Pretvorenie v zhizn' idei Lenina," *Pravda,* April 23, 1960.

LAVELLE, M. J., S. J. *The Economics of American Disarmament: A Soviet View.* Cambridge, Mass., unpublished manuscript, 1963.

LEBEDEV, Y. "Adlai Stevenson on U. S. Foreign Policy," *New Times,* No. 27, 1955.

LEBEDINSKY, A. "New Facts on Radiation Hazards," *International Affairs,* No. 7, July 1959.

————. "The Harmful Consequences of Nuclear Weapons Tests," *International Affairs,* No. 6, June 1958.

"Leninskii kurs na mirnoe sosushchestvovanie — general'naia liniia vneshnei politika Sovetskogo Soiuza, *Kommunist,* No. 11, 1957.

LEONIDOV, A. "The Making of a New Diplomacy," *New Times,* No. 14, 1960.

LEONT'EV, A. "O mirnom sosushchestvovanii dvukh sistem," *Kommunist,* No. 13, 1954.

LEONT'EV, L. "Sotsializm v ekonomicheskom sorevnovanii s kapitalismom," *Kommunist,* No. 15, 1957.

LINDEN, C. "Khrushchev and the Party Battle," *Problems of Communism,* Vol. XII, No. 5, September-October 1963.

MALINOVSKY, R. Speech of February 7, 1964, *Krasnaia zvezda,* February 9, 1964.

————. Speech of February 22, 1963, *Pravda*, February 23, 1963.

MARININ, M. "Some Conclusions," *International Affairs*, No. 1, January 1957.

"Marking Time," editorial, *New Times*, No. 15, 1957.

MARUSHKIN, B. "Post-Election Thoughts," *International Affairs*, No. 1, January 1961.

"Marxism-Leninism as International Doctrine of the Communists of All Countries," *Current Digest of the Soviet Press*, No. 19, 1964.

MENZHINSKY, E. "French-American Contradictions in the World Capitalist Market," *International Affairs*, No. 7, August 1955.

"Mezhdunarodnaya solidarnost' trudiachshikhsia," *Kommunist*, No. 6, 1955.

"Modern Revisionism to the Aid of the Basic Strategy of American Imperialism," editorial, *Zëri i Popullit*, September 19 and 20, 1962.

"Moscow Programme," Observer, *New Times*, No. 44, 1963.

"Nevada and Geneva," editorial, *New Times*, No. 7, 1963.

NOGEE, J. L. "Propaganda and Negotiation: The Case of the Ten-Nation Disarmament Committee," *Journal of Conflict Resolution*, Vol. VII, No. 3, December 1962.

NORTH, J. "On the Eve of the U.S. Elections," *International Affairs*, No. 11, November 1960.

OLIVER, F. L. "Soviet Navy Learns Value of Submarine," *The Christian Science Monitor*, January 23, 1961.

"O nekotorykh storonakh partiinoi zhizni v kompartii kitaia," *Pravda*, April 28, 1964.

"On the Eve of the Four-Power Conference," editorial, *International Affairs*, No. 7, July 1955.

"On the Threshold of 1960," editorial, *World Marxist Review*, Vol. III, No. 1, January 1960.

Open Letter from the CPSU Central Committee to Party Organizations and All Communists of the Soviet Union, July 14, 1963, *Current Digest of the Soviet Press*, No. 27, 1963.

ORLOV, I. Report from the General Assembly, *New Times*, No. 11, 1957.

"Outlaw Atomic Weapons," editorial, *International Affairs*, May 1957.

"Peace Does Not Come, It has to be Won," *World Marxist Review*, Vol. II, No. 9, September 1959.

PONOMAREV, B. "Peaceful Coexistence is a Vital Necessity," *Current Digest of the Soviet Press*, No. 32, 1960.

————. Speech of April 22, 1963. *Pravda,* April 23, 1963.

RAPACKI, A. "Socialist Diplomacy of Peace in the World Arena," *World Marxist Review,* Vol. V, No. 6, June 1962.

"Reds Boast of H-Missile," *The Christian Science Monitor,* November 18, 1959.

REIMANN, M. "Peaceful Coexistence and the Class Struggle," *World Marxist Review,* Vol. III, No. 10, October 1960.

"Resolution of the Plenary Session of the Party Central Committee — On the Anti-Party Group of G. M. Malenkov, L. M. Kaganovich and V. M. Molotov," *Current Digest of the Soviet Press,* No. 23, 1957.

RIGBY, T. H. "Khrushchev and the Resuscitation of the Central Committee," *Australian Outlook,* September 1959.

RITVO, HERBERT. "Internal Divisions on Disarmament in the USSR," *Disarmament: Its Politics and Economics.* Seymour Melman, ed. Boston, Mass.: American Academy of Arts and Sciences, 1962.

SANAKOYEV, SH. "New Type of International Relations," *International Affairs,* No. 1, January 1955.

SANTARELLI, E. "The Debate in the Central Committee and the Central Control Commission of the PCI on the XXII CPSU Congress," *L'Unità,* November 12, 1961.

"Scientists Gagged," *New Times,* No. 18, 1957.

"Secret Missile Report to Senate Revealed," *The New York Times,* February 5, 1960.

SEMYONOV, K. "All Nuclear Tests Must Be Stopped at Once," *International Affairs,* No. 10, October 1958.

————. "Marking Time," *International Affairs,* No. 10, October 1962.

————. "Obstruction Tactics Continue," *International Affairs,* No. 8, August 1959.

SERGEYEVA, N. "The Sentiment of the Ordinary American," *New Times,* No. 14, 1955.

"S"ezd stroitelei kommunizma," *Kommunist,* No. 2, 1959.

SLAVIANOV, M. "Firm Foundation of European and Universal Security: The Warsaw Conference," *International Affairs,* No. 6, June 1955.

————. "Who is Blocking Disarmament," *International Affairs,* No. 1, January 1958.

"Smoke-Screen Attempts by Anglo-American Diplomacy to Conceal its Retreat on the Disarmament Question," Observer, *Pravda,* December 7, 1955.

SMOLENSKI, L., and P. WILES. "The Soviet Planning Pendulum," *Problems of Communism,* Vol. XII, No. 6, November-December 1963.

"Soviet Bloc Reduces Armed Might Little," *The Christian Science Monitor,* January 20, 1960.

"Soviet Government Answers Statement by the Chinese Government on Nuclear Weapons Test Ban (August 3, 1963)," *Current Digest of the Soviet Press,* No. 31, 1963.

Soviet Government Statement (August 21, 1963), *Current Digest of the Soviet Press,* No. 34, 1963.

Soviet Government Statement — Reply to Statement Made by the Chinese Government (September 21, 1963), *Current Digest of the Soviet Press,* No. 38, 1963.

"Soviet Oncologists Call for Nuclear Tests Ban," *New Times,* No. 20, 1957.

Statement by the Spokesman of the Chinese Government — A Comment on the Soviet Government's Statement of August 3 (August 15, 1963)," *Peking Review,* No. 33, August 16, 1963.

"Statement by the Spokesman of the Chinese Government — A Comment on the Soviet Government's Statement of August 21 (September 1, 1963)," *Peking Review,* No. 36, September 6, 1963.

Statement of Secretary McNamara to Democratic Platform Committee, August 17, 1964, *The New York Times,* August 18, 1964.

"Statement of the Chinese Government Advocating the Complete, Thorough, Total and Resolute Prohibition and Destruction of Nuclear Weapons [and] Proposing a Conference of the Government Heads of All Countries of the World (July 31, 1963)," *Peking Review,* No. 31, August 2, 1963.

STEVENSON, A. E. "Why I Raised the H-Bomb Question," *International Affairs,* No. 4, April 1957.

TALENSKY, N. "Sincere? — Yes. Realistic? — No," *International Affairs,* No. 3, March 1963.

"The Bedrock of Soviet Foreign Policy," editorial, *International Affairs,* No. 3, March 1957.

"The Burning Problem of Today," editorial, *International Affairs,* No. 2, February 1960.

"The Friends and Foes of Disarmament," *New Times,* No. 13, 1955.

"The Most Urgent Problem," commentator, *International Affairs,* No. 8, August 1956.

"The Origin and Development of the Differences Between the Leadership of the CPSU and Ourselves — Comment on the Open Letter of the Central Committee of the CPSU, by the Editorial Departments of *People's Daily* and *Red Flag*" (September 6, 1963), *Peking Review*, No. 37, September 13, 1963.

"The People Demand: Curb the Aggressor and Ensure Lasting Peace," editorial, *World Marxist Review*, Vol. III, No. 6, June 1960.

"The Principal Problems of the Time," editorial, *International Affairs*, No. 7, July 1961.

"The Soviet Union, the United States and the Fate of Peace," editorial, *International Affairs*, No. 9, September 1959.

"The Test Ban Talks," editorial, *New Times*, No. 29, 1963.

"The Tokyo Declaration," *New Times*, No. 34, 1957.

"The U.S. 'Policy of Strength' — Its Miscalculations and Failures," editorial, *International Affairs*, No. 2, February 1955.

"The Western Powers and Nuclear Tests," Commentator, *International Affairs*, No. 11, November 1958.

"The World Breathes More Freely," editorial, *International Affairs*, No. 10, October 1959.

"Transferred to Geneva," editorial, *New Times*, No. 6, 1963.

TRIANIN, A., and G. MOROZOV. "Podgotovka i propaganda atomnoi voiny — tiagchaishee prestuplenie protiv chelovechestva," *Kommunist*, No. 8, 1955.

"Two Different Lines on the Question of War and Peace — Comment on the Open Letter of the Central Committee of the CPSU (5), by the Editorial Departments of *People's Daily* and *Red Flag*" (November 18, 1963; excerpts), *Peking Review*, No. 47, November 22, 1963.

U.S. Department of State. "United States Replies to Polish Note on Rapacki Plan," *Department of State Bulletin*, Vol. XXXVIII, May 19, 1958.

"U.S. Downgrades Missile Gap," *The Christian Science Monitor*, March 16, 1960.

"Vicious Circle," editorial, *New Times*, No. 15, 1963.

VIKTOROV, Y. "The Soviet Union and Disarmament," *International Affairs*, No. 6, June 1956.

———. "Towards a Relaxation of World Tension," *International Affairs*, No. 7, July 1957.

VOSNESENSKY, A. "Arms Reduction and the Underdeveloped Countries," *New Times*, No. 22, 1956.

WHITE, LT. COL. J. B. "The Army of Communism," *Army Combat Forces Journal*, March 1954.

"Who is Frustrating Hopes at Geneva?" commentator, *International Affairs*, No. 6, June 1962.

"Whom do N. Khrushchev's Views and Actions Serve?" editorial, *Zëri i Popullit*, March 2, 1962.

"World Peace Council Appeals," *New Times*, No. 25, 1957.

"World Problem Number One," Commentator, *International Affairs*, No. 2, February 1957.

YEVGENYEV, I. "The Nations Want Disarmament," *International Affairs*, No. 8, August 1958.

——— and P. FYODOROV. "The Way to Solve the Disarmament Problem," *International Affairs*, No. 7, July 1956.

YEVZEROV, R. "Militarism and the Uneven Development of Capitalism," *International Affairs*, No. 7, July 1962.

YUDIN, Y. "The American Business Community and the Treaty," *New Times*, No. 35, 1963.

"Za urkeplenie druzhby sovetskogo i iugoslavskogo narodov," editorial, *Kommunist*, No. 9, 1955.

"Zaiavlenie senatora Dzhorzha," *Pravda*, May 19, 1955.

ZHIVKOV, T. "Peace: Key Problem of Today," *World Marxist Review*, Vol. III, No. 8, August 1960.

ZORIN, V. A. "Marksizm-Leninizm i problema razoruzheniia," *Mirovaia ekonomika i mezhdunarodnye otnosheniia*, No. 9, September 1963.

———. "Problemy razoruzheniia i manevry Pekina," *Izvestiia*, June 30, 1961.

D. *Bibliographies*

CLEMENS, WALTER C., JR. *Soviet Disarmament Policy, 1917–1963: An Annotated Bibliography of Soviet and Western Sources*. Stanford, Cal.: The Hoover Institution, 1965.

COLLART, YVES. *Disarmament: A Study Guide and Bibliography on the Efforts of the United Nations*. The Hague: N. Nijhoff, 1958.

Deutsches und Ausländisches Schriftum zur Frage der Abrüstung, 1945–1956: unter besonderer Berücksichtigung des Schriftums zu den Problemen der Kernwaffen und der internationalen Kontrolle der Kernenergie. Frankfurt am Main: Deutsche Gesellschaft fuer Auswärtige Politik, 1957.

Disarmament and Arms Control: Selected Readings. New York: Foreign Policy Association, World Affairs Center, 1961.

"Disarmament — A Bibliography," *Survival*, Vol. II, No. 1, January-February 1960. London: Institute for Strategic Studies, 1960.

322   SOURCES FOR STUDY OF SOVIET POLICY

DOUGHERTY, JAMES E. "The Disarmament Debate," *Orbis,* Vol.
V, No. 3, Fall 1961; Vol. V, No. 4, Winter 1962.

FISCHER, GEORGE. *Soviet Disarmament Policy: A Survey of Recent Sources.* Cambridge, Mass.: Center for International
Studies, Massachusetts Institute of Technology, 1961.

"Focus on Arms Control and Disarmament," *Intercom,* Vol. V,
No. 2. New York: Foreign Policy Association, 1963.

"Focus on the Soviet Union," *Intercom,* Vol. III, No. 4. New
York: Foreign Policy Association, 1961.

HAMMOND, THOMAS T., ed. *Soviet Foreign Relations and World
Communism.* Princeton, N. J.: Princeton University Press,
1965.

Letopis' zhurnalnykh statei. Moscow: Organ gosudarstvennoi
bibliografii S.S.S.R., 1926————.

*Mezhdunarodnie otnosheniia (bibliograficheskii spavochnik,
1945–1960 gg.).* Comp. V. N. Egorov. Moscow: Institut
mezhdunarodnikh otnoshenii, 1961.

Mir bez oruzhiia — mir bez voin. Comp. Iu. L. Kusnets. Leningrad: Publichnaia Biblioteka, 1960.

RUBENSTEIN, ALVIN Z. "Selected Bibliography of Soviet Works
on the United Nations, 1946–1959," *American Political
Science Review,* Vol. LIV, No. 4, December 1960.

*Sovetskaia literatura po mezhdunarodnomy pravu. Bibliografiia,
1917–1957.* Ed. V. N. Durdenevskii. Moscow: Gosu-
darstvennoe izdatel'stvo iuridicheskoi literatury, 1959
(Sovetskaia assotsiatsiia mezhdunarodnogo prava).

United Nations. *Annotated Bibliography on Disarmament and
Military Questions.* Geneva: League of Nations Library,
1931.

————. *Liste mensuelle d'articles sélectionnés; Monthly List
of Selected Articles.* Geneva: United Nations Library,
1949————.

————. *Liste mensuelle d'ouvrages cataloguée à la Bibliothèque
des Nations Unies; Monthly List of Books Catalogued.*
Geneva: United Nations Library, 1928————.

————. *List of Selected Articles.* New York: United Nations
Library, (Bilingual English and French), ST/LIB/Ser.C/
1————. Published irregularly.

————. *Index to Proceedings of the Economic and Social Council.* New York: United Nations Library, ST/LIB/Ser.B,
1946————.

————. *Index to Proceedings of the General Assembly.* New
York: United Nations Library, ST/LIB/Ser.B/A. 12,
1946————.

U.S. Arms Control and Disarmament Agency. *A Brief Biblio-graphy. Arms Control and Disarmament.* Washington: U.S. Arms Control and Disarmament Agency Publication 22, July 1964.

U.S. Department of the Army. *Bibliography on Limited War.* Washington: Headquarters, Department of the Army, 1958. Department of the Army Pamphlet PAM 20-60.

———. *Disarmament: A Bibliographic Record 1916–1960.* Washington: Staff of the Army Library for the Office of Special Assistant to the Joint Chiefs of Staff for Disarmament Affairs, May 15, 1960.

———. *Soviet Military Power.* Washington: Headquarters, Department of the Army, March 1959. Department of the Army Pamphlet PAM 20-65.

———. *U.S. National Security and the Communist Challenge: The Spectrum of East-West Conflict.* Washington: Headquarters, Department of the Army, August 1961. Department of the Army Pamphlet PAM 20-60.

U.S. Department of Defense. *U.S. Security, Arms Control, and Disarmament, 1961–1965.* Washington, 1965.

U.S. Department of State. *Documents on Disarmament, 1945–1959.* 2 vols. Washington, 1960. Department of State Publication 7008.

U.S. Disarmament Administration. *A Basic Bibliography: Dis-armament, Arms Control, and National Security.* Washington: Department of State Publication 7193, Disarmament Series 1, June 1961.

Index

Adenauer, Konrad, 67, 134, 215, 275
Albania, 121, 128, 216
Alexayev, A., 64n
Alsop, Stewart, 38n
Anglo-French memorandum,
    see Disarmament, Anglo-French memorandum on
Antarctica Treaty (1959), 88, 151
Antiballistic missile (ABM), see Soviet Union, antimissile defense of
"Antiparty group," see Soviet Union, "antiparty group" in
Arbatov, Iu., 64n
Arbitration, international, 7, 11
Arms control, ban on war propaganda, 122, 133
    "bomber bonfire," 103
    definition of, 1n
    demilitarized zones, 8, 81, 84, 151
    exchange of troop representatives among forces in Germany, 191n, 223, 242n
    removal of foreign troops from Germany, 223
    Soviet Union and partial mea-

sures of, 12, 18, 23, 24, 27, 28, 31, 34, 44–47, 69–71, 77–78, 81, 83–84, 91, 99, 103, 134, 146–147, 190–191, 205–208, 222–224, 248, 258
    tacit measures of, 57, 69–70, 77–78, 87, 205, 207, 258
    see also Budgetary controls; Direct communications link; Disengagement; Fissionable materials; Foreign military bases; Ground control posts to prevent surprise attack; Inspection and control; Nonaggression pact; Nuclear-free zones; Nuclear proliferation; Nuclear test ban; Nuclear weapons; "Open Skies" proposal of aerial inspection; Outer space; Soviet Union
Arms race, 4, 14, 57, 119, 142, 206–208, 248, 259, 269, 279
    see also Soviet Union, arms race and
Arzumanyan, A., 122

325

Tito, Marshal (Josip Broz), 60,
73, 74
Togliatti, Palmiro, 61
Trianin, A., 64n
Trieste settlement (1954), 73
Triska, Jan. F., 11n
Tsarapkin, S., 140n
Turkey, 159, 197n
Tushino Airfield, 39
Twentieth Party Congress (1956),
17, 32, 33, 21, 55, 59, 60,
61, 62, 74, 78, 97n, 124
Twenty-first Party Congress
(1959), 149, 178
Twenty-second Party Congress
(1961), 92, 121, 128, 211,
216

U–2 affair (1960), 120, 121, 128,
135, 161, 169, 175, 180,
274
Ulbricht, Walter, 223
United Arab Republic (UAR),
138n
United Nations, 21, 24, 32, 79,
132, 138, 139, 143, 144,
146, 148, 176, 186, 187,
188n, 191, 223, 224, 293
Committee on the Peaceful
Uses of Outer Space, 191
Disarmament Commission, 29
Disarmament Commission Subcommittee, 22, 25, 26, 27,
30, 31, 48, 132, 138, 144,
147, 165, 294
peace-keeping forces, 139, 142–
143, 145, 223–224
United States, 2, 10, 12, 14, 26,
27, 32, 34, 63–65 passim,
67, 70, 84, 113, 117, 138n,
140, 151, 174, 184–188
passim, 191, 195, 200, 206,
211, 214, 224, 236, 240,
244, 267, 285, 295
Arms Control and Disarma-
ment Agency, 292, 296
Atomic Energy Commission,
71

bombers, 36, 37, 40, 94, 202,
264
Department of Defense, 38,
93n
military spending by, 107, 109,
114, 121, 228
military strategy of, 35–36, 141
missiles, 40, 96, 103, 104, 174,
183, 196, 202, 203, 223,
247, 263, 268, 278
National Security Council, 214
NATO and, 28, 65, 66, 67, 70,
192, 195, 215, 221
Senate, 212, 240
Strategic Air Command, 36, 40,
46, 49, 70, 84, 85, 96, 263,
266
strategic military balance and,
38, 39, 40, 43, 56, 58, 93–
97, 107–108, 114, 205,
247, 256, 263, 264, 269
see also Arms control; Atomic
energy; Direct communi-
cations link; Disarma-
ment; Eisenhower, Dwight
D.; Inspection and con-
trol; Johnson, Lyndon B.;
Kennedy, John F.; Nu-
clear proliferation; Nu-
clear test ban; Nuclear
Test Ban Treaty; Nuclear
testing; Outer space;
"Open Skies" proposal of
aerial inspection
Ustinov, Dimitri, 231

Vasilevskii, Marshal A. M., 39
Vesecky, John, 301
Vienna Appeal (1955), 31
Vienna meeting (1961), 121, 176
Vietnam, 214, 243, 276, 287
"Virgin Lands," 54
Voice of America, 190n
Volle, Hermann, 292n
Vyshinsky, Andrei, 21, 31

Wadsworth, James J., 25
Wallace, Phyllis, 52n, 110, 227n